SPORTS REPORT
40 YEARS OF THE BEST
EDITED BY BRYON BUTLER

SPORTS REPORT
40 YEARS OF THE BEST
EDITED BY BRYON BUTLER

Foreword by HRH The Princess Royal

Macdonald
Queen Anne Press

A *Queen Anne Press* BOOK

© BBC 1987

First published in Great Britain in 1987 by
Queen Anne Press, a division of
Macdonald & Co (Publishers) Ltd
3rd Floor
Greater London House
Hampstead Road
London NW1 7QX

A BPCC plc Company

Jacket photographs – Front (clockwise from top left): Associated Press; Gerry Cranham; Associated Press; All-Sport/Adrian Murrell

British Library Cataloguing in Publication Data

40 years of Sport Report
  1. Sports report (Radio program).
  I. Butler, Bryon
791.44'72   GV742.3

ISBN 0-356-14863-7

Typeset by JCL Graphics, Bristol
Printed and bound in Great Britain by
Hazell Watson & Viney Limited,
Member of the BPCC Group,
Aylesbury, Bucks

Picture credits
All-Sport: 56, 87, 88, 151; *Associated Press:* 83, 122; *BBC:* 10, 20, 27, 29, 34(BL,BR), 61, 72, 95(T), 105, 124, 141, 148, 154, 165; *BBC Hulton Picture Library:* 22, 25, 34(TR), 42, 73, 117, 145(T), 173, 186, 190; *Bob Thomas Sports Photography:* 8(T); *Colorsport:* 36, 64, 100, 120, 187, 188; *Gerry Cranham:* 8(B); *Daily Express:* 34(TL); *Ken Kelly:* 95(B); *LWT:* 116; *Photosource Ltd:* 40, 81, 158; *Press Association:* 69, 112; *S & G Press Agency:* 47, 50, 74, 97, 103, 110, 129, 137, 146, 177, 180; *Syndication International:* 75, 125, 170

Acknowledgements

Special gratitude to Ann Davies for her staggering industry, gentle patience and unfailing cheerfulness. Also to Robert Nothman, the kind of knowledgeable fan every sport deserves, and the rest of my impossible colleagues. And certainly not forgetting Queen Anne Press editor Caroline North for her expert handling of the reins.

Contents

Foreword

HRH The Princess Royal

BUCKINGHAM PALACE

I am pleased to write the foreword to a book that celebrates the 40th birthday of "Sports Report".

Saturdays at 5 o'clock has always been a regular date for everyone in Great Britain who enjoys their sport. Millions of others - via the BBC's World Service - have been kept in touch about who and what was making the headlines at home.

It happened to be an Olympic year when the first edition of "Sports Report" went on the air. And here we are, 40 years on, in another Olympic year, when the athletes of the World meet in Seoul in South Korea.

During those forty years the "Olympic family" has trebled, new records have been set and new sports introduced. There have been boycotts and financial problems, but the Olympic Games have survived and "Sports Report" has been there to tell us the important things, like the sporting achievements and results.

In its forty years, the programme has crossed many boundaries to report on issues and achievements of sportsmen and sportswomen everywhere. The pages of this book reflect those first forty years and long may "Sports Report" continue to cross boundaries through its coverage of sporting events.

Happy birthday. Here's to the next forty.

Anne

Introduction

Bryon Butler

BBC Radio's football correspondent since 1968, Bryon Butler previously worked for five newspapers including the *News Chronicle* and the *Daily Telegraph* and has written and talked about football in nearly 60 countries. His books include *Soccer Choice* and *The Giant Killers*. A former presenter of *Sports Report,* he is a cricket-playing, book-collecting antique-envier.

Saturday 3 January 1948. 5.30 p.m.
Announcer: 'This is the BBC Light Programme. *Sports Report*. (Music: Hubert Bath's "Out of the Blue".) Here is Raymond Glendenning to introduce a new Saturday feature for sportsmen.'

Glendenning: 'Hello there, sports fans, and welcome to *Sports Report* – a weekly programme on the air at this time every Saturday, with a roving microphone, to bring you not only the football results, but up-to-the-minute accounts of the major sporting fixtures from all parts of the country, and an "open" microphone over which we shall be airing the personal views of experts on sport on topics of the moment. Now, our aim is to bring into your home, wherever you may be, a half-hour coverage of sport, wherever it may be taking place. How well we have succeeded in this first edition, you will be able to judge after the next 29 minutes.'

Was there a note of dubiety in the voice; the merest hint of an apology in advance? Or did Glendenning punch out his little introduction as if describing the start of a five-furlong flier? We shall never know because no recording was kept of that first *Sports Report*. We have the script but not the sound. All that can be said, 40 years and around 1,500 editions later, is that the programme obviously showed promise.

It is now, unassailably, the longest-running sports programme of all, nimbler on its feet, more flexible, broader based and certainly a touch breezier than it was in 1948; but, unmistakably, it is a chip off the old block. The format endures. Measured voices up front, sweet disorder behind the scenes: headlines, results, reports, interviews, reflection, controversy, instant solutions, humour, news and more news. All sports, all countries. Evergreen and everywhere. For an hour (5.00 to 6.00 p.m. throughout the football season on Radio Two) it is part of the Saturday scene. The history of *Sports Report* is a history of sport during the last 40 years.

The programme has resolutely kept in step with the pace and spirit of its times. Television was just an ostentatious toy for the *beau monde* in 1948, its wares sandwiched into a couple of pages at the back of a tuppenny *Radio Times*. *Sports Report* was in the front line: sharing an austere New Year edition with Dick Barton, that most special of agents; the daily bran tub of *Housewives' Choice; Children's Hour* ('Are you sitting comfortably?') and Richard Murdoch's exquisite *Much Binding in the Marsh*. Radio ruled – and what radios! Stately wooden domes or powerful all-wave, five-valve jobs in trendy bakelite that 'required no aerials'.

Forty years on it is a little different. Trannies are worn like wrist-watches or stuffed into hip pockets. Studios of unspeakable complexity are understood only by masterminds. Little switches spin sound around the globe. Australia? Instantly. The moon? Dialling for you now!

Sports Report was a child of the boom in sport just after the Second World War. It answered a demand and, like all pioneers, it had to clear its own path and set its own standards, standards from which television learned much. Now, of course, television shows it all as it is, faithfully, remorselessly. Someone even calculated once that if the annual sporting output of British television and radio was stitched together into one non-stop programme it would run night and day until Pentecost. Competition only sharpens and refines, however, and *Sports Report*'s voice is still resonant, its range unequalled, its credibility unbruised.

The style of sports reporting has changed, inevitably, but so have the requirements of the programme. A young John Arlott began the first football report on 3 January 1948 with admirable sureness: 'The game between Portsmouth and Huddersfield was a magnificent one to watch because both forward lines kept up on the attack and the wing-halves of each side gave them all the support they could possibly want, bringing the ball to them along the ground . . .' Arlott told the story of the game with simplicity and reverence. There were no buttons and bows; and he was listened to carefully.

Nearly 40 years later Stuart Hall would begin a report: 'The ultimate sacrifice for your humble reporter is to leave the warm bosom of my Wilmslow shack and my frugal meal of plovers' eggs, larks' tongues in aspic, dromedary steaks washed down with '79 Chambertin, and cross the icy, desolate, bitter, unforgiving wasteland of the snow-covered Snake Pass on the Pennine Tundra . . .' But this says less about the style of modern *Sports Report* than its range. Hall, word-lover and word-ravisher, is one of a team that is allowed a long rein. Facts are still obligatory but the wrapping is optional. Dear Stuart, it ought to be added, stands alone. One marbled Hall is an adornment − two would be extravagance.

It also needs to be said that if Hall had offered his larks' tongues to *Sports Report* in 1948 a lean Scot with slicked hair, trim moustache and eyes of wrath would almost certainly have reached him in seconds, wherever he was, and garrotted him on the spot. This would have been Angus Mackay, the Godfather of *Sports Report*. Mackay was invited to produce a sports programme for the nation to enjoy with its Saturday tea, a job many considered impossible then, a job which others certainly didn't fancy, and an important part of this book is properly devoted to his drive and originality.

Mackay's sovereignty lasted until the early 'seventies, and his place was taken by others who moved the programme on swiftly. Men like Bob Burrows, indefatigable, innovative, a master of his craft; Bryan Tremble, gentle and softly-spoken but an instinctive creator and perceptive judge; and, in more recent times, the chair has been shared by Rob Hastie, Mike Lewis and Derek Mitchell: men who care passionately about their inheritance and guard the programme's standards jealously.

The men who have introduced *Sports Report* have been a gloriously mixed bunch, men of highly varied talent, experience and persuasion; but all deeply conscious that they were sitting in a special chair. Five different men were used in the first five weeks: Glendenning, Rex Alston, Geoffrey Peck, Wynford Vaughan-Thomas and Stephen Grenfell. Soon, too, there would be Stewart MacPherson, Peter Wilson, John Webster (later the supreme reader of results), Alex McCrindle, Max Robertson, Henry Longhurst, Cliff Michelmore and George Allison. Allison had delivered the first football commentary 21 years before and he later became manager of Arsenal. Nonetheless, after his one evening in the *Sports Report* chair, he dived into his taxi, mopped his brow and uttered just two words: 'Never again'.

Later came Robin Marlar, Liam Nolan, Brian Moore, Peter Jones, Desmond Lynam, Jim Rosenthal, Peter Brackley, Tony Adamson, Alan Parry, Mike Ingham, Ian Darke and Renton Laidlaw. But, above all, abidingly, there was Eamonn Andrews. Mackay and Andrews, Andrews and Mackay. They were more of a team than Adam and Eve or gin and tonic. Andrews, big man and endearing personality, also commands a handsome part of this book.

Yet *Sports Report* has always needed more than opening batsmen. Much of the programme's strength has been in its middle order, with reporters like the late Bill Bothwell, an enlightened chairman of Tranmere Rovers and for many years the authentic voice of Northern football; and his caring counterpart in the Midlands, Larry Canning, a former Aston Villa player. Men, too, like Bill Lowndes, who was once dispatched by Angus Mackay to carry out a weekly, in-depth investigation into the state of toilets at football grounds. 'This week' a hollow voice would say, 'I'm standing . . .'

Then there was Godfrey Dixey, who at moments of crisis (it can now be admitted there *are* such moments) was never far from

Mackay's right shoulder.

Mackay: 'Stop nattering, Godfrey.'

Dixey: 'But I'm not . . .'

Mackay: 'Then don't breath so loud.'

There was also William Norris Ross – 'Bill'. He was the belt and braces of the sports room for nearly 30 years, bearded, irascible, opinionated, concerned, highly professional and the zealous keeper of the 'Blue Books' which contained the day-by-day, goal-by-goal records of all League clubs. Bill produced classified racing and football results almost before finishing lines had been crossed and final whistles blown, although as Mackay once observed: 'I do wish Bill would make less noise when performing his miracles of exactitude'.

There is, too, a hardy and talented breed of auxiliaries, permanent denizens of *Sports Report*'s basement studio in Broadcasting House, who all answer to one name: 'Aveyougotbothamontheline; andcuttherugbytape; andfoundoutwhere bobbyrobsonis; andcheckedthetorquay kickoff; andclearedthetapemachines; andtimedtheforeignnews; andwritten thetenniscue; andwhythehellnot'. Without this back-up team, as well as the Mensa-folk at the control panel and the collective 'delight' of girls who are the bridge between the studio and the outside action men, the seats of the presenter and producer would collapse like old deckchairs.

Problems there are: every *Sports Report* reporter has his tales of equipment that wouldn't work, lights that went out, scripts that blew away, cars that broke down, gatemen who refused entry, keys that disappeared and lifts that stopped between floors. As Raymond Glendenning once said: 'If Sean O'Casey had ever been in the *Sports Report* studio I'd know for sure where he got the idea for his famous curtain line "the whole world's in a terrible state of chassis" '. Perfection, never, but always a good companion. We'll settle for that.

'They turned down Sloame Street, and the warm windows cast light patches on to the pavement between the blobs of the street lamps. The same tune muffled through the walls as they passed from house to house, fading then swelling between the space of each lighted window.

"Hey up, Dad, that's *Sports Report*, I'll race you" '.

(From Barry Hines' novel *The Blinder*)

Angus Mackay

Patrick Collins

The *Mail on Sunday*'s perceptive observer
of the sporting scene, Patrick Collins
worked as reporter or columnist for the
Kentish Mercury, the *Sunday Citizen*, the
News of the World, the *London Evening
News* and the *London Evening Standard*.
He was a Charlton Athletic zealot − until
they left the Valley − and is a regular
contributor to *Sports Report*.

In the beginning was the tune. Nothing special, just a few bars to establish a mood and trigger a hundred images in a million minds. Strange things, tunes. Even today, some of us cannot hear tumbling strings pour out 'With a Song in my Heart' without sniffing the roast beef of Sunday lunch and waiting for Cliff to ask Jean about the weather in Cologne; and who, of a certain age, can listen to a harp without anticipating the cut-glass vowels of Mrs Dale, eternally worrying about Jim?

So a radio programme has to have a signature tune. And at 3.30 p.m. on the afternoon of 3 January 1948, with the first edition of *Sports Report* just two hours away, Angus Mackay was still searching for his melody. He was saved by a call from the BBC Gramophone Library. Would Mr Mackay care to consider a rather catchy march called 'Out of the Blue' from the pen of one Hubert Bath? Indeed he would. Dee-dum, dee-dum, dee-dum, dee-dum, dee diddley dum dee-daaah! Thank you very much, that'll do nicely. He didn't know it then, but Mackay had just invented Saturday tea-time: burning toast, nibbled finger-nails and watching the newsprint soaking up the ink as you scribbled the football results in the columns of the morning papers (kick off three o'clock unless otherwise stated). Over the next 24 years, Mackay was to take a steady stream of decisions. Some misfired and many were inspired, but the one which secured his place in broadcasting history came out of the blue on a January afternoon. That brave little tune had set the tone. A mountain of talent, industry, original thinking and cussed determination would ensure that the tone was maintained.

Angus Mackay was not the most obvious choice to fashion the programme which would set the standard for sports broadcasting in this country. As a young Edinburgh journalist, he had run the sports department of the *Scotsman* newspaper, but when he joined the Corporation in 1936,

sport was so highly regarded by the prevailing powers that no sports news was allowed to be transmitted before 6.15 p.m. It was not until October 1947 that he was asked, by the first assistant to the Controller of the Light Programme, if he would 'care to try his hand at putting a sports programme out on the air at 5.30 p.m.' He described his reaction to the invitation in untypically lyrical terms: 'New fields to explore and profit by, risks to be met and taken; above all, something new, something with the taste of adventure to it'. He accepted immediately.

In this age of instant media miracles, we see nothing difficult or strange in assembling such a programme in such a space of time. Mackay is the man largely responsible for shaping our attitudes. In the short months of preparation he toured the BBC regions to ask for help and co-operation. 'Most certainly', they said, 'Why not? That's what we're here for, old boy.' Then they told him that he hadn't a hope in hell of getting it on the air by 5.30. They were still singing the same song on the evening of 3 January, when a gramophone record revolved and Hubert Bath's little tune blasted out and Raymond Glendenning welcomed the world to *Sports Report*.

Despite the scepticism of orthodox broadcasters, Mackay was working in the ideal era for a radio sports pioneer. In the late 'forties and early 'fifties, the public appetite for sport was at its most voracious. Never before and certainly never since were so many sports watched by so many people. The newspapers attempted to satisfy this appetite within the austere constraints of newsprint rationing, and the age saw the development of a more vital and colourful school of sports writing. But with radio's advantage of immediacy, its ability to add flesh to the bare bones of sporting legend and the scope which it offered for debate and discussion, the possibilities for a sports newspaper of the airwaves were obvious and appealing.

All that was needed to translate opportunity into reality was a man with the instincts of a journalist and the organising talents of a Field Marshal. Mackay was fortunate in possessing these gifts. He also had the low cunning of a natural politician. Cliff Morgan, who worked for and with him in later years, still marvels at his ability to cajole and persuade. 'He was amazing with the technical people', says Morgan. 'That's what made *Sports Report*, the way they made radio do what they wanted. Angus didn't really know how things worked, but he knew how he wanted to tell the story. So he used to challenge engineers. He'd say to them: "You can't do that, can you? That's not possible, is it?" And they'd go away thinking: "I'll bloody show you what's possible". It was like watching a good rugby captain at work. He surrounds himself with people who are all better than he is at their own job and he gets them at it. They know he's using them, but they love it.'

That talent was exercised repeatedly in the initial years of trial and error. Reports had to be delivered from studios, so only those grounds which were within a fast drive of a BBC studio could be considered for coverage. Mackay found himself apologising to clubs like Stoke, Preston, Derby and Middlesbrough, all of which were out of range. 'Unfortunately', he said, 'we have a few blind spots.' Those blind spots, and the primitive technology which caused them, would continue to enrage him, but he learned a little more with every passing year and every passing programme. He wanted *Sports Report* to be busier, more urgent and crammed with more information. So while he chipped away at the prevailing technology, he also began to attack reporting techniques. Every man who worked with Mackay swears that his god was his stopwatch. If people could only be trained to conform to his timings, a programme could be shaped and formed to something like his ideal. He encountered opposition, but he made them conform.

Within a very few years, he became slightly contemptuous of his previous efforts. 'I often look back on those early editions of *Sports Report* with some amusement', he said. 'In 1948 we used to think we were putting on fast, slick shows. In those days we used to give as much as two and a half minutes to a report on a soccer match, and we got what we deserved – flowery, well-padded stories which contained a good deal of wholly unnecessary information.' He used to say that in one minute anyone could tell any story about any event and he enforced the directive with complete ruthlessness. In time, a whole generation of sports broadcasters would be grateful for his insistence on being spare, lean and accurate with the language. David Coleman spoke for many when he said 'Angus built a stopwatch into my brain'.

The programme quickly forged its own personality, just as quickly reaped an audience – in the pre-television days of the early 'fifties it was regularly heard by around 12 million people – and within three years of its birth it discovered its own distinctive voice. In December 1950, it acquired a new presenter. And for the next 13 years, the sound of *Sports Report* was the gentle Dublin drawl of Eamonn Andrews.

Eamonn was regarded as Mackay's representative on earth, a brilliant natural broadcaster who understood his producer's mind, could instantly interpret his whims and collaborated to the comma with his *Sports Report* scripts. It was an unlikely alliance; the stern, methodical Scot and the affably engaging Irishman. But the chemistry was perfect and the results were stunning. The essential service of reports and statistics was never disregarded, but a newspaper of the airwaves consists of more than a back page, and one of the great strengths of the programme became its willingness to air controversy and encourage strong opinion. Mackay gleefully crammed his studio with Fleet Street's finest; Peter Wilson, J. L. Manning, Geoffrey Green and

a host of men with agile minds and golden tongues. And they would spin their stories and press their arguments while Andrews nudged the whole thing along with the chuckle of a man who knew just what a stir he was creating.

There were times when Mackay would present on a single programme four or five of Fleet Street's biggest names. The *Sports Report* staff never could understand how he worked the trick, for at that time the financial inducements were underwhelming. Mackay never revealed his secret. 'Get them on the phone', he would say. 'Tell them it's Angus. They'll come for me.' And they did. Every week.

By now, the time of the programme had expanded to an hour, between 5.00 and 6.00. The scope and stature had also expanded, and bright young men were eager to join the successful team. Vincent Duggleby, now a power in the BBC's Finance Unit, was attracted to radio sport by Mackay's reputation as a brilliant programme maker. 'The trick was to find somebody in the old guard at the BBC who was receptive to new ideas', he says. 'And Angus had been having the best ideas over the years. He was the one who pushed along the SOOBE, Self Operated Outside Broadcast Equipment. It was a briefcase which you took along to a match, plugged into a telephone point and it connected to the Post Office and thence to Broadcasting House. No more rushing for studios; you could do the job from any ground. He also cut a telephone in half and invented the system whereby the presenter could talk to the producer. Very simple, of course – once somebody had done it.

'Of course, he could be difficult. Any autocrat is difficult. We couldn't stand him at times, but we never stopped learning from him. He had his blind spots. He clung to what he knew in his later years. He couldn't stand minor sports, for instance. It was as well he departed before snooker really arrived, and I can't imagine what he would have made of something like darts! But he extended the medium, he made demands on it. And his techniques would survive today. I can't think of another programme maker of his era of whom you could say that.'

It was radio's fortune that Mackay resisted repeated attempts to involve him in the emerging world of television sport. 'Paul Fox tried very hard to take him when he was Head of BBC Sport,' recalls Cliff Morgan, 'but he turned them down. I think he loved the spoken work too much to be distracted by pictures. But Fox had a great regard for him. He always said that you know something has real class when you worry about it. You found yourself saying: "What are those radio buggers doing today?"He always made sure he knew what Angus was doing.'

Amid all the tributes to his ability, certain words pepper the conversation of his former colleagues when they speak of Mackay. Words like 'difficult', 'awkward' and, most frequently, 'cantankerous'. The picture emerges of a man who was respected, admired and sometimes even feared – but not a man who was generally loved.

Respect there certainly was and if he could not be loved then he would settle for the admiration due to a genuine innovator. Bob Burrows, now Head of Sport for Thames Television, who followed Mackay as producer of *Sports Report*, recalls with some awe the number of developments which Mackay ushered through. 'Radio cars were largely down to Angus. Now we can do pictures as well as sound from them, but it took him to come up with the idea. The first major programme from abroad was when Eamonn linked the whole of *Sports Report* from the States. Now we think nothing of putting someone in front of a camera in Sarajevo and having him say: "Good evening and welcome and here are the football results". The old boy started it and loads of other things that the public wouldn't be aware of – hot-lines in the studio so the producer could have information at his fingertips, and closed circuit screens that the presenter could read in the bowels of Broadcasting House while the information was being flashed through from five floors above.

'He was always a pioneer, always searching for ways to push back the old frontiers. And he did it all in one golden hour between five and six. You just had to be around him to pick things up. He was always coming out with little phrases, catchphrases that made his point. "Beware of the specialist" he'd say. And he was right in some ways. Sometimes the experts can start talking for other experts. The producer can't afford that. He has to aim for the widest possible audience. Angus always relied on his gut feeling. Where sport was concerned, he was a layman who wanted to be entertained and informed. He was an outstanding teacher. Sometimes I feel sorry that the young radio journalists of today don't get the same kind of training that we had from Angus.'

But even Burrows, the heir-apparent, suffered from that stubborn cussedness right up to Mackay's final show in 1972. 'He insisted that there should be no fuss, no Press, no publicity', says Burrows. 'Dick Tracey did manage to do a short interview for the PM programme with him, which may well be why they finished up making him Minister for Sport. But, apart from that, Angus wanted to slip away quietly. The problem was that everybody wanted to say goodbye. The place was packed: Alan Hardaker, Denis Follows, Fred Perry, Jim Wicks, Henry Cooper. They all turned out for him. We got a crate of Champagne in. After all, *Sport Report* was his baby. He invented it and he'd been running it for 24 years. It was the least we could do. I sent a couple of bottles upstairs to the sports room, and that really upset him. When he came in to clear away on Monday, he gave me a real rocket. 'But the lads have been working their socks off on this programme', I said. 'They deserve it.' He wouldn't have it. He didn't like drink around the place and he didn't like all this fuss and nonsense. That was the way he was. He could reduce you to tears, then be amazed to find you crying.

'Extraordinary man. He had a lasting effect on everybody who ever worked for him. You always know people who worked with Angus because they remember his rules. Sometimes I'm sitting in a television studio with Brian Moore and we're going through the final preparations for a show and we'll start bouncing the old phrases off each other: "Attention to detail . . . check and double-check . . . you're only as good as your last programme." All phrases that Angus used all the time. All bloody good sense.'

Angus Mackay now enjoys a contented retirement at his home in Middlesex. He still shuns publicity, declines interviews and wonders why anybody should want to remember a radio producer. But he has left his honourable mark on the medium. And if he should ever wish to be reminded of his achievement, then he has only to switch on a radio any Saturday afternoon at 5.00 p.m.

These radio times may have changed. Cliff has married his Jean and Mrs Dale has long since closed her diary, but Angus Mackay's baby is marching towards its half-century, to a familiar tune from the pen of Hubert Bath.

A New Way

John Arlott

The voice of cricket for more than 30 years, John Arlott's last Test Match commentary was at Lord's in 1980 – and England and Australia stopped play to applaud him. He took part in the first *Sports Report* and did football commentary the same afternoon. A former policeman and 12th man for Hampshire, he is a *Guardian* correspondent, prolific author, poet, wine expert and collector.

It is difficult for any man to think he is making history yet, in a minor way, those who first made *Sports Report* were creating radio history. The whole development of British broadcasting was now passing into a third phase.

The first had been the tentative, almost consciously upper-middle-class broadcasting from the grass roots. The number of Old Etonians and Old Harrovians of the early days indicates its respectability; and they were indeed innovators with impeccable accents. They were the people who launched the early groping attempts at sports broadcasting when the soccer or rugby commentator had at his elbow an assistant who interpolated the number of the 'square' in which play was taking place. That 'square' number corresponded to one marked in a plan of the ground printed in the *Radio Times*. Already, too, Sir 'Plum' Warner had launched his authoritatively descriptive cricket broadcasts.

The second phase of broadcasting came with the Second World War; and, if anyone asks what this has to do with *Sports Report*, the answer is everything. The men sending back the stories of battle − people of all nationalities including Ed Morrow, Frank Gillard, Wynford Vaughan-Thomas and Stanley Maxted − were not concerned with the politeness of the mannered broadcast, but with action, violence and death. They were the people who changed broadcasting, who gave it urgency, on-the-moment drama and yet also the common touch. It helped, immeasurably, of course, that they happened to be superb natural broadcasters. Essentially, though, a new way had been cut to the listener's consciousness.

So, for those who were to broadcast in time of peace, a new formula had been created. Essentially this was so in the case of outside broadcasts, of ceremonial and great State occasions but, most of all, of sport. Here a new technique had to be created, and *Sports Report* was to inherit much of it. 3 January 1948: what a mixed

bag. The first edition of *Sports Report* − in the Light Programme − appeared in *Radio Times* directly opposite the Home Programme's *Saturday Sports Review*, introduced by Lionel Marson − remember him? He could never have been on the Light Programme.

Already much was happening that was new; there were no more 'squares' in the soccer or rugby commentaries and a more informal manner was already filtering into sports broadcasting. There was now no limitation, or virtually none, on social or economic grounds to the possession of a radio, or, as we called them then, a wireless set. Sport was already the common property of all the people and the BBC − then, despite the elementary phase of television, effectively the only broadcasting voice in Britain − reflected that fact. *Sports Report* arrived because there was a social demand for it. The contributors to the first programme were a typical BBC mixture of the time, established experienced broadcasters and newcomers feeling their way, the old style and the new. To introduce it Angus Mackay used Raymond Glendenning, already known to a wide listening public as a commentator on racing and football; an extremely ample gentleman with a splendid moustache and a Welsh, sporting and broadcasting background. There were special reports on two soccer matches: Portsmouth against Huddersfield by the present writer (then wide-eyed and raw); and Manchester City against Aston Villa by Alan Clarke, a Londoner with a very quick mind well stored with soccer knowledge. He too, was a post-War broadcaster and another eager learner. In the Scottish League the match was Rangers versus Dundee; Frank Shaw covered the England-Australia Rugby Union International and that was the end of the first-hand action reports. Peter Wilson, newspaper man and son of a newspaper man, and who had lately reported the Joe Louis against 'Jersey Joe' Walcott fight, talked about events and personalities in United States sport; Alan Hoby argued in favour of part-time payments to athletes. The whole lot lasted only half an hour, and the arrangements were ad hoc. Broadcasting was not yet capable of a high standard in such activity. Neither, to tell the truth, were the performers, but the challenge was immense, and so was the excitement.

In the early days the programme and certainly its contributors, owed a vast amount to the Outside Broadcast engineers; that fine race of under-estimated men of technical expertise and often, as the broadcasters had reason to expect, psychological wisdom.

There was much to be done in the studio itself. The first introducer, Raymond Glendenning, was a highly professional broadcaster, but there was always a suggestion that he did not enjoy the part of introducer or compere so much as that of performer. Angus also hauled in George Allison, one of the first and best of football's broadcasting voices, later Arsenal's manager, and a wise man of the game. He was not, though, an accustomed broadcaster and he was lost – as he admitted – in the attempt to direct the somewhat frantic hurly-burly of ad lib broadcasting as part of a team. There was, too, Stewart MacPherson, whose Canadian accent gave

George Allison, BBC Radio's first football commentator in 1927, Herbert Chapman's successor as manager of Arsenal in 1934 and – just once – presenter of Sports Report.

an air of liveliness to his broadcasting. He went back to North America, having done much to increase the tempo of this type of broadcasting in Britain.

Eamonn Andrews, however, was exactly the man Angus needed. They were friends from the start. In Broadcasting House they would bet on which lift arrived first to take them to the studio floor, and they found Saturday nights hectic, but fun. Eamonn could take, relish, interpret and carry out everything that Angus barked into his earphones and still retain the ability to grin back at him through the glass wall of the goldfish bowl. This was undoubtedly the partnership that established *Sports Report*. It was based on understanding and quick thinking in the studio, which was essential.

Out on the road, life was different. In those learning days, the contributor used to chase from his football match to – if he was lucky – an established studio; he was relatively lucky if he could use a minor, unmanned studio like the one in the back of the Civic Building at Portsmouth. He could, though, find himself baffled when he had to find the New Forest transmitter. Perhaps, however, even that was preferable to being told to make it from the Charlton Athletic ground at The Valley, or from Millwall, to Broadcasting House at an alarming speed. So far as memory serves, no one was ever pinched for speeding. Indeed, when the pressure was intense, the police used to be raked in to provide an escort for the hard-pressed reporter.

There were several different types of contributors: the outside reporter, dashing to a microphone to hustle his hot news over the air; the talker who would discuss a situation authoritatively; and, finally, the personality, from a world champion at any kind of sport to a man who had just made news.

As time wore on Angus, above all, but everybody concerned in varying degrees found some sort of confidence, a professional certainty. The whole programme ceased to be a tentative if stimulating struggle and began to look and feel like a professional operation. Many of the contributors – certainly this writer – had a baptism of fire and learned some highly salutary lessons. The first of them was about time-making after matches, perhaps best described as the 'getaway'. A match with a 3.15 kick-off, frequent at that time, would finish somewhere about five o'clock. That left half an hour, at best, to get to Broadcasting House. The only way to do that, however good your car, was to have a perfect parking place – and there are precious few of those outside London football grounds – and to run on the last kick and be away before all the other motors in the district. Often that meant more work before the match than afterwards. It was part of the stress and the excitement of the job.

It is all too easy to look back on the advance of the programme without realising its growing pains. It is not simple, either, to allocate or evaluate the credits for the achievement; for achievement it was, the creation of an instant report on the day's sport every Saturday evening. Nobody knew quite how it was to be done, but Angus Mackay was determined it would be. The BBC's reporters were not used to this kind of haste. The complete report delivered in minutes was something new. No single person can take credit for the fact that it eventually became a smooth and balanced exercise, but in the beginning was Angus Mackay.

He was determined, flexible and at heart, a perfectionist. He respected professionals of all kinds, and it may be that his major triumph was his equal acceptance of professional broadcasters and professional journalists. He himself had one advantage: unlike many producers he never had, or at least never showed, any ambition to broadcast himself. Thus he was always an objective critic of those who worked with him. He listened to the programme as it was made, and afterwards to a recording, and he knew exactly what he was putting out. It was broadcasting in the making, though it is doubtful if Angus himself ever saw it quite in that light or indeed as anything more than a job. It may sound silly now, but this was the first example of 'instant' sports news being broadcast in Britain and it attracted a very considerable audience. The ultimate evaluation of *Sports Report* is the simplest possible: it succeeded.

The Mackay made no gestures nor postures. He simply wanted a good programme, and because of that he made one. It must also be remembered that he was a good 'picker', and in Eamonn Andrews he unerringly put his finger on the person he needed. From that point onwards *Sports Report* prospered. It is many years since Eamonn asked this writer in Dublin if there was any point in coming to London as a broadcaster. Having heard him there was no doubt that he had a natural broadcasting talent. 'Come!' was the only possible response. Surely enough, he turned up, modest, but quick and perceptive; a natural talker, a man who talked to people not at them. He took the best that people offered while filtering out the rough. He made his interviewees and reporters feel at ease and among his regular colleagues he made many friends. The Mackay-Andrews partnership was the foundation of *Sports Report*. Many others were picked up, and some lost along the way, but this pair sustained the programme at its centre. The two, Scot and Irishman, conferred, deeply and generally perceptively, and it was their joint judgement – with Angus having the final word – which maintained the form of this indestructible programme.

One of the programme's greatest achievements was its blend of broadcasters, a mixed bag that proved highly satisfying to the consumer. There was splendid and intuitively balanced variety, often with unexpected surprises. Joe Davis came to talk about snooker and to hand out splendid

invitations to come and play with him on one of his tables at Chesterfield, which seemed like an accolade to a struggling and indifferent snooker player.

There was Donnie – H. D. – Davies, 'Old International' of the *Guardian* (he won amateur international soccer caps for England) who, with no broadcasting background (he was a schoolmaster and spare-time journalist) became a master of the short broadcast. More often than not he did his reports on Manchester United or City or international matches. Between ground and studio he would create a splendidly poised and polished essay which, unusual in such efforts, sounded right. He was one of the unlucky people killed in the Manchester United air crash. The other Davies, A. T., was a Newcastle man who reported soccer, often with an unhappy story about his local side, with a splendid sense of humour and, when the opportunity presented itself – as with the great Newcastle triumphs – in an absolute paean of triumph. Arthur Appleton was, in age at least, his junior as the voice of north-eastern soccer, a thoughtful reporter with a passionate feeling for his region and a generous understanding of football and footballers.

Teddy Eden was the wise man of the soccer discussions. He was a member of the FA Council and he spoke with authority, understanding and immense wisdom not merely about the players, but about those who strove to administer the game.

Rex Alston covered cricket, rugby and athletics. He had been a Cambridge athletics Blue, a minor county cricketer for Bedfordshire and was highly knowledgeable about rugby; a courteous and thoughtful man with a most kindly broadcasting voice. Max Robertson, one of the doyens of broadcasting, began in Australia in 1938 and he still continues with his immensely informed talk on lawn tennis, and, of course, he branched out many years ago into highly informed broadcasting about an

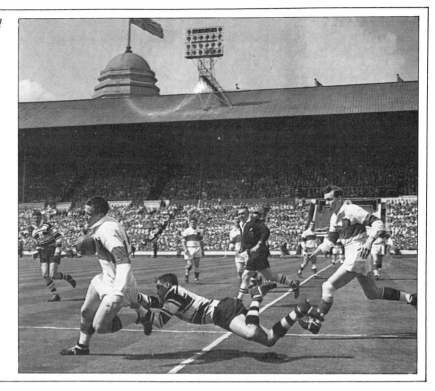

Neil Fox of Wakefield Trinity in full stride, but about to lose his shorts, during the 1960 Rugby League Challenge Cup final at Wembley. Wakefield beat Hull 38–5 and Fox contributed a record 20 points (seven goals, two tries).

extremely wide range of antiques. Henry Longhurst was the ultimate natural sports broadcaster. He talked without effort or condescension, with utter ease and friendliness, about golf and life. He was a great asset to after-broadcast sessions when every man drank his own tipple.

Freddie Mills sometimes came as something of a shock with his gritty voice and New Forest accent but he talked a lot of good sense, especially about boxing, and he had, too, a fine if acid sense of humour. Bill McGowran, for many years joint occupant of all too small an office at the *Evening News*, had a splendid Derbyshire accent, a dry wit and a wide knowledge of sport. He was a good friend and a wise man.

One of the major figures of after-programme parties was Peter Wilson. He had been to university yet retained a common touch, a man who maintained enthusiasm magnificently. It took little to spark him off and wherever he went he illuminated the scene. Another early recruit to the programme was Peter West,

courteous, keen, sincerely interested, especially in cricket; one of those who serves the game well through his sympathy with those who play it. Like Brian Johnston, he became deeply involved in the game which does, above all, offer involvement in depth.

Jim (J. L.) Manning was consciously and always a news man. He would argue a case for a cause but never go back on his own, often passionate, beliefs. He could sometimes seem a hard-boiled journalist but much of his heart lay in sport. The same was true of Bill Hicks, a sympathetic, creative and helpful sports editor of the old *News Chronicle*. His splendid West Country accent echoed superbly round the *Sports Report* studio and for years afterwards his wisdom in sporting journalism helped young writers in their careers.

One of the oldest and sagest of them all was Charlie Buchan, who in his day had been a world-class football player. By the time he came to *Sports Report* he was an elder statesman of the game and sometimes, after a programme, he would talk with the rest about players and matches not only before their experience but, in my case, before their birth. He was a perceptive but kindly critic who would say contentedly enough: 'You see the game has gone on since my day but, you know, there are some standards you can never forget, however modern you are'. His wisdom helped many and added depth to the entire programme. Jack Crump was another of the wise elders. He had been long enough in British athletics to savour many of its great triumphs but also to suffer many of its setbacks. He assessed his sport without bitterness and with infinite understanding.

So the programme ebbed and flowed; contributors came and went but, because broadcasting always reflects the society it records, *Sports Report* changed as the rest of broadcasting – and life – caught up with it. Many of the early contributors used to think themselves hard done by when they were allowed only two and a half minutes to describe a football match. Soon, though, the Mackay operation perceived that many even of those 150 seconds consisted of padding. So, instead of four two-and-a-half minute reports they took in eight one-and-a-quarter minute pieces, cutting out the fluff but still maintaining the standard of information.

Let us face it and enjoy it. *Sports Report* has been value for money: hard, early and well-selected news above all but also good talk and good entertainment. It has changed now in length and placing but it has never forsaken its original purpose or quality. We raise a glass to it as the old contributors used to do every Saturday night in the 'Gluepot', encouraged and accompanied by Angus Mackay, Eamonn Andrews and many more of us who no longer have to make those furious after-match journeys.

Heavenly Hell

Eamonn Andrews

'*Sports Report*: introduced by Eamonn Andrews and produced by Angus Mackay' – a renowned partnership for a dozen years. Eamonn Andrews was also BBC Radio's boxing commentator. He is now a household television celebrity and the central pillar of such popular programmes as *What's My Line* and *This is Your Life*.

When to the sessions of sweet silent thought I summon up remembrance of *Sports Report* things don't stay silent for long. The earpiece of memory begins to crackle with the hoarse baritone of Angus Mackay and, very often simultaneously, with one of dozens of other voices of less measured tread and the upward pitch of front-line reporting.

Rumour had it, when I was Angus's marionette (I prefer Action Man) fronting that famous programme, that I not only had two earpieces during the live transmissions but that Angus was researching the practical possibilities of a third. Certainly it was no rumour that, in addition to the electronic input, he would also send in, from his control panel position, scribbled notes containing cryptic information, or an instruction to be prepared to change direction. Latterly, he conceded one tiny inch to visual advances in communication and installed a screen on my desk on which he could scribble even more messages.

If there could be such a thing as heavenly hell, this was it; and, although my sufferings at times were enormous, my happiness was immeasurable. You will read elsewhere about that impatient, intolerant, dictatorial Editor with the prudishness of his Scottish forebears and the ruthlessness of his English empire-building colleagues. For he truly built an empire in sports information and, with knowledge and cunning and sometimes bluff, he coaxed to our microphone the keenest sportsmen and sports writers of at least four continents.

It seemed to me that every Fleet Street reporter of note was pushing in the queue to get on *Sports Report*. It certainly wasn't for the money (Angus took good care of his masters' purse) so it must have been the pleasure or the pride or both. Angus treated them all as if he was a tough but benevolent headmaster, maintaining a strict discipline in the classroom but quite prepared to relax and become one of the boys in the pub or the club afterwards.

I can still see Peter Wilson of the *Daily Mirror* – the Man They Couldn't Gag – most reluctantly handing over, before transmission, his script on some set piece (as opposed to the free-wheeling discussions) and hovering over Angus's shoulder, fists clenched tightly, wincing theatrically but realistically each time Angus's sharply-pointed pencil struck out a word or a sentence or a phrase. It was the first time I ever realised that moustaches *do* actually bristle. Afterwards, if the surgery had been too great for Peter's dignity, we would have the pop, pop, pop of argument in the pub and Peter would soothe his jumping ulcer with his one-time favourite drink, a Velvet Hammer (whiskey and milk).

Picturing that pub now, I can see another prima donna of *Sports Report*, a boxing writer rival of Peter's, Bill McGowran of the *London Evening News*, both, alas, no more. Bill and Peter would vie with each other on many counts but, very often, on who had travelled further in search of his sporting lore. It was considered a measure of one's importance in the Street how ready your Editor was to send you to the far corners and spurn the wire services, no matter how prestigious. Peter and Bill would face up to each other in The Cock Tavern, or wherever, moustache to moustache – Peter, the deceptively benevolent-looking walrus, Bill, the dandy with the waxed ends and the knowledge that the *Evening News* budget could never hope to match the *Mirror*'s. One evening in the pub, Bill casually placed his travel bag on the floor. It was covered from stem to stern with labels from around the world – or seemingly from around the world. Peter eyed the bag. His pale, plump cheeks squeezed into crumples of contempt, the cigarette-holder trembled as he pointed to the bag.

'You were never in Nicaragua. I recognise that label. You bought it in Smith's!'

I think Bill left and refused to drink with any of us for at least a week.

Sports Report 1960. Left to right: Jacob de Vries, Bill Hicks (Sports Editor of the News Chronicle), Angus Mackay, Gerald Sinstadt, Barrington Dalby (steward of the British Board of Boxing Control and BBC expert summariser), Eamonn Andrews and Cliff Morgan.

The *Daily Mail* produced two Sports Editors who became very closely identified with *Sports Report*: Bill Hicks and Jim Manning. Bill Hicks, whose main interests were soccer and golf, professionally and personally in that order, probably broadcast on *Sports Report* more often than any other reporter. (They were all 'reporters' to Angus. Lord Reith could have checked in a piece on 'Ladies Hockey except on Sunday' and have received no greater nomenclature.)

I don't have any records from which to check but I'm pretty sure I'm right about Bill Hicks. Certainly, had he been less independently-minded, there could be no doubt. They were both good Sports Editors and Bill would not be browbeaten by Angus. When they disagreed about angles or interpretations, it would frequently result in a silent impasse. Bill would, therefore, in effect be barred from the programme because Angus would not pick up the telephone to invite him the following week. How long Bill was off the airwaves would depend upon whether it was a matter as passionate as the Football Association versus the Football League, or something less fundamental and soul-searing, such as Rugby League's relationship with Rugby Union, or professionalism at Wimbledon. Frequently, in this and other such disputes, I would quietly play the role of peacemaker, bound, in the long run, to get thanks from neither side but, at least, to get some such respected pontificator back on the air without wounding anybody's dignity and without impossible kiss-and-make-up routines.

Jim Manning – J. L. Manning to his readers and his voters – was a different kettle of quills. Jim was always full of causes and Welsh passion. Angus used to sneer at him about leaving his White Charger outside the pub and Jim would never, ever rise to the bait but accept it all with a flow of rhetoric as if he had just been tapped upon the left shoulder by a royal sword. Jim and his lovely wife Amy (most of those guys had beautiful wives, now that I come to think of it) used occasionally to drop in with their daughters, one of whom grew up to be that talented and delightful actress Katy Manning. Jim, who as Sports Editor of the *Sunday Dispatch* sent me to Moscow to cover the first English amateur boxing team that went there, is someone I remember with a great deal of affection and amusement. I remember that when television was beginning to move into sport in a serious way the BBC was still clinging to the outward belief that horseracing was the Sport of Kings and not of punters. Therefore, some idiot upstairs decreed that, while BBC viewers could see the races and read the results, they could not be made

Daley Thompson, perhaps the finest all-round athlete of all. He dominated the decathlon in the Olympics and World and European Championships during the 1980s.

aware of the prices. This continued for some short time after the advent of ITV, who, of course, ruthless, commercial and realistic, gave *all* the prices. The effect of this was that it was possible to watch a race on BBC, switch to ITV, who would be covering a rival track, and who in addition to giving results and prices at that track would also flash up the prices at other meetings – including those covered by the BBC. In other words, by adroit channel-changing, you could get all the races and all the prices despite the BBC embargo. Jim's description of one afternoon so spent, sitting in his armchair and leaping up to change channels (there were no remote controls in those days), was priceless. His complaint against the BBC was bitter and piteous.

'Three times in the one day', he said, 'I was savaged by my own dog!'

Hardly have I stopped chuckling at J. L. M. than into focus comes the face of Clifford Webb, one-time *Daily Herald* soccer writer, silver moustache, fresh cheeks, bright eyes, head cocked to one side and a racy – was it Cockney? – accent that could come only from a true sports reporter. Round that barrel in the old Cock Tavern, Cliff (dammit, he had a beautiful wife too!) was always ready to chip in his anecdote and send the laughs billowing up.

My favourite featured Lord Beaverbrook, in the latter days when he spent most of his time in the South of France and had his newspapers flown over daily so that he could bark back by telephone criticism or praise. On this particular day, the sports page caught his eagle eye and the mood was good. A soccer writer, let us call him John Smith, had written a dynamic story on a thrilling Cup semi-final. His Lordship summoned the Sports Editor to the phone in Fleet Street and was lyrical in his praise of the piece.

'That guy John Smith is the kind of reporter we need. Not only does he describe the game in the kind of dynamic way that takes the reader with him but he's able to get into the dressing-room afterwards and, as he says, into the very shower-bath itself. He can call Stanley Matthews by his first name and, what's even more important, have Stanley address him as John. That's the kind of thing the readers love. Give him a rise.'

'I'm sorry, sir, but I fired him this morning.'

'You *what?*'

'Yes, sir. He got the score wrong.'

During that time – as in the case of actors in a movie or a long-running play or explorers on a journey – sports reporting almost became our whole lives. We did everything to keep ourselves and the programme fresh. We hiked out to Pinewood Studios to interview Bob Hope and Bing Crosby on golf. I hammered on Gregory Peck's door at the Connaught Hotel on the rather slim grounds that he had an interest in a horse running in the Grand National and got a delightful, droll interview from that charming gent of the silver screen. Any connection, however tenuous, was jumped at by Angus. When the Ambling Alp, known to boxing historians as Primo Carnera, was cast by Carol Reed in the Wolf Mankowicz film *A Kid for Two Farthings*, Angus didn't care that he could hardly put together four words of English. He was invited to *Sports Report* and I was told to go and interview him. I can't remember what we got, but we got something, and even persuaded him to come round to the Tavern afterwards and try a half pint of bitter. He was a huge but gentle creature, not all that long for this world. In the course of conversation, I discovered that my old friend, the comedian Harold Berens, had been cast as his manager. Now this was good news. I'll tell you why. Harold, like so many funny men, tends to look on the greyer side of life when he's off stage. He's the one whose glass is always half empty. We were neighbours in Bayswater at that time and he shared parking facilities below the block of flats where I used to live. Frequently, returning home late on Saturday night, I'd bump into Harold and, at this particular time, he was going through a lean period and was more depressed than ever. Once or twice (Heaven and Harold forgive me) I actually made a point of dodging him. This particular Saturday night I had no fears. I was full of good news and, sure enough, there was Harold parking his car as I arrived. 'Great news, Harold. I've just been interviewing Carnera and heard about it. Carol Reed has cast you as the Manager. Congratulations. What a break.'

'Yes', said Harold, his black, liquid eyes surveying me mournfully, 'gotta be up at five o'clock every morning next week.'

Angus was one of the first to spot the young Cassius Clay in his capacity as poet. More than once, when we might have been short of light relief on *Sports Report*, he would start chasing the young fighter (and, when Angus started to chase, he never gave up) and get him on the end of a 'phone in Pittsburg or Pennsylvania or New York or wherever, have me interview him and talk him into delivering one of his seemingly effortless, if not exactly literary quatrains. It was all wonderful go. We were so naively enthusiastic that, at one stage, we corralled Kenneth Adam, boss of BBC Television, and tried to persuade him to install television cameras in Studio 4A on Saturday evenings, since we firmly believed there was no other sports programme in the world that mattered except *Sports Report* and that television shouldn't be deprived of it. I'm quite certain we felt deeply resentful when Peter Dimmock eventually headed BBC TV's own *Sports Review* from studios designed for such incidentals as cameras and lights and dollys and booms.

They were heady times. One of our ideas got me into a strange spot of bother. On the Saturday nearest the end of the year, we would clear out the furniture save for a stand microphone and my earpieces. Angus would feed in a continuous stream of sportsmen and women who had hit the headlines in the previous year. Once we had dealt with the hard news, they would form the rest of the programme. Coming forward at one stage, I saw the smiling, happy, innocent face of featherweight boxing champion Sammy McCarthy, who in later years, alas, had contests with the Law that kept him out of circulation. Lovely lad, nevertheless. We touched on his successes during the year and I asked what was next on the agenda, knowing full well that the answer was a contest in Belfast against Billy Kelly some time in February, at which both the British and Commonwealth titles would be at stake.

'Thank you and good luck, Sammy', and next came the smiling face of dear old Denis Compton with Tom Finney's elfin triangle just behind over his shoulder.

By the time February rolled round, December was little more than a blur. Barrington Dalby and myself headed for Belfast by boat because of a blizzard that hit most of the country and the airports. We got to the King's Hall, Belfast, with very little time to spare and, as we entered, I was greeted by a group that included many of my former colleagues from my amateur boxing days. I smiled a big smile and hailed a loud hello when, to my astonishment, one of them stepped forward and said 'You're a right . . . ing Irishman!'

'What *are* you talking about?'

'You wished Sammy McCarthy good luck!'

I had completely forgotten December's *Sports Report*.

Inside, I even had a few programmes thrown at me. They take their boxing very seriously in Belfast. Mind you, with a name like McCarthy, you'd have thought I'd have got away with it. As it was, they forgot about me later and turned their fury on Jimmy Wild, the Welsh wizard of yesteryear, The Ghost with a Hammer in His Hand who, having had a few balls of malt too many, climbed into the ring after the fight and said 'I could have beaten either of them with one hand'. Most of us had to hide under the ring after that while Jimmy was escorted out by the police.

Back to *Sports Report* the following Saturday: do you think there was a word of sympathy from Angus? You know, I would have blushed if there had been. It was never a place for soft talk. Ask any of the secretaries. Leaving to get married was about the only forgiveable excuse for desertion, and then only just.

40 Years of Football

Jimmy Armfield

Dashing full-back for Blackpool (1952–1971) and England (43 caps between 1959–66), and a former manager of Bolton and Leeds, Jimmy Armfield now works for the *Daily Express* and as expert summariser and reporter for BBC Radio.

Trevor Brooking

An inside forward of style and character for West Ham (1967–84) and England (47 caps), Trevor Brooking is now a businessman and an expert summariser for BBC Radio and Television. He is one of the most popular 'Happy Hammers'.

Ron Greenwood

Ron Greenwood is a former manager of West Ham United (1961–74) and England (1977–82) and was a sterling centre half for Bradford Park Avenue, Brentford, Chelsea, Fulham and England B. He is BBC Radio's expert at international matches.

Denis Law

One of Scottish football's folk heroes, Denis Law scored 30 goals in 55 internationals. His clubs were Huddersfield, Manchester City, Torino, Manchester United and Manchester City again. Now a BBC Radio expert summariser and a certifiable 'character'.

Football, when *Sports Report* first cast an eye on the game, was enjoying a wonderful boom. The total attendance at Football League matches in season 1947–48 was 40,259,130. Arsenal were the League champions and were followed by Portsmouth, who won the title twice. There were 88 clubs in the League with more than 4,000 players – on a maximum wage of £12 a week. The FA Cup was won in 1948 by Manchester United who beat Blackpool 4–2 in one of the most entertaining finals of all. The 40 years since are discussed by BBC Radio's four regular experts: Jimmy Armfield, Trevor Brooking, Ron Greenwood and Denis Law.

Greenwood:

Those 40 years are full of memories and, in fact, the 1947–48 season gave me one of the most marvellous afternoons of my life. I was captain of Bradford Park Avenue and in the third round of the FA Cup – on the second Saturday of *Sports Report* – we beat Arsenal 1–0 at Highbury. We were just a middle-of-the-road Second Division side and Arsenal were a great outfit, with players like Joe Mercer, Archie Macaulay, Jimmy Logie and Leslie Compton, and went on to win the championship by seven points. It was the first time most of us had been to Highbury but we had 1,500 Bradford fans there, all singing 'On Ilkley Moor Bar Tat' at the top of their voices, and we played the game of our lives. It seems unreal now, but on the day we were the better side. That's the beauty of the FA Cup.

Armfield:

I'd have loved to have been in that Blackpool side at Wembley in 1948, but Stanley Matthews and Stan Mortensen were still going strong when I joined them in the early 'fifties. I remember playing for the A team on the day Blackpool beat Spurs in the 1953 semi-finals, and somebody had a radio which stole the show. Everybody was listening

and we might have been playing on the moon for all the attention that was paid to us. I was playing on the wing to start with and actually scored a couple of goals, but then our right back got injured and limped off (probably to listen to the radio!) and I switched to his position. And from that day on I never played anywhere else. I stood on the terraces with one or two other Blackpool youngsters for the final itself, the great 'Stanley Matthews final' and when it was all over and Blackpool had come back from the dead to beat Bolton 4–3, I clearly remember thinking to myself: 'if this is football I want to be in it'.

Law:

1953 was a bit special for me as well, because I got my first football boots for Christmas. They were Hotspur boots with big ankle protectors and as hard as brick, and I remember sitting on the sink with my feet in a basin of water to soften the leather. I was only 13 and I could hardly believe my luck because there was no money to spare at home; and, in fact, even though my father was dead against credit, my mother had secretly joined one of those credit schemes with one of the big Aberdeen stores and I got my boots that way. The boots had to be hidden from my father, otherwise he would have found out about the credit. That was the best present I ever had.

Brooking:

I've got to admit I didn't listen too carefully to *Sports Report* early on because we were both born in the same year, 1948, but I remember the early days of television. We had a little black and white set at home with just BBC1 on it. No football, though, which was probably why I didn't watch very much. But I always saw *Quatermass*.

Armfield:

I played in the first League match which was televised live. It was Blackpool against Bolton on a Friday evening in

35

1960, with Billy Wright doing the commentary, and it was such a bad match, really awful, that plans to do a 'live' game every Friday were promptly forgotten. We lost 1−0 and I think for just about the first time our gate dropped below 20,000. They'd love a crowd that big now, but in those days it wasn't very good. Football and television live together all right these days, but I think it was television that took away a bit of the mystique from the game. Television drops the game into everybody's front room. Players are like regular visitors.

Greenwood:

In the old days the supporters never saw a visiting player unless they went along to their local club to watch him. They saw the big stars once a year. Now, on the box, they see them regularly. It's all part of the social change. When I was playing for Chelsea in 1955, when we won the Championship, I used to travel from South Harrow down to Stamford Bridge by train and I got to know a lot of our supporters. Players were just ordinary members of the community then. They were known as individuals. These days, though, players turn up in their big cars, do their job and then drive off to their big homes. It's split the community.

Armfield:

You're going to laugh at this but in my first two or three seasons as a First Division player with Blackpool I used to go to the ground on my bike. Except on Saturdays − when I used to walk! We lived about a mile from Bloomfield Road and I just used to join the fans on their way to the match, squeeze over the bridge with them − sometimes so many

Blackpool's Cup, 2 May 1953. Captain Harry Johnston and hero Stanley Matthews are chaired around Wembley. Stanley Mortensen, who contributed a hat-trick to the famous 4−3 defeat of Bolton, is on the right.

went over they had to stop the traffic − and then go off to change. That was the way it was.

Brooking:

I played my first senior game in the mid 'sixties and we used to travel everywhere by train, most clubs did, which meant that going up and coming back there was a chance to chat to supporters. But there was a gradual change later on and certain players and directors began to experience one or two heated exchanges with fans . Fair enough in one sense: if you'd had a bad game you'd be sure of getting some stick. So in the 'seventies clubs started travelling most places by coach. Economics was one reason, and hooliganism was another. Crowds became more demanding and, in a sense, this is why the modern players need a lot of character. They've got to suffer their bad games and all the stick and still look for the ball, still want it. There are lads now who're reluctant to go out at half-time because they're having a bad patch and the crowd is on their backs. It was all part of the hooligan thing which gradually deteriorated. Police, security, fences, video cameras, membership cards, the Heysel disaster in Belgium and so on. It's not just a football problem but a wider social issue. In the 1986−87 season there were signs of progress being made.

Law:

There has been a lot of other changes, too. Some big, some bigger than they seem, like the change in the ball. The old leather ones used to soak up water and mud and become so heavy that if you could make a corner reach the penalty area you were in the team.

Greenwood:

Stanley Cullis up at Wolverhampton used to soak the ball in water before a game.

Law:

Yes, you had to give the ball a tremendous whack to get it anywhere but now it's water resistant and lighter and

37

you can get the ball to go 40 yards with just a flick. It came in a bit later in Scotland – probably because we had a supply of the old balls to get rid of first!

Armfield:

Floodlights were one of the biggest steps forward. They started to be used in the middle 'fifties and I remember the difference they made very well. We used to play Cup replays on Wednesday afternoons, but floodlights meant night football and bigger crowds because people could get to a game after work. It seemed a bit strange at first and the lights weren't always brilliant, and there were arguments about it all. But everything in football is argued about before it's accepted and now, of course, it would be impossible to get along without lights.

Brooking:

The commercial side of the game has come on a lot. Sponsorship, lotteries, advertising and the rest. Clubs need money to survive: that's a fact of life. And so is television. We've got to be careful about over-exposure but, done the right way, television gives tremendous promotion to the game. The Americans discovered this a long time ago. It's all a question of balance.

Greenwood:

We mustn't forget the football itself. That's seen more changes than anything, almost season by season. Different methods, different techniques, different trends. And I've got to say that I don't like the way our professional game has gone. I spent my whole time as a manager doing my best to send out teams that gave pleasure. I've always believed, strongly, that football is as much about entertaining as winning and losing. I'm not going to claim that football isn't what it used to be – it never was! – but I do wince at a lot of the games I see now. There's too much pace, pace for the sake of pace, and not enough imagination and touch and control. Speed is essential, of course, especially in attack; but everyone's fit these days – they have to be – and more important qualities are change of pace and quickness of mind. Football is a battle of wits or it's nothing.

Armfield:

Our game has always been a bit parochial, I think, and that goes back to the 1950 World Cup, when England became the first British nation to take part. England got beaten then, in Brazil, by the United States, but I don't think it was looked on as the national disaster it would be today. The World Cup wasn't as important then. It was a trial and error thing.

Greenwood:

We were very insular and this was basically because our knowledge of what was happening across the water was limited. There was no coaching here, either, after the War. Kids simply played football until the lights went out and developed plenty of skill which was tremendous. But what they were short of was knowledge of how to play alongside other players. When I started I learned a lot from older players during games, but there was no collective coaching off the pitch. Not until Walter Winterbottom mainly, and one or two others, took a grip of things did it begin to change.

Brooking:

If you take youngsters for a session now and start teaching them the basics I can guarantee that after about five minutes they'll all be asking 'When are we going to have a game sir?' And when you start a game you find they can't string two passes together. Playing is important but you've got to learn the alphabet before you can start writing.

Law:

All we used to do was play in the streets, and all we had was a tennis ball. Even going to school we'd be knocking it against a wall and what we were doing, of course, although we didn't realise it, was developing our skill. It doesn't happen like this anymore. The first thing kids get now is a full-sized ball. Some of them haven't even got the strength to kick the thing. The old tennis ball was much more difficult. Control one of those and you could control anything. There's no substitute for skill and that's why I think the old players would do well in today's game. They were masters of the ball. There wasn't any coaching when I started playing. The woodwork teacher or the metalwork teacher looked after us, and, the two goalkeepers apart, we'd have 20 little guys running around after the ball wherever it went. Now it's 'I want to play in the middle' or 'I prefer up front' or 'don't wander over to the left'. It happens so early to kids it's ridiculous. Where's the fun in it?

Greenwood:

I agree. I'm a great advocate of coaching, but coaching now has gone over the top. It's got a lot to answer for because there's nothing worse than bad coaching. Too many people are using it as a platform for themselves.

Brooking:

There's no doubt that the style of our game has changed dramatically. The emphasis used to be on skill. Now it's on fitness. Even when I first got into the West Ham side − which isn't much more than 20 years ago − you could look around before kick-off and almost every one of the outfield players you'd see would be capable of swinging the game. It was just a case of whose skill came out on top on the day. It was end-to-end stuff. But gradually I noticed there were more and more players whose job was simply to prevent the opposition playing. Two, three and sometimes four of them. They weren't players. They were just athletes − stoppers.

Armfield:

Most changes in the game have been gradual but I think the crucial period was from the early 'fifties to the mid 'sixties when everything happened in a rush. We had Hungary beating England in 1953, the first foreign side to win at Wembley; and not long after that there was the start of European competition for clubs. Then, in 1961, the maximum wage was removed and in 1966 England won the World Cup. The Hungarian defeat proved we had a heck of a lot to learn, but England's World Cup win proved we could still do it. In between the European tournaments opened up all sorts of new doors and the wages free-for-all changed everybody's attitude. It was all a bit of a shock to the system.

Greenwood:

The Hungarians were certainly very important to me because I'd always had a vision of the way the game should be played, and, perhaps without realising it, I was waiting for someone to show me it could be done. There were hints of it in Arthur Rowe's push-and-run Tottenham side that won the Championship in 1951, but it was the Hungarians who really opened my eyes. And, remember, the England side they beat − 6−3 − was a very good one: Stan Matthews, Stan Mortensen, Alf Ramsey, Billy Wright, Jimmy Dickinson . . . they were all there. But the Hungarians simply played a different kind of football. The England side kept to their numbers, five looked for nine, two looked for eleven, but the Hungarians pulled them all over the park. Their movement was tremendous. They knew how to use space, they were free agents, they were never predictable, the man with the ball always had alternatives. They had some marvellous players, Puskas, Hidegkuti and so on, but it was the way they played that was the real eye-opener. Walter Winterbottom, who was England's manager and in charge of coaching, saw it the same way and he called a meeting of managers soon afterwards and asked for constructive

Hungary's sixth goal – and Hidegkuti's third – against England at Wembley in November 1953. Hungary won 6–3 and obliged English football to accept that it was not the best in the world. Jimmy Dickinson of Portsmouth (left) and Harry Johnston of Blackpool (right) are the nearest England players.

comment. A lot was said but not much happened. One manager actually got up and said: 'What do you expect? All our players care about is combing their hair in front of a mirror before they go out'. Very constructive! Later on I would hear people say: 'Ah yes, the Hungarians. Very good, but not for us'. I'll tell you, it was certainly for me. It was a big moment for me when West Ham beat Munich 1960 in the European Cup-winners' Cup final in 1965 using the same basics as the Hungarians.

Law:

It was the same when European football came along. It wasn't rated in England at all to begin with and it took Matt Busby to say, right, Manchester United are going to give it a **go**. And, of course, they were doing marvellously in the European Cup when the Munich air disaster happened in 1958. It was terrible . . . terrible. Duncan Edwards, Eddie Colman, Tommy Taylor, players like that, all gone. It gave United a different place in the game, a new kind of meaning, and when Matt Busby built the team again everybody cared about them and everybody wanted to see them. Celtic won the European Cup in 1967, with Jock Stein in charge: a great performance. But United won it a year later, the first English club to make it, and I was part of the scene then, although, unfortunately, I couldn't play in the final against Benfica because of cartilage trouble. It was the one I would really love to have played in. But it was the breakthrough for English clubs in the Champions' Cup and since then we've seen Liverpool and Nottingham Forest and Aston Villa all win it.

Armfield:

I think it often takes time for the significance of something to show through, like the removal of the maximum wage. Money was obviously important to me when I was getting £20 a week but playing football was even more important. That's absolutely true. When the wage ceiling went, of course, gates still weren't bad, getting on for 30 million a season, but since then wages have been going up and crowds have been going down, and what has happened is that the main power is now in the hands of a few clubs who can afford to buy and pay the best talent. Twenty or 30 years ago there were always a lot of clubs who fancied their chances but now you say Arsenal, Tottenham, Liverpool, Everton and Manchester United, and you're talking about the winners. The reason is simple economics.

Law:

The change after the World Cup in 1966 was pretty quick. The win was good for English football's opinion of itself but, unfortunately, it didn't do much good for football generally. England won it without wingers, and a lot of managers looked at the system and copied it. No wingers meant a decline in excitement in the box and that was a big shame.

Greenwood:

The game certainly suffered afterwards. The big ambition became to close space down instead of opening it up and using it. Football became very defensive.

Brooking:

Since I finished playing, the most frustrating thing about all the games I've watched is the way the offside game has developed. It's become a big feature. It never used to be a real factor in team-talks at all. We didn't used to worry about it. But there are a lot of teams now who rely on it heavily. You get one side moving up to the half-way line and then the other lot are offside from their goalkeeper's kick-out. That's shocking.

Law:

Absolutely disgraceful. The offside game is part of football but when it's overdone it just drives people away from the game – and any manager who does that should be struck off the list.

Greenwood:

People are talking about changing the offside law, but the fact is the rest of the world don't want it changed because they don't play the offside game. We didn't see it played in the World Cup in Mexico and most of the football played there was a delight. Here, though, you get the ball in the goalkeeper's hands and you suddenly have 20 players either side of the half-way line, about ten yards apart. It shows a lack of imagination on the part of managers and, make no mistake, it's their responsibility. They're the only people who can put it right.

Armfield:

I wonder if managers will ever put it right when there's a chairman standing over them, saying 'you're going to be out of work if you don't win on Saturday'. There's security in the odd club but I've always said that if a manager like Bill Nicholson can be sacked they'll sack anybody.

Brooking:

I was certainly influenced by Bill Nicholson's Spurs but if we're going to talk about favourite players then George Best comes into that category for me. His individual ability was incredible. Remember that goal they always show on television: he took a short corner against West Ham and then jinked past three defenders before slipping the ball into the net. Unbelievable really. I'll always remember the great Brazilians, the team that won in Mexico in 1970, and, most of all, Pelé himself. I thought their style was out of this world. Everyone just watched them with awe. Franz Beckenbauer of West Germany is another one for me — I thought he had that special arrogance about him — and the other player I really rated was Johan Cruyff, the Dutch lad, who was fantastic and probably as good as anyone at his peak. I thought he was superb.

Greenwood:

I think I'd put Cruyff at the top of my list as well. He was more than a great player — he was an orchestra leader. He'd put his foot on the ball and dictate the game. He'd tell the rest what to do. Alfredo di Stefano, the Argentinian who played for Real Madrid, was another who did this and so was Johnny Byrne who we bought from Crystal Palace. I used to call Byrne 'the di Stefano of British football' and praise can't be pitched

higher than that. They shaped games but they also scored goals. And I agree with Trevor about Beckenbauer. Such cool elegance! I used to say to my youngsters: 'Watch Beckenbauer play. He makes it look so easy you'll believe your granny could play the same way'. And I'll give a vote, too, to Bobby Moore; and not just because he played for me and helped England win the World Cup. At his best he was alongside Beckenbauer.

Armfield:

Di Stefano was my favourite player, the most complete footballer I ever played against. Tom Finney was the most complete British player. Tom literally had everything. But I think Stan Matthews was the greatest attraction. He used to double gates just by turning up. He was 36 when I started playing with him but he was absolutely phenomenal,

Jimmy Armfield of England (right) and Alfredo di Stefano (Rest of the World) lead out their sides before the FA Centenary match at Wembley in 1963. England won 2 − 1. Bobby Moore is behind Armfield and next to di Stefano is Ferenc Puskas.

so fit and dedicated when it came to diet and training. He was so good at taking people on that he was regularly marked by two players. There's only been one Matthews.

Law:

The votes are going for di Stefano, aren't they? Mine, too. He ran all over the place, never stopped, and he'd defend as well as attack. And what about Ferenc Puskas, the Hungarian he had with him at Real Madrid? The greatest goal-scorer, I think, was Jimmy Greaves. I doubt if there's ever been a cooler scorer. He didn't do much outside the penalty area but, by jove, when he got into the box there was no one who was more clinical. I would also mention George Best and Bobby Charlton, my old United team-mates. Best, especially, had everything. Brave, a good header and skilful, he tackled and scored goals. It was a pity that at a certain time in his career he just went on the blink.

Greenwood:

We haven't mentioned any modern players but I'm sure that in ten years or whatever from now they'll still be talking about Gary Lineker. He's exceptional, great ability on the spot. Ian Rush is the same. He guarantees goals.

Armfield:

I'm very tempted to include Kenny Dalglish who is one of the best of what I call 'all-purpose' players. He knows the game and could play almost anywhere. And – at the risk of embarrassing him – I must add this chap Denis Law, and with him Jimmy Greaves. They are the sharpest players I ever played against in the penalty box. And I don't think I could ever select my best England team without Bobby Charlton. In my opinion his shooting power won us the World Cup in 1966.

Brooking:

The teams I've admired most have been Liverpool's. They've had several outstanding sides, going back to the days of players like Ron Yeats and Ian St John. Then there was Kevin Keegan and John Toshack and when Keegan went, Kenny Dalglish arrived. There was never a break in step. It was all so smooth. I used to love the Manchester United side that Denis played for along with George Best and Bobby Charlton. Tremendous individuals, lots of excitement. But if I'm putting a team of honour on the shelf it's got to be Liverpool.

Law:

The best I've seen was definitely the Tottenham side of the early 'sixties who also did the 'double'. I thought they were the equivalent of even Real Madrid. They had everything. Dave Mackay and Danny Blanchflower in midfield, Jimmy Greaves up front with a perfect foil in Bobby Smith, and poor John White who was killed by lightning. He was one of the best. Spurs first but, at the risk of sounding biased, I'll save a vote for our Manchester United side of the mid 'sixties as well as for Liverpool later on – and we mustn't forget the Celtic side which won the European Cup under Jock Stein in 1967. I thought they were very exciting. But above all, Bill Nicholson's Spurs were the best.

Greenwood:

This may surprise you but I pick Leeds United when they were at their best under Don Revie. At one time they looked fantastic and went more than 20 games without defeat. They started a bit dubiously but when the final product emerged they were a complete side. You had to admire them.

Armfield:

I believe Manchester United's pre-Munich side would have been great, but I agree with Ron: I think the best group of players any club has had since the War was at Leeds. They were on top for nearly ten years with practically the same players. I also agree that Spurs were excellent, a really top-class side, but if we're talking about a club, well, Liverpool's record over the years stands on its own. Nobody can match what they've done. Bill Shankly started it all for them and would be at the top of any managers' list, though I think Matt Busby would have to be up there with him for what he did for Manchester United. People inside the game all rate Bill Nicholson very highly and among those who influenced me tremendously were Walter Winterbottom and Ron Greenwood. Ron when he was my manager in the England Under-23 team was one of the first people to make me think about the game.

Brooking:

Obviously Alf Ramsey must be on any list. He wasn't everybody's cup of tea but he won the World Cup for England, and nobody can do more than that.

Greenwood:

And we certainly mustn't forget Brian Clough. He's an exceptional man, a bit unusual but he's his own man and I admire him for the teams he has put out. His teams always play good football and that has been a stamp of his authority.

Law:

Clough took two clubs who weren't amounting to much, Derby County and Nottingham Forest, and won the Championship for them both. And he also won the European Cup twice for Nottingham Forest. That's something!

Armfield:

The one thing I wouldn't like to see in the next 40 years is the disappearance of the small clubs. It's better for everybody when there's a big pyramid. It gives the game strength. I certainly hope there's no Superleague breakaway. I'm also totally against artificial pitches. The game was meant to be played on grass. I know people have been trying to come up with an artificial surface that plays just like grass, but God has been the winner so far. The lovely thing about grass is that it's always changing. It can be dry or wet or muddy or hard. It's part of the game.

Law:

I'd like to see chairmen and directors take the fear away from managers to enable them to let their players go out and play entertaining football. I know that's easily said and not so easily done; but there must be an answer.

Brooking:

The offside game is the thing that's still bugging me. FIFA have looked at it but they say it's up to us to sort out our problem. So it's really a case of coming up with something within our own game. It really is frustrating. Something's got to be done.

Greenwood:

If the offside law can't be changed then it's up to the people in football to find a way to destroy the offside game. That's what I mean when I say football should always be a battle of wits. And football has got to be looked upon as an entertainment instead of a commercial venture. People want to be entertained, and if they're not entertained they just won't come. What's left then?

On Reflection

Cliff Morgan

One of the great figures of Welsh Rugby,
Cliff Morgan won 29 caps at fly-half, was
a member of the immortal British Lions in
South Africa in 1955 and also played for
Cardiff and the Barbarians. A former
Editor of BBC Television's *Sportsview* and
Grandstand, Head of BBC Radio Sport
and Outside Broadcasts and Head of BBC
Television Outside Broadcasts.
Commentator, presenter, disc-jockey and
soul of a thousand parties.

Islwyn Evans, who taught English at Tonyrefail Grammar School, made listening to Dylan Thomas on Radio – the Welsh Home Service in those days – compulsory. He claimed that by doing so, we valley children would experience an excitement in our examination of a rich language and an appreciation and respect for the noble style of delivery that marked the poet's every performance. 'Evans the English' was dead right. My abiding regret is that I never met Dylan, whose mastery of the visual and evocative power of words brought a glow to those early morning broadcasts and to our lessons.

Dylan Thomas once said that the memories of childhood have no order and no end. I have exactly the same feeling about *Sports Report*. For nearly 40 years, in one way or another, it has been a constant factor in my life; first as an interviewee; then, when I retired from International Rugby in 1958, as a reporter; and finally, with Bob Burrows, as Editor, in the mid 'seventies, when the peerless Angus Mackay retired. There is no doubt that Mr Mackay, as we all referred to him at first, left a glorious legacy and the joy is that the people who make *Sports Report* today have maintained, and often improved on, the standards set.

It all started for me at 5.35 p.m. on Saturday 8 March 1952 in Dublin. Wales had beaten Ireland to win the Triple Crown and the BBC commentator, Sammy Walker, who had captained Ireland and the 1938 British Lions, came to ask if I could spare the time to be interviewed by Eamonn Andrews for *Sports Report*. Little did he know I would have given my Welsh jersey to speak with Eamonn. That interview I remember clearly. Having asked me about the run of play and my opinion of the legendary Irishman, Jackie Kyle, Eamonn asked what I would remember most about that afternoon. 'My father losing his teeth', I said, 'and he wasn't even playing!' What actually happened was this. When Ken

Jones ran 50 yards at Olympic speed to score a try, my father leapt to his feet and shouted with joy, but he spat his top set ten or 12 rows in front of him. He never got them back!

Now I suppose I told that story on the air because I had been influenced by the philosophy of the Head of the BBC in Wales, Hywel Davies, who believed that broadcasting not only had the job of reflecting news and facts, but it also had an obligation to amuse and make people think and laugh.

There was also a policy, which I tried to follow as an Editor and broadcaster, that we should clearly understand the essential difference between the written and the spoken word. The way you would carefully and perhaps painstakingly write for a newspaper, with perfect punctuation and a cold eye on syntax, was not the style you would adopt in preparing a talk for broadcasting. It meant thinking in a fresh way about clarity and lucidity. For radio, complicated sentences were taboo and the aim was to write in an idiom that would be understood immediately by the listener, using a vocabulary that would not confuse or, indeed, frustrate. Simplicity was the order of the day.

There was one other aim: to produce a surprising line or two that would live in the mind of the listener. Not an easy task, but I recall with ever-increasing pleasure some memorable contributions to *Sports Report* over the years.

It was, beyond all reasonable doubt, the late J. L. Manning who was the master craftsman at writing a radio column. Week after week and year after year, he produced scintillating copy in Fleet Street that made sport take itself seriously. He inevitably touched a nerve. His writing was never dull. As a regular contributor to *Sports Report* for over a quarter of a century, his powerful words and forthright delivery gave the programme editorial clout. It was compulsive listening for he always said

The changing face of motor racing. (Above) Stirling Moss in a Maserati (bearing his lucky number, seven) in 1954, and (below) Graham Hill in the Embassy Lola, 20 years later.

something which would cause people to stop and think, or to be angry or to laugh.

Four days before he died, in January 1974, he telephoned from his hospital bed to say that he would like to record for us some of his thoughts about sport and people and issues which had dominated his life as a sports writer. Peter Jones and I were privileged to sit at his bedside and share what proved to be a celebrated broadcast – arguably one of the best ever in sport – by a man who had given so much to so many. As we celebrate the 40th birthday of *Sports Report*, it is proper to record here, for those who did not hear that J. L. Manning interview with Peter Jones in 1974, some of the opinions and memories of a giant of the written and spoken word.

It was the longest contribution ever to *Sports Report*, lasting for 24 minutes and five seconds of the programme time of 59 minutes and 40 seconds. The broadcast contained some pretty hard stuff, for Jim was a sports writer who went out of his way to find a campaign to fight for.

'I feel about sport that people are always arguing over it. It doesn't matter what pub or what club you go into, they argue about it and it seems to me that sport is something you can argue about without losing friendships, and you can't do this, as far as I know, about any other aspect of life. So I became argumentative about sport because the people I was working for were argumentative. And so I looked for campaigns.

'I remembered what my father had been told in 1919 by Lord Hawke – regarded as the High Priest Tory of Cricket, a blimpish sort of figure. "You've got to remember, Lionel" he said to my father, "that Ministries for darned sillier things than sport have been set up and Governments and industry have their full part to play in the reconstruction of sport." That was in 1919, and here we are in 1974 with the full consciousness that we have not yet got the right sort of relationship that Lord Hawke

envisaged, and we are spending 2,000 million pounds on gambling and gaming in this country every year and yet we haven't enough for sport. That racing gets more than Dr Roger Bannister's Sports Council and CCPR is nonsense.

'We've got to scrap the privileged Levy Board – not only what racing has, but what football now wants – and have an across-the-board levy so that gambling money is put into sport because then you will keep party politics out of sport and you'll keep sport out of the departmental queues and we shall know what slice of the cake we can have. Given the money, we shall produce the champions.'

Jim's most memorable campaign was fought against professional boxing. 'It began before the War when I was in Leicester and there I lived in a marvellous sporting town. Ben Ford, Larry Gains and Reggie Mere, all heavyweight boxers of ability, were around and I began to see the squalor which was behind the boxing game. It didn't seem real in the sense that cricket and football and tennis seemed real and, I decided to make a distinction. Immediately after the War came the tragedy of Freddie Mills.

'I am not blaming anyone. There was no one about at his weight for him to fight. Freddie wanted fights and he gave away an awful lot of weight against men like Baxi and even Woodcock in this country; and he took these fights at very frequent intervals. When he finally committed suicide I felt that I had to stand up and say that this was not suicide at all but death from an industrial disease and it should not invalidate insurance policies. I felt exactly the same about Randolph Turpin when he committed suicide, and so I began to look into the fatalities that there were in boxing – and not only fatalities, but the irreversible cerebral injuries that came to men ten years after they retired. And when my journalistic colleagues asked me why I was anti-boxing, I said to them, I have never seen you at the inquest of a boxer!'

Jim Manning was a regular on *Sports Report.* He told of one broadcast in the company of Bill McGowan and Peter Wilson: 'We were in the studio discussing the issue of why Oxford sank in the Boat Race. Now Bill McGowan was an ardent Catholic and he always wore his Derby rowing cap. I think he wore it in bed! He thought that the umpire, who was the Protestant Bishop of Willesden, was completely wrong and that the race should have been awarded to Cambridge instead of being re-rowed on the following Monday, and he said "I believe in the infallability of the Pope but I'm damned if I believe in the infallability of the Bishop of Willesden". That was way-out stuff in radio in those days.'

Jim had clear memories of his early days: 'After leaving school, I wanted to go up to Balliol College, Oxford, because I knew I was certain of getting my running Blue, having been trained, not only by Harold Abrahams [many times a contributor to the programme and a man who really popularised athletics] but by Tom Whitaker and Herbert Chapman at Highbury when I was on holiday from school. People talk about discipline. I was sitting in the dressing-room at Highbury with all the great players – Cliff Bastin, David Jack, Alex James – one day, and Chapman crossed the dressing-room and saw a piece of cotton wool on the floor and said "James, pick that up. This is not a pigsty, this is Arsenal Football Club". And Alex James picked it up and not a word was said. Can you imagine that happening today?

'No, I didn't go up to Oxford. My father said he wanted me educated properly! So I joined a weekly paper called the *Lymington Times* or *Chronicle.* I got fired from there for going off to play cricket when I should have been covering a Conservative Ladies' Conference. When my replacement arrived, I asked him if he played cricket. When he said no, I told him that he'd be all right. And that young man was Richard Dimbleby, who later became a renowned and much-loved commentator.

'My father wouldn't let me be a sports writer while he was a Sports Editor because he felt that people would accuse him of using his influence. I saw Ken Farnes – I had been at school with him – take five wickets for England in his first Test Match against Australia and Trevor Wignal, then the doyen of sports writers, offered me a job. But my father said no, because I didn't know enough about inquests and city councils and that sort of thing and so I didn't get to Fleet Street until after the War. Nevertheless, I made it in a sense in that there has been, continuously since 1919, a Manning column published in Fleet Street and I apologise to the public for this quite outrageous dynasty.'

On the greatest sports personality he met or had written about:

'No doubt about that. It was Charles Burgess Fry. He was a fine cricketer who played for Oxford, Sussex and England, held the world long jump record and won an international soccer cap. He missed a rugby Blue because of injury but won a Cup final medal with Southampton. On top of that, he was a better scholar than F. E. Smith, who became Lord Birkenhead and Lord Chancellor. He was senior scholar to him up at Wadham. His influence on cricket, his influence on everything and his devotion to the Mercury Training School – and because he came in and out of my house when I was a boy – I was very greatly impressed by him.

'I was also impressed by him because of his failings. With all those marvellous attributes, he made the great mistake of writing a book – even as late as 1939 – recalling a visit to Adolf Hitler in 1934, and still in 1939 finding that there was some merit in the Hitler Youth Movement. On top of that, he also fully intended, but for the intervention of Ranjitsinhji, his greatest cricketing pal, to accept the Crown of the

Jim Laker of Surrey, Essex and England is considered by many to have been the best off-spinner of all. He will be remembered forever for taking 19 for 90 against Australia at Old Trafford in 1956.

Kingdom of Albania. Well, to make that mistake and the Hitler Youth mistake is the other side of a truly great man. But he had a Noel Coward gallantry about him and during this Christmas when my mother, who is 82 next month, came up, we did a little teasing because we dug this up.'

At this point Jim handed us a poem. 'Get my actress daughter, Katy, who's starring with Derek Nimmo in the West End, to read this poem for you'. So off we went to the theatre. Katy Manning said 'It's actually a love poem written by C. B. Fry to my grandmother – my father's mother:-

Dear one – no capital save love may pay
  the toll of strife.
So mine, of now and every year, would
  bring you back to life,
No wintry woe shall ever dim the golden
  joy you bring,
Your daffodils are here again and my
  perpetual spring.

  (signed) C. B. Fry'

And then Katy capped it with a typical comment worthy of her father: 'Lord love us Grandma, if you'd gone on flirting like that we might not have been little

50

Mannings, but very small Frys!'

The last words in what, sadly, was J. L. Manning's last broadcast, referred to a letter he had received, offering congratulations on his inclusion in the New Year's Honours List. The letter was written on the headed paper of The British Olympic Association.

J. L. said 'I shall find it difficult not to be in tears when I read you this letter. I hate to be emotional'. He then read the letter. ' " I spent yesterday – New Year's Day – out behind the Christchurch Beagles and this morning was back into my sculling boat for a five-mile stint on the Henley Course etc. etc. Happy New Year, yours ever, Jack Beresford." Now Jack Beresford is 75. Doesn't that make us all feel humble?'

J. L. Manning's last contribution was memorable and unassuming. For us it was a remarkable experience and the memory of that broadcast will never fade.

Fourteen years ago, listeners to *Sports Report* were treated to a catalogue of nouns and adjectives from the distinguished Welsh author and humorist Gwyn Thomas, who suggested on the programme that rugby was the absolute combination of opera, ballet and murder!

'In the Rhondda, we played our games in back lanes in poor light and with very little reference to a ball. I remember falling on my face on that concrete-hard ground and suffering concussion ten times before I was 12. Then when we got to play at the grammar school on a posh, lush, green, grass pitch and fell on our faces, five boys in my class suffered chlorophyll poisoning – they were intoxicated by the smell of grass because we didn't know that sort of vegetation existed.

'There's no doubt that there were three distinct periods of significance in rugby history during the 20th Century. During the first 20 years many a talented player never made it to Murrayfield or Twickenham or Lansdowne Road or Cardiff Arms Park because he was chained to the chapel wall by his mother in case he would forfeit a seat on the Deacon's bench or a place in Paradise.

'Then the second 20 years of lunatic political fever when the zeal of many a great forward was blunted on a long route march to London to tell the Government to do its Christian duty. And that must have surprised a few Governments!

'And the last 20 years of Barry John and Gareth Edwards and Gerald Davies and J.P.R. and Mervyn Davies. They all march in spirit alongside the great Celtic heroes of the past who tried to remove the iron dentures from the mouth of Edward the First in the 13th Century. And you hear all kinds of tales. I know of a man in Llanelli who claims that he cured his shingles by touching the boot of Phil Bennett when the leather in his boot was charged with miracles after kicking six goals in an International.'

Yes, on *Sports Report* there were, on occasions, massive lies and stupendous exaggerations, and that is right and proper for sport inspires flights of fancy and romance. Down the years, few people matched the style of the scholarly Geoffrey Green, football correspondent of *The Times*. His infectious laughter and wit; his love of sweet music and inspired lyrics; his passion for our national game brightened the studio and everyone around him. His contributions were unique. He believed in the importance of telling a story.

Many years after the horror of the Munich air disaster of 1958 when a nation mourned the death of so many members of the glittering Manchester United team, Geoffrey went with the England team to Belgrade and a happening there inspired the story, about Manchester United, which only he could tell. 'The England boys went into a shed to change and suddenly we were surrounded by swarms of schoolchildren. Bernard Joy and I sat on a little wall with these giggling, excited bubbling kids. We didn't understand Yugoslav and they couldn't understand our lingo but we made magic, jumping rabbits and disappearing coins and they thought the circus had come to town.

'It was magic and we kept amusing them somehow or other and suddenly, through the crowd pushed an old man with a sort of crabapple face, a crumpled, marvellous brown face. He had a framed coloured photograph of the Manchester United team which had fallen at Munich, and on each of the red shirts of the boys who had lost their lives, he'd put a little black cross. He showed the photograph to me and he said, in stumbling English, that he was a great friend of Manchester United and Matt Busby and as he talked some tears began to ripple down his old face and it became, really, rather embarrassing.

'The kids were all laughing – they didn't know the little drama – and the old man pushed out of the crowd and then came back again and produced out of his pocket a faded photograph of himself. He had been a groundsman at the new Red Star Stadium where the England team were going to play the next day. On the back of the photograph he'd put his name and address in Belgrade and said he was a great friend of Matt Busby and would I give this to him when I got back to England. By this time the England team had finished training and were back in their changing-rooms. I wandered off to an asphalt pitch where the schoolboys had started a game and, suddenly, alongside me appeared Bobby Moore. And once again the crabapple face was behind me, pulling on my coat, and he beckoned me to follow him.

'So I got hold of Bobby Moore and we both followed and we got to his home, in fact it was like a little hut on a corner. I introduced Bobby as the England captain and the old man was delighted and very proud. In his hut was a wooden bed and an oil lamp and all the walls were plastered with pictures of football teams and international players, and he and Bobby were pointing out players and suddenly the old man dived into an old chest of drawers. He brought out one of those pins which the Continentals are so proud of, the Red Star lapel pin: "Please will you give this to Matt Busby". And then, as an afterthought, he dived into another drawer and brought out an old packet of cigarettes – goodness knows how many years old they must have been – and then said "give them to Mr Busby too". So I had photographs, a snapshot with his address on the back, a lapel pin and cigarettes to take back to England for Matt Busby. I eventually gave them to him.

'Well, that is the end of the story, except I wonder if there is an end. Surely there can be no end to the admiration and respect that Manchester United have inspired wherever football is played?'

On the subject of self-respect and good manners in sport, it was an inspired thought by Bob Burrows to invite the celebrated Alistair Cooke to contribute a story from America in 1974. The thought was prompted by a deep concern about the outrageous behaviour of certain sportsmen and women who had, seemingly, forgotten the meaning of sportsmanship. As ever, Alistair Cooke produced a gem for the show.

'Whatever happened to Frank Merriwell? Let me explain. He was the fictional hero of all American boys a couple of generations ago. He played to win but he played fair and he lost with grace. And it does seem so many years ago since we had a character like that looming large on the American sporting scene. In tennis it used to be that a champ, no matter how glamorous, got a severe reprimand and a threat of disqualification if he so much as dropped his racquet in anger. Today we not only tolerate two-hour long tantrums but we pay to see them and leave the umpire and linesmen to seem like foolish squares stuck with the rule book.'

The broadcast went on to tell of how the true tone of sport in the 'seventies was set by the elite corps – the rich – of basketball and football and tennis. It went on to point the finger at money and commercial exploitation as the root cause of loutish behaviour by some overpaid 'stars' in so many sports. His final thoughts were on the game which is close to his heart, the game of golf which, he claimed, remains an oasis in a sporting desert of gold and scruffy manners.

'I keep my fingers crossed, but so far the public spectacle of golf still seems to be ruled by Bobby Jones' remarks. Win or lose, the game has no meaning if you don't play by the rules.'

And I suppose that last line sums up the approach of Angus Mackay's *Sports Report* which has, for 40 years, reported and reflected and interviewed. It aimed at the best interests of sport and the audience. It has made people laugh and cry and think and react. There's no doubt in my mind that *Sports Report* is by far the best team I ever played for.

40 Years of Cricket

Christopher Martin-Jenkins

BBC Radio's authoritative cricket correspondent, Christopher Martin-Jenkins is also Editor of *The Cricketer* and the author of ten books, including *The Complete Who's Who of Test Cricketers*. A talented cricketer who once scored 99 at Lord's—'the most bitter-sweet moment of my life'—he has played for Surrey Second XI and is an accomplished mimic.

'We have passed a lot of water under the bridge', as Sam Goldwyn once said, since my first broadcast for *Sports Report* in 1969. 'We're calling you Chris Jenkins, OK?' said Angus Mackay with an icy stare just before they cued to me. 'No,' I cockily replied, 'I would prefer my full name, please.'

It seems a lifetime ago since my first ball-by-ball commentary for Radio Three (excluding one for a computer Test, which was fun) in August 1972 when England staged a one-day International for the first time, at Old Trafford. Dennis Amiss made a hundred and I worked with Jack Fingleton after dining with him the night before at the Swan at Bucklow Hill.

Time . . . an ever rolling stream; and 'Fingo' is one of many friends who have since moved on. He was a brilliant cricket writer and a good broadcaster with a twinkling, mischievous sense of humour. He did some work for Angus Mackay and I can still recall his slow, compelling drawl delivering one of his weekly observation pieces: 'The team played in Somerset this week. I visited the men's room in the village pub and thought I would pass on to you a notice on the wall: "We aim to please – you aim, too, please."'

Talk with friends like Fingo – the anecdotes running into hundreds – have enlivened many a meal after a day's Test cricket. Broadcasting, especially in overseas heat, can be a tiring business; and I would add that I have carried my microphone virtually from the start to the finish of three tours of Australia, two of the West Indies and one of India as well as reporting on three other occasions in Australia and once each in India and South Africa. I am well aware of my good fortune, because there is still much romance surrounding the performance of an England team battling for national honour in some foreign clime in the depth of a British winter.

Broadcasting commitments these days are heavy, with 20-minute commentary stints, hourly reports and close of play interviews, so one looks forward to a beer and a bath and then dinner; and personally I never tire of talking cricket with those who, in H.S. Altham's phrase, 'love and understand it'. Brian Johnston and John Woodcock come especially to mind as the most entertaining of dinner-table companions. No wonder they have given so much pleasure, one on Radio Three, the other in *The Times*.

Brian, of course, was my predecessor as a roving cricket reporter overseas. My first assignment after his retirement was the MCC tour to the West Indies in the early months of 1974. Mike Denness was in charge and it was a tour for 'stories', starting with the extraordinary incident at the end of the first day of the opening Test Match at Port of Spain. Bernard Julien played the day's final ball just to the right of the rapacious Tony Greig at silly point. He picked up the ball and, with his back to Alan Knott, who was already removing the bails, he saw that Alvin Kallicharran, eager to get back to the pavilion with a not-out hundred to his name, had carried on walking without having grounded his bat after backing up as the non-striker. Greig took deliberate aim and fired down the stumps. Douglas Sang-Hue raised a reluctant finger. Kallicharran hurried to the pavilion, eyes ablaze. His feeling of shock and anger was reflected in the large crowd. There was an indignant, menacing roar.

Up in the commentary box at the southern end, with the wooded hills behind, I was called on by 'Raffy' Knowles, the voice of Trinidad radio, to give an instant judgement. I said that a dismissal like this was against the spirit of the laws and the interests of the game. Noticing that Mike Denness was talking animatedly to Sang-Hue as he came off the field at the other end of the ground, I added that the England captain may well have been asking for the appeal to be withdrawn.

This may conceivably have averted a riot. The scoreboard operators and many of the crowd were listening to the CBC broadcast on their transistor radios, and the scoreboard immediately changed back the number of wickets fallen from six to five, putting Kallicharran's score back in place. Almost immediately, the vast majority of the crowd went home. For those who remained, including, of course, myself, anxiously trying to keep the news and sports desks in London in touch with what was happening by telephone lines which were much in demand, there was a long wait in the humid heat of the pavilion while officials discussed what should be done. Eventually the normally genial, but now tense, drawn-looking England manager, Donald Carr, and the urbane, cool, diplomatic Jeff Stollmeyer called a Press conference and announced that the England team had indeed withdrawn their appeal; and that, with the umpire's reluctant agreement, since he had merely applied the law, Kallicharran would be reinstated. Greig's South African background added to the racial tensions which were stirred by his unfortunate piece of opportunism.

Greig proceeded to dominate the England team's performances for the rest of the tour, culminating in his extraordinary *tour de force* as an off-spin bowler in the final match, the return game at Port of Spain.

Perhaps because it was my first tour and everything about the experience was new and exciting, I recall it better than any other: Amiss's heroic 262 not out at Sabina Park after he had survived a legitimate appeal for a catch behind the wicket off his glove when the innings was in its infancy; Boycott getting caught off bat and boot at Barbados; Lawrence Rowe's cool, masterful triple hundred at Bridgetown; the beauty of the Bourda ground at Georgetown, but the depressing run-down, faded atmosphere of the old Dutch capital with its heavy humidity and mosquito-infected evenings; the joy on Jack Birkenshaw's face when he won an lbw decision against Rowe in the First Test; Boycott's determination to make something of lasting worth in that same

game; the sadness of Gary Sobers' failure in his final Test innings; the overall pleasure of watching the joyous smiles on a thousand faces in the crowd when a memorable stroke was played.

The West Indian love for cricket was once perfectly demonstrated during that tour. My wife had come to Barbados for a fortnight and we wanted to hire a Mini Moke so that she could see something of the island while I was away all day at the Kensington Oval. We were told that we must first get a driving permit from the local police station. Alas, neither of us had brought our driving licence with us.

'I'm sorry', said the local inspector with a firm shake of the head, 'if you haven't got no licence I can't give you no drivin' permit.' We were leaving the room disconsolately when he called us back. 'Hold it a moment. You de fella who talk on de radio 'bout cricket? Chris Martin-Jenkins, eh, your voice not bad, man. What you think of Collis King?'

I said I was most impressed by him. Also with a chap named Nolan Clarke, who had just made a dazzling hundred against a struggling MCC attack. We talked also of the Test Series and of other matters of mutual interest and importance. I heard a bit about the fortunes of the Barbados police team. I became aware of my wife clearing her throat. 'Good to talk to you', I said, 'but I'm afraid we must be going now.' We turned to do so. 'Hold it a moment, man. You can't go without your driving permit!' The broad smile told everything. Cricket is a passport anywhere.

Before 1974 was out I was on my travels again, this time to Australia; first port of call, Brisbane. Even after a seemingly interminable flight I had to go to see the Gabba before getting to the hotel for a

One small step for England. Ian Botham on the way to his brilliant 138 in the First Test against Australia at Brisbane in November 1986.

shower and a sleep. It is a relatively intimate ground, full of character. I love the days of uncertain speculation before the start of an overseas Test Match, especially those before the opening Test of the tour.

In that November of 1974, a young fellow called Thomson, Christian name Jeff – not to be confused with the one who had bowled in-swingers at Ray Illingworth's team four years previously – bowled rather fast and well in the Queensland match which preceded the first match of the rubber, but it was still a surprise when the selectors announced his name in the 12 for the Test.

Two days before the match a tropical storm made the Gabba's square a quagmire. The city's Lord Mayor, Clem Jones, who had sacked the groundsman and taken over preparations himself, was walking across it in wellington boots when I went to have a look at the Test strip. With a white helmet in his hand he looked like the foreman on a building site. A few days later Thomson became an overnight sensation, Dennis Lillee started his rehabilitation and England were hustled to defeat despite a barnstorming hundred by Greig. Not long afterwards they had a cyclone in Darwin and Jones, a human dynamo if ever there was one, was sent up to the north to organise the rebuilding of a shattered town. Modern Brisbane, with its bustling new city centre, owes much to Clem Jones even if the 1974–75 England team owe him nothing.

The MCC touring team that year never really got over 'Cyclone Lillian Thomson'. The two big guns were marvellously supported by big Max Walker and by their close catchers: the Chappells, Walters and Mallett were all outstanding. There has seldom been a tour like it for injuries. Colin Cowdrey, veteran of five previous Australian tours at four-yearly intervals, joined the team at Perth, white from an English winter, smilingly polite to everyone. I gave him some net practice at the WACA; hardly a preparation of what was to come!

'Come on Thommo, rattle out a tune on his false teeth!' yelled a bloodthirsty modern 'yabba' as the venerable old gentleman walked out to bat, round backed and padded from chest to toe. These days he would be helmeted too, of course, and such was the flak which flew from Lillee and Thomson on that tour it was surprising that the idea of protecting the head waited another three years. After Lillee had hit Keith Fletcher on the forehead at Sydney, the ball rebounding almost as far as Ross Edwards at cover, a defeated but still cheerful England team travelled to Tasmania the following day. At the airport someone asked Fletcher for his autograph. David Lloyd of Lancashire could not resist intervening: 'What are you signing, Keith – Nat Lofthouse?'

My next trip to Australia took place after the MCC tour of India in 1976–77. Denness, the first perhaps to feel the full heat of the critical scrutiny now applied to every England captain overseas by television pundits and the tabloid newspapers, had left the Test scene and Greig was now in charge. He had a wonderful tour of India and hard, demanding grind though it was at the time, in retrospect I cannot think of a tour I have enjoyed more. Greig himself, of course, was a 'media' dream, always willing to communicate and, like Richie Benaud before him, skilled at using microphones and newspaper columnists to put his own, and his team's, point of view across.

I probably made a rod for my own back during this tour. No BBC man had ever, I think, played quite so many interviews across from the sub-continent but this was a friendly, happy and successful team and the demand from home was high for news of their exploits. There was many a difficult moment from a technical point of view. I shall never forget the successful experiment of a recorded phone-in programme with Greig from a studio near Gauhati, high up in the Assam Hills. I had asked the taxi driver to convey us to All India Radio and half an hour later he despatched us with a triumphant smile at the headquarters of Oil India.

On another occasion I had a terrible time trying to get my reports and interviews across from a half-finished studio at Jullunder. The attempt to get a line to London had lasted more than two hours and alternative efforts to get even a telephone call through had failed. Then, miraculously and at last, a thin voice answered my despairing call of 'Hello London' just as *Sports Report* was going out on the airwaves. But my smile of pleasure and relief was quickly wiped away by the entry into the studio of a very important and stern looking Sikh, bearded, beturbaned and clearly in no mood for any argument. It was the Chief Minister of the Punjab and his party political broadcast would not wait!

On the field there was much to savour, especially the startling and well-deserved success of J. K. Lever in his first Test Match at Delhi. Swing bowling of the highest order gave England a joyous success just before Christmas on a pitch which had been expected to suit the venom of Chandrasekhar and the sinewy guile of Bishen Bedi.

At the end of the tour, weary as walkers in a desert, we moved from India's unforgettable decadence, beauty and organised chaos to the clean-cut modernity of Perth in Western Australia, prior to the Centenary Test. I was whisked away from Perth to Canberra by the BBC to cover for the World Service the opening of the Australian Parliament by the Queen. I was introduced to Her Majesty at a cocktail party the night before, an honour which made well worthwhile another long plane journey at the end of which the normally highly efficient Ansett Airlines had mislaid my suitcases!

Then to Melbourne, for the greatest assembly of cricketing talent in the history of the game. No event has equalled it for its sense of occasion and camaraderie. Round every corner one saw the face of a former English or Australian cricketing hero, some famous, some forgotten, and familiar only to the enthusiast. Even as England and Australia were engaged in their classic Centenary Test Match before huge emotional crowds at the vast, ugly but loveable MCC, moves were being made to tear international cricket asunder. The 'Packer Revolution' was at hand.

When next I travelled to Australia, in 1978–79 with Brearley's team, Australian cricket was involved in a bitter civil war. It is still sorting out the consequences as I write this, nearly a decade later, at the end of another England tour of Australia under Mike Gatting. The limited-overs Internationals with which the tour concluded became, to me, numbingly monotonous after a while, for all their spectacular staging and moments of high excitement. But the Test Matches for the Ashes remained the centrepiece of the tour and England's retention of the urn, followed by a noble Australian victory in the Fifth Test at Sydney, helped to keep things in proper perspective. What luck to have been again the one to say over the air to eager early-morning listeners in the cold of a British winter, those magic, timeless words: 'England have retained the Ashes'!

Sports Report was born a year after one of English cricket's most wonderful summers, 1947. I was in only my third year when Denis Compton and Bill Edrich were blazing their happy-go-lucky trail across the cricket grounds of Britain watched by large, jubilant crowds still constrained by the economic stringencies imposed by Stafford Cripps, yet profoundly relieved to be free of the shackles and anxieties of the War. Compton and Edrich never quite equalled their extraordinary deeds of that year. Who ever could? Over 3,500 first-class runs each, Compton 18 hundreds, Edrich 12. But they played on long enough for me to see them bat and both, of course, were together when

England regained the Ashes after the long, long wait either side of the War in Coronation year. So I saw Len Hutton, too, the quiet master, and Cyril Washbrook and Godfrey Evans and quite a bit of Alec Bedser, whose cricketing home was The Oval where my father had kindly made my brother and I junior members.

In the 'fifties this was the best place to watch cricket, for all its smuttiness and brown bricks, for here it was that Surridge, May, Clark, Constable, Fletcher, Barrington, McIntyre, Loader, Lock and the mountainous Bedser twins (to name only those whose pictures spring to the front of the mind when the subject is recalled) forged their way to Championship after Championship.

It is my regret that knowledge of some of the great players of the immediate post-War era comes only from books and broadcasts. I cannot boast that I saw the immortal Don Bradman; nor the commanding New Zealand left-hander Martin Donnelly (though I played with him years later); nor some of the bowlers of genius: Doug Wright, for example, who spun his leg-break so fiercely that it frequently beat both batsman and wicket-keeper; or Ramadhin and Valentine in their prime on the 1950 tour. In 1957 Ram and Val toured again, along with Walcott, Weekes and Worrell, as, in 1953, did Lindwall, Miller, Harvey and Hassett, four of the pillars of Bradman's undefeated team of 1948. But from that 1948 side Sid Barnes did not tour England again and the same was true of the prolific Merchant and Hazare from the 1949 Indians and of the peerless George Headley and three others of the powerful 1950 West Indies team: Gomez, Stollmeyer and Rae, all of whom I have since had the privilege of getting to know well. Incidentally, talking of Vijay Merchant, did you know that he stands second only to Bradman in the best of those with career averages over 50? Merchant's was 72: useful!

Once English cricket got back on to a winning trail again in the 'fifties, life was sweet for a patriotic, cricket-mad youngster listening to programmes like *Sports Report* and making the most of the wonderful new phenomenon of television. Under Hutton the Ashes were retained in 1954–55, three superlative strokemakers in May, Cowdrey and Graveney each having his day of glory, though the headlines went mainly to Tyson and Statham.

This was a rare era indeed in English cricket, for with the great Trueman and Loader also in contention for places there were four bowlers not only of genuine all-out pace but also of genuine quality, with Bedser, huge of heart and frame, in reserve and Trevor Bailey too. Again, there was Johnny Wardle as an alternative to Tony Lock when it came to choosing a partner for Jim Laker who, in 1956, almost beat Australia on his own. His performance at Old Trafford that year warmed the nation's heart in a way equalled since only by Botham's extraordinary deeds at Headingley in 1981.

If the West Indies, bristling with brilliance, got a nasty shock when they lost to England in 1957 after Cowdrey and May had broken Sonny Ramadhin's spell at Edgbaston, England themselves, and all their supporters, got an even more unpleasant surprise when Australia under the enterprising Richie Benaud defeated May's invincible-looking team in 1958–59. A batting order starting McDonald, Burke, Harvey, O'Neill, Mackay, Simpson, Benaud and Davidson was the main reason, along with the bowling of Davidson – his shoulders broad as the stern of an ocean-going liner – of Benaud himself and of the controversial Ian Meckiff, fast and suspect, but a man of much charm.

It is commonly thought and often stated that in the 'sixties cricket lost its way a little in its upper reaches and to some extent this is true. There was some fairly dull Test cricket played, even with players around as brilliant as Garfield Sobers, as explosive as

Gary Sobers – later Sir Garfield – scored 8032 runs (57.78) and took 236 wickets in 93 Tests. At the age of 21 he made the highest individual Test score, 365 not out, against Pakistan at Kingston in 1958. A Glamorgan bowler called Malcolm Nash will also remember Sobers as the batsman who struck him for six sixes in an over at Swansea in 1968.

Wes Hall and as devastating as Ted Dexter. If any side captured the imagination among those who came to England in that decade it was probably the 1965 South Africans. They included a cover fielder, Colin Bland, whose grace and speed simply took the breath away; a competitor as tigerish as any who has ever pulled on a cap in Eddie Barlow; and a batsman of such poise and majesty in Graeme Pollock that one can only count oneself as extraordinarily fortunate to have seen even a little of his sadly brief time on the international stage.

My own life as a commentator, reporter and writer was starting just as the political storm was breaking around South Africa's ears. Barry Richards and Mike Procter were to be deprived of much. But there has been a good deal, nonetheless, over which to enthuse in international cricket in the last 20 years of *Sports Report*'s 40-year existence.

On the Road

Stuart Hall

Television and radio presenter, host,
reporter, interviewer and *Sports Report*'s
resident Bohemian for 30 years, Stuart
Hall introduces BBC Television's nightly
North West Tonight in Manchester and
laughs his way into every corner of the
land in *It's a Knockout*. He is an
antiquarian horologist and a failed
footballer – he was once on the books of
Crystal Palace.

When I was asked to contribute to this erudite tome 'twas instant flattery to me. Writers, you see are categorised thus: if one can really write, one writes novels. If one can write a little, one writes biographies. If one aspires to writing, one writes a newspaper column. If one can't write at all, one becomes a television critic. If one should never, at any time, put pen to paper, one becomes a sports reporter.

Dear reader, I am, come Saturdays, a football reporter. A somewhat different animal. The BBC permits flights of fancy, all colours of the rainbow in the prose, and licence enough to hang me but keep them from the well of the courthouse. I have been ostracised from Old Trafford. Cauterised by City. Lampooned by Liverpool. Bastinadoed at Blackpool. Spurned by Spurs. Shunned at Sheffield. Curmudgeoned at Carlisle. Bludgeoned at Burnley. Gurgitated at Goodison.

Bill Shankly was a great personal friend and he told me once of his latest international signing. I awaited the usual jargon – he's got everything: catches pigeons, two great feet, the style of Matthews, speed of Eusebio, the majesty of Denis Law. 'He's got everything,' grunted Shanks, 'bed bugs, lice, trench foot and clap.' Hooray for humour. The reason is simple. I refuse to accept football as a matter of life and death.

To me, most things in life have to be enjoyed. Latterly, and by that I mean in the 'decade' between my 21st birthday and my 49th (well, what lady ever told the truth about her age anyway?) there has been a decline in humour. Legions of journalists spawning words like frogspawn, and to

'Shanks'. Profession: football manager. Clubs: Carlisle, Grimsby, Workington and Huddersfield. Also Liverpool.

similar effect, have turned our national game, the finest entertainment in the world, into intergalactic warfare. They, football management, and the poor deluded players, have driven laughter from their stage, and replaced it with robotic football which stupefies the mind, induces severe boredom and stimulates the moronic, baying loonies into kicking hell out of anyone for any excuse. Oh, for the huge grin of Joe Mercer, the japes of Len Shackleton, the rough-hewn humour of Bill Shankly.

Tell me reader, that you too miss the jokes, the time when 'footers' used to be *fun.* That's why I shall always look for what's lost, cherish Frank Worthington for ever. A Don Quixote black-maned romantic Romany who tilted his boots for loot and laughs. When he smiled t'other night in a battle 'twixt Southampton and Liverpool why, the telly screen lit up. It didn't last for long, though − he was substituted!

Mind you, I've had my come-uppance oftentimes. Recently I described Michael Robinson, the erstwhile Liverpool number nine, as a 'dyspeptic water buffalo grazing with a herd of gazelle'. Clumsy, awkward, a yard behind the play and a thousand yards from Dalglish's analytical surgical football, he just didn't fit. The following week he smote a hat-trick at West Ham. My next Liverpool visit was awaited by all. Then, at a Huddersfield Town soirée, a voice enquired 'Do you remember describing a certain Steve Kindon as a "lumbering runaway wardrobe?" ' 'Yes', I perked. 'Well, he's 'ere and looking for yer.'

Many years ago Don Revie, possibly the prickliest, most over-sensitive manager ever, rang the BBC; discreetly mind you. 'About last Saturday. We listened to your broadcast and the lads didn't like it. Mick Jones isn't a heaving sweating Lincolnshire dray-horse. Billy Bremner isn't fed on raw meat and iron filings, the Mafiosi capo with a contract on his opposite number. And Johnny Giles isn't the arch assassin with the Mona Lisa smile.' 'But my dear Don

Corleone,' said I, 'when you've picked up the severed limbs of the opposition hacked off by Norman's left boot, isn't Giles the most feared in football; Jones the honest artisan; Bremner, though vastly talented, the ace hit man?' 'Pah', said Don Corleone, 'Elsie didn't like it either.'! Elsie is the wife. Elsie, the Queen Victoria of football. Her stentorian tones shrilled above the rest. Once at Wembley she stood up and bellowed 'Show yourself, Hunter! Show yourself!'. Norman was suitably taken aback, if not affronted. He adjusted his codpiece, and played on.

What has all this football to do with industry, you entrepreneurs are demanding? Well, buried deep in us all is pride, which manifests itself in diverse ways. My wife is always 'doing' her face. I'm forever cleaning my motor cars. My son, Danny, a fledgling graduate, is forever at 'Lord Jim', an advanced boys' boutique flogging clothes that Grandad wore. My daughter, Francesca, an actress, is constantly polishing her vowels − yes vowels. But we all support the local footie team.

When it wins we rejoice − lose and it's a mini disaster. A football team is, or should be, a barometer of goodwill within the community. From factory floor to office to boardroom runs the *Fil Rouge* of pride. Take time out to study not the Stretford End at Old Trafford but the stands. A typical animal was an old pal, Frank. A staid company accountant, intractable, insular, introvert. Yet on Saturdays he'd be on his feet, arms akimbo in rage, disgust, triumph − you name it, every emotion was manifest. Referees were the butt especially. None of them had parents. All should have a white stick, not a whistle. Bent as nine-bob notes, mentally deficient geriatrics. For 90 minutes Frank vented his spleen, then reverted into a nice peaceful law-abiding member of society. For Frank, that 90 minutes was the umbilical cord that united him with the lad on the shop floor. I'm positive that United's European victory in

1968 boosted ego and profits, that City's distinctive championship win of 1969 lifted the workforce morale. And where would the city of Liverpool be without the teams of Bill Shankly and Bob Paisley?

For the last 12 years I've travelled Europe denying what eurovision cameras have propagandised. Film crews from France and Germany have focused on the dreadful and ignored the good. I have tried to explain that when hordes of drunken fans invade the pitch waving broken bottles, railway carriage doors, half bricks, flick knives and flails, they are really only seeking to exchange gifts. And when they engage the foreign police in running warfare, they are simply testing EEC defence plans for Mrs Thatcher. After all, she has scant regard for a Froggie – the fans just carry it a stage further. At least our footie teams win in Europe. Unlike our white flannelled fools – until, that is, the invasion of Abboland in 1986–87.

But seriously, readers, away from the headlines, can we win back the whimsy, let the old visage crease into a smile. Hand me my bovver boots, cosh and Mohican wig. I've some friends to win over!

Liverpool Football Club has played a well-defined formative role through the years. 'Shanks' once allowed me to record the Kop in full voice. The Real Kop of the 'sixties, when 'You'll Never Walk Alone' was the inspiration. Scarves akimbo, tonsils quivering, a united hymn from genuine fans determined that, despite Merseyside's slow descent into industrial decline and decay, aspiration would still flow with each tide. Armed with tape recorders and sweating technicians, I posted my team at the back of the Kop goal. I conducted the 'Kop Choir' through a succession of chants and anthems. The hype was at fever pitch. Steam rose from bodies packed tight, furled up copies of the *Echo* doubling as urinals. How do 24,000 folk obey calls of nature trapped on the terraces?

The final anthem was 'You'll Never Walk Alone'. Sung as never before. The nape hairs bristle. Emotion overflows. Tears course down my cheeks. Through the public address I thank the fans. The cheers resound, from all bar one urchin perched on the retaining wall. 'Hey mister', he calls urgently. I hurry to him, thinking him overcome by this incredible occasion. I looked into his narrowing eyes and found truculence. 'Sod off you short-arsed git' he said, and shot off into the maelstrom.

Iconoclastic, divine, and so Liverpool. Collapse of short-arsed git.

When Shanks quit the club he did so because he lost faith in Britain. He believed that our country was on the verge of bankruptcy, that the currency would, overnight, become as the German mark of the 'twenties, worthless and devalued. He visualised mounds of notes being carted in wheelbarrows to buy a bunch of bananas. He even lost faith in the pension funds, and promptly withdrew his. He was a huge man in every way. A sage but, like all great men, he was flawed. Bob Paisley, his successor, quietly assumed greatness. The build of a farm labourer in Gray's *Elegy*, visage like a pickled walnut, the gait of a broken-kneed cab-horse. Kind, witty, avuncular, lover of the simple and honest, hater of pretension and pseud. Let me unfold a story never told before.

The year was 1977. The setting Rome. The event the European Cup final against Borussia Mönchengladbach. I persuaded the BBC to film the massive exodus to the Eternal City. Forty thousand trekking to the event of their lives. By jet in style. By motor car and motor coach. By thumbing lifts. Travelling steerage. By passenger and goods train, sleeping rough without food or drink. The Scousers took over Rome. They occupied bars and *trattorias*. Swarmed the streets with cacophony and wit. They even pimped for the ladies of easy virtue who throng the Via Veneto. Always with low-key style. No rioting, no vandalising, no head-breaking. I was proud to be with them.

Stuart Hall, with electric razor, shaves Bob Geldof.

My second camera team was to film in the Olympic Stadium. I required passes to gain access. The day before the match Peter Robinson, that truly magnificent administrator, and I loaded a taxi with 40 pieces of silver and set off for the headquarters of the Italian FA. 'Gifts', said Peter, 'will always sweeten labour.'

On the Via Veneto we stopped at a red traffic light. On instinct I peered through the rear window to observe a light lorry bearing down at great speed. It tore into the rear of our taxi, crumpling the boot and the driver's temper. He leaped out: 'Basta, basta, molto cattivo'. His temper evaporated as from the back of the lorry jumped 40 *carabinieri*, armed to the teeth and threatening instant access to heaven for us

all. 'Tell 'em you were reversing and apologise for God's sake', I implored. He acquiesed, acquired a jemmy, opened the boot, transferred the silver to another cab, and we were off and away.

Inside the building the gifts were distributed. The passes smilingly issued. Just then, Gigi Peronace, 'Mr Big', strolled in, silently viewed the passes and ripped them to shreds. 'Only Italian cameras inside the stadium.' He was adamant – we withdrew, abashed, but undaunted. Back at the ranch, our hotel, Bob Paisley drew up the master plan. 'Disguise yourselves as players, hop on the team coach, the rest is up to you.'

Joe Fagan carried the camera inside a team bag. Ronnie Moran and Tom

Saunders carried the lighting equipment, Phil Thompson and John Toshack the rest of the gear. Police escorts, lights flashing, sirens screaming, hot-foot to the stadium. Up the marble staircase into marble dressing-room one. Hastily Terry Wheeler, the film director, and the crew were hidden in the treatment room. Come the kick-off, I had nowhere to sit! 'File out with the team', suggested Bob. 'Sit on the sub's bench.' Cool, matter-of-fact, still smiling – the phlegmatic Bob Paisley, on the eve of his finest hour. No histrionics, arm-waving, cigar-chewing, gum-munching, heavy sweating, foul-mouthed behaviour synonymous with some football management. Bob could have been a bank manager on his way to the Toxteth branch.

Imagine the scene. Bringing up the rear of this great football team, carrying the dressing-room key, I was last to leave. And I was two yards from the most gripping, exciting, dramatic match I have ever seen, clad in my Liverpool tracksuit. Keegan played out of his shirt; and as Bertie Vogts was up that shirt most of the time, butting, punching, reaping and binding, Keegan's performance was heroic. Heighway was leaping down the left with that high-stepping style. Crazy Horse was at the battle of Little Big Horn. Tommy Smith was Mafiosi. Jimmy Case layered in sweat.

For Borussia, Simonsen stopped my heart with skill at speed. Steilike was Rommel, the total general. We were one up at half-time. I dashed to the dressing-room. I'd lost my voice in the sheer tumult. The cameras turned as the team trooped in. Nerves jangled, limbs twanged. Bob moved among them, quiet words here, a pat on the back there. Ronnie Moran was like a staff nurse ministering to his charges. Joe Fagan smoked through his third pack of the match. The bell for the second half. Suddenly the players began stamping their boots. The cavalry on the charge, the drum beat of the Balaclava, the most dramatic 45 minutes of their lives. The pitch the battling ground in the blazing sun. A mass of hysterical red and white, a crucible of noise. I locked the door behind me and filed out with the team.

Borussia equalised. Steilike was hurt and rolled over the line to our dugout. A torrent of pure Scouse and anti-German invective so terrified him that he rolled back on the pitch. Tension gripped me in a paralysis like a child's Christmas Eve, a thousand of them encapsulated in one. Tommy Smith smote the goal of the century. Phil Neal's penalty. Uproar. Joy such as I've never seen. Voiceless I hared back to the dressing-room. My crew, with handkerchiefs over their faces, enquired after the score. '3 – 1 to us', I croaked. 'Stand by to roll. Lights, action, scene 32, take one.'

But trudging towards us were the Germans. Tearfully led by Vogts, shirts in their hands. They congratulated us. In faltering German I tried to explain we were not club officials but the BBC. They still parted with their shirts and disappeared into the marble bowels. Crazy Horse on the jig led the joy, prancing, kissing, holding the European Cup aloft. The camera rolled and made history. The first time a European Cup Winners' dressing-room had been filmed.

As the junket reached its zenith, Peronace entered, light raincoat draped over the shoulders, Italian style. His mouth, prepared to mouth congratulations, dropped open. He couldn't believe it. We were here, arc lights illuminating his beloved scene, working in defiance of his sole authority. He shrugged his shoulders, gave me a withering stare and stalked away. As the stadium emptied, the supporters, wending from the dazzling amphitheatre of the Eternal City through Europe back home, would carry the moments of that match through their lives.

The players departed, leaving Bob Paisley, Tom Saunders, Ronnie Moran and Joe Fagan in the elegant marble edifice of dressing-room one. 'Evans the coach', the young back-room boy schooled for management, cast me a look that said 'Do you appreciate exactly what you've had today?'. There we were, sitting on the team skip, sipping warm Coca-Cola. Anticlimax hung in the air. I humbly, voicelessly, thanked Bob Paisley and his 'Boot-room Boys'. Bob smiled enigmatically. 'It's the second time I've been to Rome and beaten the Italians'. Laughter pealed round the marble hall. Men of quality, that on this, their proudest day, they had shown such patience and kindness to me and my team. The film was a mega-success and now lies in the archives. A mighty effort.

Oh! I almost forgot. I locked the door of dressing-room one at the Olympic Stadium leaving behind golden memories. I still have the key. It's a treasured possession.

As you will have detected Liverpool has a special place in my affections. But down the years I have cherished golden memories and spurned the dross. Who can forget the boardroom at Blackburn Rovers? A cavernous mahogany palace of Waterford glass and rounded friendly warm vowels. Hot, real meat pies, apple crumble and cheesecake made by the plump, twinkling-eyed gals who serve it. And the boardroom at Burnden Park. I always put on my best suit to visit Bolton. Matching tie and pocket handkerchief. My routine is set. Arrive at 2.00 p.m. precisely. Meander to the room. Knock on the door of the tea-room. The door is opened by a slim lady of mature years. Hair permed in grand manner. Her chum is of more robust build – imagine the great Norman Evans and his hilarious 'Over

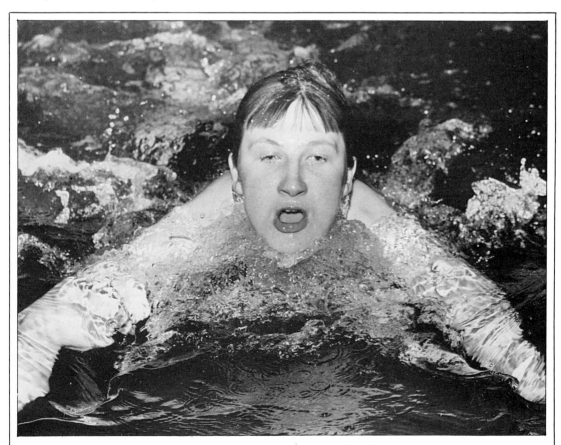

Anita Lonsborough of Huddersfield winning Britain's first gold medal in the 1960 Olympic Games in Rome. Her time in the 200 metres breaststroke was also a world record. She later became BBC Radio Sport's regular swimming expert.

the Garden Wall' sketch, and you will visualise the scene.

'Oh! Alice, look who it is.' I kiss both ladies on the cheek and stand back to be admired. 'Oh! isn't he luvly.' 'Who got yer ready?' I smile whimsically and reply 'Me Mam'. The screenplay never varies, long may it, and the spirit that moves it, live.

I revere nostalgia. The days of Joe Mercer and Big Mal at City. Matt Busby and United. Leeds United with the fabulous Bob Roberts and Don Revie. When the Don gave the team its head the play was inspiring. They won the championship with a 0-0 draw at Anfield. The reception from the Kop was so emotional that most of the players were reduced to tears. I remember, with joy, Eric Taylor of Sheffield Wednesday. Pert as a sparrow, deadly in adminstration. John Harris's Sheffield United with Joe Shaw the immaculate.

Down the years it has been my pleasure to bring you the delights of this wonderful football game. I submit to you, dear reader, two reports at random.

Sheffield United 3
Brighton 0

The ultimate sacrifice for your humble reporter is to leave the warm bosom of my Wilmslow shack and my frugal meal of plovers' eggs, larks' tongues in aspic, dromedary steaks washed down with '79 Chambertin, and cross the icy, desolate, bitter, unforgiving wasteland of the snow-covered Snake Pass on the Pennine Tundra. I observed a solitary blue tit nibbling a half coconut. Beside the storm-tossed waters of a reservoir, a herd of yak searching for fodder. Until, at last, on the grey horizon the concrete finger of Bramall Lane, the Taj Mahal of Yorkshire.

I clambered from my Snow Cat, clad in yeti boots and mangy fur, to ascend 120 steps to my eyrie, buffetted by gales and Yorkist vowels. Diminutive players cavort on a tacky pitch. Spread thin the 7,000 frozen faithful.

We endured an excrutiating first half, noting some neat but inconclusive Brighton play, and Peter Withe - the 'Big Daddy' of football - 'putting himself about' somewhat. Hail to thee Withe spirit. Little bird thou never wert on eagle's wings, this day inspired a barnstorming Sheffield onslaught in the second half. Colin Morris took a penalty on 55 minutes. Digweed saved the power shot, but Morris himself lashed in the rebound. Keith Edwards, with a classic header from a deep cross, scored the second goal. Peter Withe sealed a meritorious win with a mighty shot from a corner kick. Brighton came on the riposte. Danny Wilson casting off the South Coast effete, lathering himself with Yorkshire sweat. The eccentric Burridge in Sheffield's goal denied them. Yorkshire spirit had triumphed. A drop of spirit from further North will revive me as the ice is chipped from the ballboys.

Manchester City 2
Queens Park Rangers 0

Snowflakes fell gently from Moss Side's azure grey industrial pollution. But Stanley Gibson, the groundsman with a visage like burnt cork, grinned and pronounced his heated pitch perfect for football. Alas, much of the fare smacked of 'end of term'. End of term in early February, the price of no European soccer - what's a game without a prize?

City began with a fortunate goal. On nine minutes Mark Lillis, foraging right for Reid's through ball, looked yards offside. No linesman's flag, no referee's whistle, so he punted over a centre which Paul Simpson obligingly rattled past an astounded Hucker in the QPR goal to give City the lead. Subsequently, instead of heeding the lesson, QPR persisted with this mad offside trap. Without Steve Wicks to orchestrate it, the QPR penalty area was like a chicken run with a fox running amok. Hucker lived dangerously as City could have amassed a healthy goals bag.

Just before half-time Gordon Davies, running swiftly again on to a Reid pass, struck a lovely striker's goal. Reid was dissecting the left-side weakness of QPR with exploratory probes. The second half was a mix of artisan and pantomime. I enjoyed Mark Lillis, the City centre forward, a large red-headed flailing lad, a bit like a stevedore in a *corps de ballet*. But occasionally he revealed Astaire footwork that took one's breath away.

But, in truth, this match was somewhat tainted by an insanitary tom-cat.

He micturated over the six telephone directories that serve as my seat in the Press box here at Maine Road. The stench of stale cattery put me in solitary. As I was wearing my Granny's mangy old mink coat, there were dubious stares and downright rancid comment. Next time here I'll bring a bag of mothballs, if I can capture the moths. I'm miffed – yes *miffed*.

The Royal Year

Brian Johnston

BBC Radio's first cricket correspondent and godfather of the *Test Match Special* team, Brian Johnston was a television cricket commentator for 24 years. Host of *Down Your Way* for 733 programmes, and the author of *It's Been a Lot of Fun* etc., he is an expert on cream cakes, gaffes and friendship.

The splendour of 1953 always comes back to me when I watch television replays of the Fifth Test against Australia at The Oval that year when England regained the Ashes after 19 years. I hear myself shouting hoarsely: 'It's the Ashes, it's the Ashes!'.

That was obviously important to me; but even a cricket buff must concede that one or two other things happened that year. The cup overflowed. It was the year of the Coronation, the conquest of Everest, Gordon Richards' Derby, Stanley Matthews' FA Cup final and that famous victory by Hungary at Wembley – the first time England's footballers had lost to Continental opposition in the old grey stadium.

I was still a comparative new boy at the BBC, having been in the Outside Broadcast department for only seven years. I had just completed 150 *Let's Go Somewhere* broadcasts, a four-minute 'live' spot in Radio's *In Town Tonight* programme. Every Saturday night I did a stunt that was meant to be exciting or amusing. Some were. Some definitely were not. But it was a live spot, there were no re-takes and every Saturday was a first night. We either got it right or it flopped. Things like riding a horse bareback at a circus or being shaved and shampooed by the Crazy Gang in a barber's shop sketch at the Victoria Palace. Not easy to keep talking nor to keep to exactly four minutes. But it was all tremendous experience and I suppose it made me a fairly versatile broadcaster.

My time was divided equally between radio and television, with television having first call on me for cricket commentary, and radio for everything else. I was therefore quite surprised to be chosen by television as one of the commentators for their biggest outside broadcast occasion yet, the Coronation. For the first time there was commentary from *inside* Westminster Abbey, and there were commentary positions all along the route. I had been at Hyde Park Corner as television commentator for the late King's funeral procession in 1952. Now, in more cheerful circumstances, our commentary position was in Hyde Park itself, roughly half-way between Marble Arch and Grosvenor House. I shared the commentary with Bernard Braden. We had to get up at some unearthly hour in order to get through the crowds to our position.

It was a filthy day, everyone got terribly wet, and we had to wait for hours for the procession to reach us after the Coronation

The climax of the Coronation, 1953: the Archbishop of Canterbury is about to place the Crown of St Edward on the head of Her Majesty.

Sir Gordon Richards winning the Derby – at his 28th and final attempt – on Pinza in 1953. He had received his knighthood shortly before the Epsom meeting. Sir Gordon was Champion Jockey on 26 occasions (1925–53).

ceremony in the Abbey. There was the usual job of identification and information about the various formations as they passed us. It was all very impressive, but my outstanding memory is of the friendly and buxom figure of Queen Salote of Tonga in her open carriage. It was pouring with rain but there she sat – sometimes even standing – waving and blowing kisses to the damp but cheering crowds. She discarded her umbrella and earned a tremendous reception. Alongside her in the carriage sat a small man. When asked who he was, Noel Coward is reputed to have said: 'Her lunch'!

There was one great disappointment. Sir Winston Churchill (created a Knight of the Garter on 24 April) never reached us. To his annoyance he was in a closed carriage and could be seen by the crowds only if he stuck his head out of the window. He did this for a while, but evidently got fed up and ordered his driver to leave the procession and go back to Number Ten.

Yet there was even more to this great day – 2 June – than pageantry and ceremony. On the morning of the Coronation there was an extra fillip for national pride. Colonel Hunt, leader of the British Mount Everest expedition, sent a beautifully-timed message to announce that E. P. Hillary and Sherpa Tensing Bhutia had reached the summit of the mountain, more than 29,000 feet high, on 29 May. The message ended 'All is well', and the British people had one more reason to rejoice. Colonel Hunt and Edmund Hillary were both knighted five days later, and Tensing received the George Medal.

What a June it was! Fast on the Coronation and Everest came the Derby, where vast crowds hoped to cheer on the Queen's colt Aureole to give Her Majesty a Coronation victory. It was not to be, but the next best thing happened. In his 28th Derby, Gordon Richards, recently awarded a knighthood in the Coronation honours, rode his first Derby winner, Pinza, to beat Aureole by four lengths. Although the crowds – and the Queen – were robbed of a fairytale finish, they cheered the Champion Jockey all the way to the winner's enclosure.

Charlie Smirke on Shikampur led from the start and rounding Tattenham Corner was five lengths clear. But coming down the hill Pinza was nicely placed second with Aureole not far behind. In the straight for home Pinza caught and passed Shikampur who began to fade, and to the renewed cheers of the crowd Aureole ran on gamely to pass him and take second place. Although disappointed I don't suppose the Queen grudged Gordon his success after 28 attempts. Three weeks later she was to knight him at an Investiture at Buckingham Palace. Also knighted at the same time was an equally popular figure in another sport and just as great a master, Jack Hobbs.

How the crowds loved their heroes – and what heroes they were! Even before the Coronation the nation had crossed its fingers for Stanley Matthews, the old 'wizard of dribble'. Matthews was 38-years old and had never won a Cup-winners' medal but in 1953 he got to Wembley again with Blackpool and the whole country sensed that this would be his last chance. He was everybody's idea of a footballer, a chap who could toy with defenders like a cat plays with a mouse. I used to feel sorry for his victims as he invited them to go one way, and then went the other. He made them look such fools!

Blackpool's opponents at Wembley were Bolton Wanderers, and with 20 minutes to

Stanley Matthews receives his FA Cup winners' medal from the Queen at Wembley in 1953. Blackpool, 3–1 down against Bolton with 20 minutes to go, had fought back heroically – inspired by the 'wizard of dribble' – to win 4–3. Sir Stanley Rous, secretary of the FA and later president of FIFA for 13 years, smiles approvingly.

go Matthews' hope of a winners' medal were not very bright. Bolton were leading 3 – 1 and looked certain winners. But then Matthews took over. He used all his tricks and know-how, his great partner Stan Mortensen completed his hat-trick to make it 3 – 3 and then, with just a few seconds left, Matthews danced his way up the right wing again before sending across a perfect pass – and Bill Perry was there to whack the ball into the net. 4 – 3 to Blackpool, the whistle went almost immediately and Matthews had earned his precious medal.

I interviewed Bill Perry on *Down Your Way* a few years ago and he still warmed to the memory of that fabulous finish and was unstinting in his praise of the genius of Matthews. Plain Stanley became Sir Stanley in 1965, following in the footsteps of Sir Jack Hobbs and Sir Gordon Richards. Distinguished men!

I have always followed football closely and have supported Arsenal since their great days in the mid 'thirties. And, as it happened, 1953 was another great year for them. They won the League Championship for a record seventh time with a side that contained some old favourites of mine: George Swindin in goal; Jimmy Logie with his 'dummies' and twinkling feet; Wally Barnes, who became such a good television reporter; and, of course, the loveable Joe Mercer. Joe joined Arsenal after the War from Everton and the idea was that he should play for one or two seasons before he called it a day. But here he was, at the age of 38, still going strong despite a few creaking joints. An inspiring captain, a master craftsman and a lovely chap who always had a twinkle in his eye.

I did not play soccer myself but I am probably the only Rugby Union player who has ever scored a try in a mackintosh! It happened at Oxford when New College were playing Trinity. Someone tackled me and tore off my shorts. I went to the touchline where someone kindly lent me his mac to cover my 'confusion' while

somebody else nipped off to find me some new gear. As I stood there, the ball came down the threequarter line, and when it reached the winger on my side of the field, I couldn't resist it. I gave a shout, he passed me the ball and I sprinted away to touch down under the posts. It was really an illegal try, because I had not asked the referee's permission to return to the field. But like everyone else he was laughing so much that he couldn't blow his whistle!

But I digress. As I said, I have always followed soccer and even tried to become a football commentator. One Wednesday I was sent to Loftus Road to do a test on a Queen's Park Rangers mid-week match and taking part was a centre-forward called McGibbon who had scored three goals the previous Saturday and been described by the papers as 'Three-goal McGibbon'. During my test I noted he was number nine in my programme and gave him the full treatment. 'There he goes, a typical dribble by McGibbon' – 'a great shot by "Three-goal" ' – 'can pick him out anywhere with his bald head' etc. etc. That evening I read in the evening paper he had withdrawn at the last moment. I'd been talking about his replacement! The result was no soccer commentary for me. But that did not prevent a feeling of great shock when at Wembley on 25 November Hungary became the first-ever national side from across the channel to beat England at Wembley.

They won by 6 – 3 in front of an amazed crowd of 100,000, who saw England outplayed in every facet of the game. The Hungarians were Olympic Champions and gave a magnificent display of short and long passing, speed in execution and powerful shooting. In the past, for all their skills and technique, continental teams had generally been weak in front of goal. But on that grey winter's afternoon Hungary shot with great accuracy and led 4 – 2 at half-time. They were soon 6 – 2 and only a penalty by England made the score look a little more respectable at 6 – 3.

Looking back, it is still very difficult to believe when one notes some of the famous names in the England side, captained by Billy Wright. There was Ramsey (Alf) at full-back, Dickinson at half-back, Matthews and Mortensen in the forward line, to mention just a few. There was also a centre half called Johnston from Blackpool, but even with a name like that he was unable to stop the flood of goals!

The Hungarian I remember most of all was the great Puskas, their captain, at inside left. His wonderful ball control and passing were responsible for most of the six goals with their centre forward Hidegkuti scoring a hat-trick. So there it was. A great shock for England supporters but obviously the start of a new era. I have often spoken to Bill Wright about it. While obviously disappointed at being the first England captain to lose at home, he is always full of praise for the skills and flair of that great Hungarian side.

In 1953 there were two outstanding performances in the golf and tennis worlds, both from Americans. Ben Hogan won the Masters, the US Open and also the British Open. And in tennis that amazing little bundle of energy Maureen Connolly achieved a Grand Slam – all four major championships: Wimbledon, French, American and Australian.

And now I must return to my first love: cricket. England had regained the Ashes during Douglas Jardine's famous bodyline tour of 1932–33. But a year later in England, Australia won them back again and still held them when Lindsay Hassett's team arrived for their 1953 tour of the United Kingdom. There was a feeling of optimism among England supporters. Their master batsman Len Hutton was still playing beautifully and was in his second year as England's first professional captain at home. Peter May was fulfilling his early promise and Denis Compton's knee seemed to have recovered. Alec Bedser was still the world's best medium pace bowler, and

young fiery Fred Trueman was keen to have a go at the Aussies after his success against India the previous summer. In addition, the redoubtable pair of Jim Laker and Tony Lock were just beginning their long partnership together.

All looked to be set fair for England, in spite of the presence of old Australian favourites such as Arthur Morris, Neil Harvey, Keith Miller and Ray Lindwall. As it turned out it was an extremely level series, and the first four Tests were all drawn. England had the advantage at Trent Bridge where Alec Bedser bowled superbly to take 14 for 99 in the match. At Lord's England were saved by that famous four-and-a-half hour stand for the fifth wicket by Trevor Bailey and Willie Watson. Maybe the Australian team had celebrated their 'victory' too well the night before.

Headingley and Old Trafford were close struggles with England getting a shock or two at Headingley. In fact, once again Trevor Bailey played an important, if not entirely honourable, part in preventing an England defeat. First of all, on the first morning he and Jim Laker had a back-to-the-wall partnership. At 1.28 p.m. Trevor in order to prevent another over before lunch – told Jim Laker to appeal against the light. It was a brilliantly sunny day, so Frank Chester was naturally surprised at the appeal. But the Laws decreed that he had to go across to consult the other umpire. By the time he had done this, Hassett got fed up and led his team off for lunch. On the last evening of the match when it looked as if Australia might just snatch victory, Trevor 'persuaded' Hutton to let him bowl defensively wide outside the leg stump!

So to The Oval where once again Hassett won the toss. Thanks to some showers which freshened up the pitch and some superb bowling by Bedser and Trueman (his first Test against Australia) Australia were all out for 275, due largely to a hard-hit 62 by Lindwall after half the side were out for 118.

England replied with 306, with Hutton at his best for 82, and a last wicket partnership of 44 between Bailey (64) and Bedser (22). In Australia's second innings it was the turn of Laker and Lock and they took four and five wickets respectively to bowl Australia out for 162, leaving England needing 132 to win.

There was a scare when Hutton was run out for 17 going for a second run. But on the last morning Edrich and May added a miserly 24 in the first hour and at 88 May was out. This brought the Middlesex twins together and, amid mounting excitement, they slowly added another 35 runs. Hassett then conceded defeat by bringing himself on to bowl. Four runs were scored off his over and with five runs needed for victory he called Arthur, his vice-captain, to bowl what was the final over. A single from Edrich: four to win. Arthur Morris was bowling his left arm chinaman from the Pavilion End. Compton played the next two balls with exaggerated care. The crowd were all set, like sprinters at the start of a race, to run on to the field.

In the television commentary box I was lucky to be the commentator and rarely have I felt more excited. The next ball was outside the leg stump and Compton typically swept it for what the crowd thought would be the winning four. But no. At backward short leg Alan Davidson shot out an enormous hand and stopped it. (He was not known as 'The Claw' for nothing.) The crowd had begun to run on to the field, and back they had to go. The tension was terrific. The next ball was the same, and this time Compton swept it past Davidson down towards the gas holders. Whether it ever reached the boundary for the four runs needed for victory, we shall never know. The crowd poured across the field and converged on the pavilion. As I said at the start, my cry 'It's the Ashes! it's the Ashes!' went up as Edrich and Compton fought their way back to the pavilion through the crowd, bats held aloft like submarine periscopes.

Can you wonder that 1953 was such an important year to me? It was a moment I shall always savour. Nineteen years is a long time, but the Ashes were ours again.

Just two final memories. As you can imagine there was much celebration in the dressing-rooms, and the dressing-room clock suffered a wee bit of damage! Jim Laker always recalled that he and Peter May were whisked off to the Palace Theatre to see *South Pacific*. Much later, at about 11 o'clock, when he was back-stage after the show, he suddenly remembered he had promised to meet his wife at the rear door of the pavilion at the end of the match!

And finally, that very occasional left-arm bowler Arthur Morris became the most televised bowler in the world. The film sequence of that final dramatic over was used as a demonstration in every television shop in the land. To most people 1953 will always be the year of the Coronation. With no disrespect or disloyalty to Her Majesty, to me it will always remain the year of the Ashes.

40 Years of Athletics

Sir Roger Bannister
and Sebastian Coe

Sir Roger Bannister and Sebastian Coe are two of the grandees of British athletics. Sir Roger earned an immortal place in the record books by running the first four-minute mile at Iffley Road, Oxford, on the evening of 6 May 1954; and Coe − in a lustrous track career of medals and records − became the world's fastest miler three times (in 1979 and twice in 1981). Sir Roger's mile record: 3 minutes and 59.4 seconds. Coe's best: 3 minutes and 47.33 seconds. They talk with Derek Mitchell.

D.M.:

Is there an affinity between you?

Coe:

Yes, I think there is. Funnily enough, we've been thrown together in various circumstances, particularly since 1979, though I didn't have a great sense of athletics history as a callow youth. I didn't even realise that when I first broke the world record for the mile it was almost exactly the 25th anniversary of Sir Roger's wonderful feat. I'm a great admirer of his athletic achievements, which I think we tend to be rather blasé about now. We tend to look back at the four-minute mile and say, ah well, they're ten-a-penny now − and yet since that first one back in 1954 it's only been bettered by something like 280 individuals. Four minutes is still a very, very high standard. We tend to be slightly overawed at the moment by what's happening in the marathon and its great strength in depth. But it's still harder to run a four-minute mile than it to run a sub-two-hour-30 minute marathon.

Bannister:

I've watched Seb's career with admiration and great interest. He's had the difficult problem of having to race much more frequently than I did. He takes part in heats and finals, 800 metres and 1500 metres, and the times he produces require much harder training. I trained for about 30 or 40 minutes five days a week, and I think I raced only five times in my last year. He has problems with fitting in the rest of his life, which I didn't have.

D.M.:

Sir Roger, were you conscious in the early 1950s of being part of the heritage of British middle-distance running?

Bannister:

Yes, I was, because at Exeter College in Oxford, where I started my medicine, there had been Jack Lovelock, the great New Zealand runner who had won the Berlin Olympic 1500 metres final in 1936 and also held the world record for the mile at 4.07. There was also Sydney Wooderson, so certainly I regarded myself as part of this very curious tradition of miling which goes back to A. N. S. Jackson in the 1912 Olympics.

D.M.:

You call it a 'curious' tradition?

Bannister:

I think it comes from the English tradition of cross-country running − the harriers and so on − which gave our runners a background of strength at a time when cross-country running in America was not very popular. It was allied with this feeling of drama in the mile which is not a race that becomes tedious in the way that a 5,000 metres or 10,000 metres can, because you know nothing is going to happen for a few laps. In the mile you can watch runners jockeying for position, you can concentrate on whether they are attempting even pace running and when the moment is coming for a sprint for the finish. You wonder if somebody will try to strike out from the bell and jump the rest of the field. This is what gives the race its particular fascination for the spectator − and for the runner.

Coe:

I suppose I only started to become interested in this heritage after I had become a world record-holder. It's quite a

Sydney Wooderson, Britain's star miler from 1935 to 1947 and the man Sir Roger Bannister says was his schoolboy hero. Wooderson is shown winning his first AAA mile at the age of 20 in 1935, sensationally beating the mighty Jack Lovelock, in 4 minutes 17.4 seconds. And in 1948, a year after retiring from top-class athletics, he won the National Cross-Country Championship.

thought that only 11 people since Sir Roger have actually held the mile record, the latest being Steve Cram. It's a very select group of athletes, a great tradition.

D.M.:

Yet, as you say, it wasn't tradition which drove you on. It was your own ambition and competitiveness.

Coe:

Yes, I hadn't a clue what the world mile record was the night I broke it. I knew it was under 3.50, and when I finished the race in Oslo and people started to tell me I'd run 3.48 and whatever it was I still wasn't sure whether it was under the existing world record.

D.M.:

That's amazing. In the 40 years of *Sports Report* track and field athletics have always been one of the country's most popular sports. Sir Roger, can you account for that?

Bannister:

It is well taught, I think, at school level.

Most schools have some facilities for athletics and those who are not able to shine at games, such as soccer and cricket, will find somewhere in the athletic programme a sport or discipline which they can successfully have a go at. If they are very heavy or big they can throw things; if they are very small they can do endurance running; if they are fast they can sprint. I think it offers a spectrum of opportunity for young people to take part in sport which the traditional ball and team games may not provide.

Coe:

I think, without being patronising, that BBC Television and Radio have shown great loyalty to athletics. The sport has had little to offer at times and here I'm thinking back to some of the lower periods we had in the 'sixties, when good individuals were thin on the ground. Even back in 1976, when we had a very useful crop of runners, we won only one track medal at the Montreal Olympics. Not many years before that Dave Bedford was being hailed as the saviour of British athletics in terms of bringing the crowds back to Crystal Palace. A good crowd in 1969 was 500 or 600. So I think the media generally, and the BBC in particular, have been very supportive of the sport and have made sure that at those times when we could have drifted into being a 'Cinderella' sport we always had healthy exposure. Why the media have always tended to support athletics I don't know, but I hope it will always continue.

D.M.:

What about public interest, though? That's slightly different.

Bannister:

Public interest centres on the creation of the star because you get a very clear picture of someone's ability. It's not diluted by seeing someone in a rowing crew with seven other men and a cox.

You don't have to wait an hour and a half for a goal-less draw. There is always a definite result, and if it's a full athletics meeting then there are many interesting highlights to be edited and shown on television. The excitement is transmitted by the commentator who is able to provide information of a technical kind, which means all the time the audience is becoming more involved and more interested.

D.M.:

It also helps that, basically, the sport is all about individual excellence.

Coe:

That's true. There are some very nice features about athletics, particularly the growth of crowds since the mid 'seventies. I don't think it is any coincidence that at a time when people have been turning their backs on some of the excesses of the more professionally minded sports, like football, which has suffered massive losses to its gates, athletics has gained considerably.

D.M.:

But always middle-distance running has been the big attraction.

Coe:

I feel it's simply more interesting. The 100 metres is a great event, it's explosive, but it's over very quickly; and 400 metres is exciting with more to it than gun to tape running. But, by and large, it's only at 800 metres and above that a race can actually unfold in front of a crowd, and more at 1500 metres than 800. I think 5,000 metres is a great distance and there have been some marvellous races at 10,000, but (and I'll probably get shot down for this) it can drag a bit. Look at these features and we begin to understand what television likes. They don't want something that's over too quickly and they don't want something that drags on for 28 or 30 minutes unless they are showing it in its entirety in an Olympic final. Middle-distance running is very

Roger Bannister, Iffley Road, Oxford, 6.07 p.m., 6 May 1954. Distance: one mile. Time: 3 minutes 59.4 seconds.

good for a packaged evening of athletics. It's not too long, it keeps the interest going and there's a definite crescendo.

D.M.:

Can you see a broadening of interest now?

Bannister:

Oh yes. I think the Crystal Palace hop, step and jump, which didn't used to be considered a serious event, has become popular. Daley Thompson has made the decathlon popular. Watching decathletes run a 1500 metres has become part of the scene. Pole vaulting has become very dramatic and so has high jumping. Almost every event has become popular, including the field events whose competitors used to feel they were neglected.

Coe:

I believe people are realising there's a lot of skill in the field events. People say the media treats these events rather harshly, 30 seconds of high jump, 30 seconds of long jump and so on. But they are as traditionally valuable as middle- and long-distance running. All I would say to field events people is that if you find winners you will also find media interest. There's no lack of interest in Tessa Sanderson, Fatima Whitbread and David Ottley when they're after Olympic medals. And if we found another Lynn Davies then he would be as popular now as any runner.

D.M.:

You suggested, Sir Roger, that athletics were right for those who couldn't shine at ball sports. Is that what started you running?

Bannister:

No. I ran largely because it was very easy to combine with my work. It didn't take as much time as other sports and, indeed, even getting to school was a form of training. I was so physically active that until I came up to University I never trained in any consistent way and then, once at University, I always knew I was going to give up running once I qualified as a doctor. But, one way or another, I found I had the time to reach the various targets I had in mind.

Coe:

I always ran as a kid, long before I knew the implications of what I was doing. I found it easier to run than walk. We used to live in Stratford, two miles from the town centre, and I would think nothing of running from our house into town and then back again. In fact, I was an absolute pain in the neck to my mother, because when I should have been walking along holding the pram at the age of three or four I was running. And when we drove out into the country I would run in front of the car and open gates before it got there. There was obviously something inside me that loved the physical pleasure of running. Then, when I started secondary school, where P.E. was reasonably highly thought of and everyone started settling on sports, I discovered running was what I did best. I was winning races and getting immediate feedback from it. I enjoyed playing football but it was obvious I was never going to play it at the level I was probably going to run at.

D.M.:

Running for pleasure is one thing but when did winning become important?

Bannister:

Running wouldn't be much fun if you never won anything. The competitive side became important when I was up at

Oxford and I was expected to win for the University. Then I set myself targets in international competition and this required various preliminary races to be run at a certain pace, practising finishes in different circumstances and so on. It all emphasised the importance of success.

Coe:

Winning became important for me as soon as I started competing. A natural thing. If you compete you want to win. I don't believe in the modern educationalists' attitude that winning isn't important. We compete for houses, jobs, everything. Sport is no different.

D.M.:

Do you still enjoy the sport as much as you did?

Coe:

There are aspects I don't find particularly enjoyable. Most of what I do I enjoy because I don't get too wrapped up in it. What would have killed me − certainly mentally − would have been competing year-in year-out around the clock, coming off a track scene, going into an American road scene, then an American indoor scene. I couldn't do that. I prefer to set targets; and those targets are always the traditional championships: Olympic, European and Commonwealth.

Bannister:

I had a target of a gold medal in Helsinki in 1952 but I failed because I didn't plan my training in a sufficiently vigorous way to cope with heats, semi-finals and finals on consecutive days. It was entirely my fault. I was exhausted by the semi-final though in trials I'd run a threequarter mile in 2.52 which was a four-minute mile pace. If I had won that Olympic title I would probably have retired because I had already started clinical work at St Mary's Hospital in London. It was getting more and more difficult to find time for even the little training I did. I was so disappointed that I then made my targets the Empire Games (which are now the Commonwealth Games) in Vancouver in 1954 and, if possible, the four-minute mile. I knew a four-minute mile would be necessary to be sure of beating John Landy, who was to be in the Empire Games, and other runners who were to be in the European Games which were also in 1954. So really I had three targets of which the Empire Games and European Games were most important – although the four-minute mile, if it came, was obviously going to be quite welcome. And it all worked out right, of course.

D.M.:

Were you alone at the time in having this finite aspect to your career?

Bannister:

Probably yes. There was no reason why anybody who wasn't pursuing a medical career should have been tied by time in the way I was. In those days, once you'd qualified, you took up a resident hospital post which meant responsibility for about 45 patients. You were woken up pretty well every night because there would always be something wrong with some patient. So there was no possibility of my continuing after August or September 1954.

D.M.:

Let's make some comparisons between then and now. What do you think have been the most significant changes? Things that immediately spring to mind are tracks, shoes, training and diet.

Coe:

This is one thing we forget about Sir Roger's era, and one reason his feat was so staggering. I would challenge anybody now to run a four-minute mile on 28 miles a week as he did. I doubt if many would make it.

D.M.:

So you'd say hindsight makes Sir Roger's performance even more impressive?

Coe:

I believe it was one of the great physical achievements of the 20th Century. Just think: they used to run on suet pudding tracks. The spikes on their shoes alone weighed more than my road shoes do now. They'd been brought up on a wartime diet and they had just a smattering of work physiology and scientific knowledge as it applies to running. Nobody can take anything away from his achievement.

D.M.:

What would you say 3.59.4 would be worth now?

Coe:

Well, when we did a television programme together called *The Supermilers* the opening and closing scenes were of us together walking round the old cinder track at Hurlingham, and that's what we were discussing. A cinder track isn't bad, in fact, on a warmish day when it's not too hard and not too wet. But Sir Roger's race was in May, it was heavy and it must have been easy to pick up half a pound of muck on each shoe. It had to be worth around three or four seconds a lap.

D.M.:

That's bringing it down to close to what the record is now.

Coe:

Let's say that with the right shoes and on the right track he ran one and a half seconds a lap faster. That's bringing the time down by at least six seconds – and 3.54 is still winning a lot of European class races. And that's only a conservative estimate.

Bannister:

The speed that runners run now must be a second a lap faster purely on the basis of tracks and equipment. Especially with the all-weather track into which the shorter spike dips just enough to get a grip as opposed to the five-eights of an inch spike that went into ash or cinder. Techniques have also become much more sophisticated – the use of altitude training and so on – and these are obviously of benefit.

D.M.:

Seb called your four-minute mile one of the great physical achievements of the 20th Century, Sir Roger. How do you react to that?

Bannister:

I believe you can only compare world records with previous world records, and when a record is broken you can only say that at that particular time no one has run faster. It is as simple as that. The four-minute mile appeared to be a physical barrier as much as anything. Gundar Haegg and Arne Andersson of Sweden had been trying to break it throughout the whole of the year and Haegg's best, 4.01.4, the then record, had been there for around nine years. But they just didn't seem to be able to break four. It didn't seem logical to me, but there you are.

D.M.:

How conscious were you that runners like John Landy and Wes Santee had their sights on the record, and was this a spur for you?

Bannister:

Oh yes. I knew that Landy had already left Australia to break four minutes. He went to Finland and I knew the Finns could establish the right conditions for him because they have always been experts at organising pacemakers. I was in no doubt that my attempt would have to be made fairly quickly so I took the first opportunity in 1954, even though 6 May was very early from the point of view of conditions. And, in fact, I didn't make a final decision about the attempt until 20 minutes before the race. The wind seemed to slacken. I decided it was possible. I was ready. And, of course, it went to plan. I remember shouting 'faster' early on, but Chris Brasher, first, and then Chris Chataway were perfect pacemakers and together, as a team, we

got it right. A lot of things happened afterwards, of course. I went up to London after the race and appeared on television; the Press were on my trail; I needed a suitcase to carry my telegrams and letters and there was even a 'goodwill' trip to New York. But most of all I felt free, in a way, of the athletic ambition I'd been carrying round for years.

D.M.:

Seb, Sir Roger mentioned that the challenges of John Landy and Wes Santee were a spur for him. Did you have any similar spurs?

Coe:

I always had several reasons for wanting to run quickly. I enjoyed running; from the age of 15 or 16 I'd known only success; and running at world record pace seemed to me to be a natural development. Plus the fact that in 1970 my old man, with his analytical mind, set down a ten-year plan for me right up to 1980. It was a pretty bold thing to do for a 13-year-old kid in 1970. It had a page for every year on what he thought I was capable of doing with the right development and right nurturing. There was also the sheer naked rivalry with what was coming out of Brighton, though I deliberately tried not to get involved. I consciously told myself that it didn't matter what other people were doing, that the only important thing was what I was doing.

D.M.:

You mean that on and off the track you were always conscious of Steve Ovett?

Coe:

You can't live in a vacuum. I would look at the back page of the newspapers in the morning and I would read that Ovett had won this or that. I remember watching television in 1977 straight after *Match of the Day* and saw him run what I still say is the greatest 1500 metres I've ever seen as he won the World Cup in Dusseldorf.

Sebastian Coe (right) heading for gold, an Olympic record and the distinction of being the first man to retain the 1500 metres title in Los Angeles in 1984. Steve Cram (centre) took the silver medal and Steve Ovett (left) was forced to drop out when well placed on the last lap.

I thought, I'm 17 now and I've got three years in which to run like that.

D.M.:

Are you saying that but for Steve Ovett you might not have been the runner you are?

Harvey Smith – riding Sanyo Music Centre – show-jumping's most colourful and controversial personality. Also a professional Yorkshireman, farmer, cabaret entertainer, after-dinner speaker and wrestler who was billed on tour as 'Harvey Smith of Ilkley Moor, Super Sportsman of the Seventies and a great character'.

Coe:

I wouldn't go that far. But there have been times in my career, and in Steve's career, when life would have been easier and we could have run with a lot less constraint had we not been about at the same time. There was a period when we both seemed to be saying 'OK, he did it last week – I'll do it this'.

D.M.:

Ovett is on record as saying 'I'm a racer against people. I don't race against the clock'. That changed, of course.

Coe:

Yes, it became very important to him. My intention has always been simply to run quicker than anyone else, and the only genuine guide is the clock so, yes, in this respect, time was the real enemy. My sole ambition during the record-breaking years, 1979 and onwards, was to be able to sit back at the end of the day and say that nobody else in the history of athletics has ever run quicker.

D.M.:

Sir Roger, there is a lot of criticism these days about pacemaking – the job that Chataway and Brasher did for you in 1954.

Bannister:

We were running for the Amateur Athletic Association against Oxford University. We were a team – first, second and third strings – and it was perfectly orthodox and acceptable in those days for the second and third strings to work for the first string. It is a tradition which has disappeared but it was absolutely normal then. Chataway and Brasher were certainly there to ensure the pace was right for me and I didn't have any worries about it.

Coe:

The only difference now, arguably, is that we don't have pacemakers who take one lap easily and then come again, the way it happened at Iffley Road in 1954. There was a period in the early 'eighties when virtually only one runner would still be going at the end of a race. It was like a space launch with bits being shed right up to the lunar module – or Cram or Ovett were the only people standing up. Now I don't approve of that. I don't like to see runners pulling off the track every 50 or 60 yards. But in any case it's up to you in the end. Pacemaking helps, of course it does, but you've often got to plough the last 400 or 500 metres by yourself – and it's only your speed that counts then. There's nobody to carry you, no piggy-back for threequarters of the race. As long as pacemaking doesn't destroy the pleasure of quality of an event I don't see it as a problem. I have no moral hang-ups about it.

D.M.:

We've talked about the valuable projection the media gives athletics. But that's only part of it.

Coe:

There's what happens on the track and off it – or what is claimed happened off it. Some papers are responsible, some reasonable, but when you read an athletics report in others you discover it's not an athletics report at all. It's about how much money was made or who slagged who off or about Cram's dislike for Ovett and myself. This is a worrying aspect because it's the way football went from the 'sixties onwards. But by and large I'm not a media knocker. I think their job is a difficult one. They are in an environment that's as competitive as ours on the track.

D.M.:

It was different in the 'fifties.

Bannister:

There obviously wasn't the same media attention in those days, although I used to take part in quite a lot of broadcasts. But I was regarded as someone who was not always available. I didn't feel I had an obligation to take part in everything people had in mind which led to some criticism of the frequency of my racing. I regarded athletics, and still do, as an activity in which the individual has the right to decide for himself whether or not he'll run. Of course, there are other factors now, sponsorship and other commercial activities, which determine what happens.

D.M.:

Was there ever any talk of money?

Bannister:

Never.

D.M.:

But were you happy with that?

Bannister:

It was a totally different scene. I was fully engaged as a medical student and knew that I was just about to become a doctor.

Coe:

We've tended to become media personalities these days which means some hard knocks, some below the belt. But the money that can be earned now is important. Of course it is. I wouldn't be honest if I claimed otherwise. It's made life a lot easier. I've been in a position, through my own ability, to secure some kind of financial future. I will add, though, that I've never strayed off the path just because someone has offered me so many thousand dollars to compete when it hasn't suited me. I've always picked races that would give me the best launch pad for the major championships. The classic example was just before the

Los Angeles Olympics when I cut out all racing – except for one outing for my club – and went across to the States for four weeks' acclimatisation. I came back with a gold medal. Other athletes went across only a week beforehand because they didn't want to lose the pickings of the European circuit.

D.M.:

Has money created the great divide in athletics that so many feared?

Coe:

I don't think so – although you could argue that's easy to say for someone who has won two Olympic gold medals and the European Championship. I've always deliberately maintained my grass root links, I'm an active club athlete and when I come back after, say, a Grand Prix meeting and the newspapers have been talking about payments I never encounter any bitterness or jealousy. It's just accepted that I run a little better and because I do there is financial reward. There is probably a bigger divide at the top end of the sport. I'd love to see shot putters and discus throwers and javelin throwers getting as much as middle-distance runners, but I know that can't be the case. There are too many financial restraints, and – commercially and in media terms – middle-distance events are the attraction.

D.M.:

In the 40 years of *Sports Report* the record for the mile has improved by around 15 seconds. What about the next 40 years?

Coe:

There is no limit.

D.M.:

There has to be. We're never going to see four laps at ten seconds a time.

Coe:

Who is to say that might not be possible in 3,000 or 4,000 years' time? I think there are athletes around now who are quite capable of running 3.43 and I believe in the next ten years or so it will be down to 3.40. There are some fairly delicate physiological problems to be considered but, as Filbert Bayi said, 'I think by the year 2000 man will be flying'.

Bannister:

I have a feeling the limit will be around 3.30. That's the time I consider will be very difficult to better in terms of the known structure of the heart and the lungs and body. And the curve of improvement is bound to diminish as runners get closer to what is a medical barrier. It could take much longer than 40 years for the record to lose its next 15 seconds. Yet if one runner manages 3.30 it's illogical to believe there won't be another who, in certain conditions on a certain day, won't be able to beat him by a couple of inches. And, who knows, there may well be changes in the structure of the heart and lungs which are the result of different ways of training during the growth period. We can't be certain of anything.

The Best Seat in the House

Peter Jones

Peter Jones is BBC Radio's senior football and swimming commentator and a versatile presenter at Olympic Games, Wimbledon, Royal occasions and big boxing matches. The chairman of quiz shows such as *Sporting Chance* and *Brain of Sport*, he is a former presenter of *Sports Report* and a Cambridge soccer Blue.

'The best seat in the house' signifies, among other things, theatre. And that sums it all up for me. When thinking of all the broadcasts I've done over the past 20 years all around the world, the word 'theatre' comes most immediately to mind. Whether it's the Cup final or the European Cup final or the World Cup final in football; the Opening of Parliament Ceremony in the House of Lords or the Lord Mayor's Banquet at the Guildhall; the Olympic Games or the Commonwealth Games. The seat is quite definitely the best in the house.

The first World Cup I covered, as a very new sports assistant, was back in 1966. Our senior commentators then were Brian Moore and Maurice Edelston. I was sent to the qualifying group in the north-east of England and my first seats in the house for the BBC were at St James's Park, Roker Park and Ayresome Park. The group consisted of Italy, Chile, the Soviet Union and North Korea. Italy were the hottest of hot favourites and looked magnificent in training, but my biggest headache was collecting facts and figures about the totally unknown North Korean squad. Information was sparse and when the names did come up they were a nightmare. Not only did the players all look alike, but their names — tongue-twisters indeed — all sounded alike. Not that it would make much difference, for North Korea would surely be on the first 'plane home after the qualifying matches. They were up against the strongest opposition and the fruits of all my industry in collecting a North Korean dossier were going to be short-lived. The rest is football history. North Korea played some dazzling, if at times naïve, football and were through to the quarter-finals, and it was Italy who were on the first 'plane home. Suddenly I was one of the most popular men in the sports room, all because of that North Korean dossier. The commentators were grateful after all.

Facing Portugal in the quarter-finals North Korea took a handsome lead and their star was shining. But, when 3 − 0 ahead, they decided to go for more plunder. Disaster struck in the form of one Eusebio. Their defensive naïvete was exposed and they were finally beaten 5 − 3. A few weeks of glory, but whatever became of North Korea?

Perhaps my worst seat in the house in that 1966 World Cup was for the final on 30 July, England against West Germany. After covering the Group Four matches in the north-east I was brought back to the sports room in London for the rest of the tournament. We listened to Brian Moore and Maurice Edelston commentating from Wembley and watched the television screen to a background chatter of typewriters and teleprinter machines. In the end there was glory for England and we raised a glass, but I had had my first taste of live World Cup action in those Group Four matches in the north-east and felt frustrated within four walls when the story was unfolding, with all the drama and excitement and joy and despair, not far up the road at Wembley Stadium. I have felt the same ever since.

Four years later we were in Mexico, and by then I was part of the main commentary team with Maurice Edelston, Brian Moore having moved on to pastures new. The Azteca Stadium in Mexico City is one of the most dazzling in the world. A huge bowl of glittering colours and soaring grandstands. Pure theatre. England, sadly, went out to West Germany in the quarter-finals in Leon. After leading 2 − 0 England's fate seemed a cruel one and it was agonising listening to the commentary from our base in Mexico City. But if England's fall was depressing, there was a major consolation in covering the final on a hot June day in the Azteca. Brazil, playing some of the most beautiful and creative football I have ever seen, beat Italy 4 − 1. Pelé, Rivelino, Jairzinho, Tostao: great players all. They spun rainbows that day and I was there in the best seat in the house.

In West Germany in 1974 I had two best

seats. First in the Olympic Stadium on the afternoon of 7 July to see West Germany beat Holland 2–1 in a thrilling match and then in the evening to sit at the West German team table at the banquet in the Hilton Hotel in Munich. I had known the Beckenbauer family for some years and Franz had invited me to the banquet as his personal friend. It was an experience to be among the euphoria of victory. A few feet from where I sat stood a small gold statue. The biggest prize in football – the World Cup. It was some seat that night.

It was theatre time again four years later in Argentina when the host country beat Holland after extra time in Buenos Aires. Again we had some wonderful football on the pitch and all around was the noisy cauldron of the huge stadium, festooned with pale blue and white streamers and showered with a rain of confetti. A memory to live for ever.

In Spain in 1982 we had the disappointment of England falling at the second stage after qualifying the hard way for the finals for the first time since 1962. There was an even greater disappointment for West Germany. They had played well to reach the final but Paolo Rossi destroyed them on that July afternoon in Madrid and Italy won 3–1. We were staying in the same hotel as the West German team, along with a number of their supporters. As the team coach left for the stadium there was a mood of high optimism and talk of much festivities later. It didn't work out that way and that night – in contrast to the Munich celebrations I had attended in 1974 – I'm not sure I should have accepted Franz Beckenbauer's invitation to a seat at their table. West German gloom is formidable.

So the wheel turned full circle for me and it was back to Mexico in 1986. This time, apart from seeing the genius of Maradona (despite the 'hand of God' goal that helped knock out England), we also saw the ugly scars left by the horrendous earthquake which preceded the World Cup. But it is

still a beautiful country and one of the seats I enjoyed most during our month's stay was in a small executive jet hired by the BBC to take commentators and directors to the various centres for matches. Because of the long distances involved, the comprehensive coverage of the World Cup would not have been possible without that little 'plane. But the joy of flying to Guadalajara or Leon or Saltillo was in being able to watch the map of Mexico unfold beneath you. Great blue and white cloud formations over the Sierra Madre, rivers like silver snakes below and the occasional electrical storm to make you hold on to that seat.

With English clubs still banned from Europe at the time of writing we miss some of the outstanding European Cup finals we have seen over two decades. My first was in 1968 when that brilliant Manchester United side triumphed over Benfica 4–1 after extra time at Wembley – even without the injured Denis Law. That night I sat in a seat high up over the Wembley pitch, a seat that's become almost a second home over the years.

That night, too, I tasted the excitement of a European final. Since then there have been many. I remember, in particular, Liverpool's 3–1 win over Borussia Möchengladbach in the beautiful Olympic Stadium in Rome, with a rare goal from fearsome Tommy Smith. There was Nottingham Forest's 1–0 win over Hamburg in 1980 in the colossal Bernabeu Stadium in Madrid, home of the great Real Madrid. And Liverpool's 1–0 win over that same Real Madrid in Paris, in the Parc des Princes, a magnificently constructed stadium breathtaking scene of so many memorable Rugby Union Internationals. For excitement there was another triumph for Liverpool in 1984 – again in Rome – but this time it was penalties that beat the local team AS Roma. The one seat I would like to forget but cannot was the one in the Heysel Stadium in Brussels on 29 May 1985, a day of cold horror, awful tragedy and black despair. A day where you could smell fear in the air. A day when it didn't matter that Juventus beat Liverpool to win the Cup. A day when football died.

Before I move on to other seats in other houses that I have known I must mention dear old Wembley again and in particular Cup final day. Over the years I have seen some very good matches, some very indifferent matches, but the day is still very special. I have covered every Cup final since 1968 and that year recorded my first Cup final goal when Jeff Astle scored the only goal of the match for West Bromwich Albion in extra time to beat Everton. Since then much drama has unfolded on the Wembley pitch, but without doubt the most dramatic final came in 1979 when Arsenal beat Manchester United 3–2. Two goals behind, United came storming back to equalise in the last five minutes, only for Alan Sunderland to win the Cup for Arsenal with seconds to go. The other day we played the recording of that goal to Alan Sunderland. 'I still,' he said 'get a lump in my throat when I hear that.' I know what he means.

In the four Olympic Games I have covered there are so many scenes to remember. But it didn't begin well for me. In Munich in 1972 the black shadow of terrorism clouded the face of sport with the murder of members of the Israeli team. It was a hard two days as we waited and watched that apartment block where the Israelis were being held captive. Then came the confusion and the darkness and the bullets and the bloody end to it all. The memorial service held in that Olympic Stadium in Munich was a scene I shall never forget. A sunny morning with enough breeze to flutter the flags of the nations, as spectators and athletes from all over the world stood in silence, as the Israeli team manager read out each individual name of those who had died.

Four years later we were in Montreal on a never-to-be-forgotten night in a packed swimming hall where David Wilkie won his breaststroke gold medal. In a wonderful finish Wilkie held off the challenge of the Americans, turned as he touched at the finish, looked back down the pool at the scoreboard and knew he was the Olympic Champion. We did live commentary on the race, followed by the medal ceremony and shortly afterwards David joined us in the commentary box to talk to listeners back home: radio at its best and most immediate.

In Moscow in 1980, apart from the Olympic achievements, I remember the very impressive opening ceremony with Soviet athletes holding up coloured cards and with perfect precision changing shapes and colours and patterns around the stadium like wind through a cornfield. It ended with a huge replica of Misha the bear, the Olympic mascot, floating upwards into a blue Moscow sky. But despite the welcome and the friendliness, there was another shadow: the boycott of the Games by the United States for political reasons. The Soviet Bloc showed their disappointment by taking the same line in the Los Angeles Olympics four years later. The Americans, although saddened, went ahead, made a huge profit by careful and experienced management and as far as their opening and closing ceremonies were concerned it was pure Hollywood. Some thought them over the top. From where I sat I loved it all.

One seat I wasn't too sure about, at least when it started, was at the last Winter Olympics in Sarajevo – the first I have covered. The plan was for me to sit in a ski-lift chair with a microphone and record my impressions as we swung up towards the top of the slalom course. There was a swirling mist that morning and as we started off, swaying and bumping, I wasn't sure that it was such a good idea after all. But then we cleared the mist and below us was a scene of majestic splendour. The snow slopes sparkled like diamonds in the sunshine, towering fir trees lined either side of the course, touched by an occasional

Above: the commentary box at Lord's: Left to right:
Brian Johnston (with microphone), Trevor Bailey
(half-hidden), Alan McGilvray (with binoculars),
BIll Frindall (with beard), Peter Lush of the
TCCB (behind pillar), Christopher Martin-Jenkins
(with cup) and Henry Blofeld (with papers).

Below: the commentary position at Twickenham.
Left to right: producer Ken Pragnell, Peter West,
Ian Robertson, and actor Oliver Reed.

streak of colour from a ski-suit as a competitor tried his or her luck on a practice run. Finally our chair reached the station at the top and clanged into a locking position. I made my way through to the exit on the other side where skiers wait their turn to leap out into nothing and race their way down the course to what they hope will be glory. I crouched there and looked down. At the start it looked like a sheer vertical drop before it swung away into the wide curve of the first slope. It was terrifying. After my brief inspection I was asked if I would move aside for another competitor, a real competitor. He fastened his goggles, slid his skis on the snow-covered ledge a couple of times, looked straight ahead and then with a whoosh was gone. After that our seat in the ski-lift going down again seemed a much better place.

The Commonwealth Games are known as the 'Friendly Games'. In most cases this is true. My first Games took me to a rainswept and windy Edinburgh in 1970 and then − as had happened with the World Cup for me − the wheel turned full circle and took me back to Edinburgh in 1986. It was still windy. In between the two Edinburgh Games there were trips to New Zealand (Christchurch), Canada (Edmonton) and Australia (Brisbane). In Christchurch I had the most vivid geography lesson I have ever experienced. Our hotel was a couple of miles away from the studio. Each morning we would set off in the cars we had at our disposal. I would usually go on ahead of the others, stop the car at the beach, go for a swim then on to the studio. As it was there was usually no one around. One morning I was swimming in what seemed to be an empty sea, half a mile or so from shore. Suddenly a voice called out. I looked up. It was a lifeguard in a canoe. Was I all right? Yes I was. He pointed out that the currents were stronger a little further out and didn't advise going on. Later I passed his watchtower on the beach and thanked him for his trouble. 'Not a bit,' he said, 'but if you keep swimming over that horizon there's a long way to go. You won't hit land until you reach Chile.' Now the world really was round in the simplest terms, as opposed to the flat atlas picture I had retained from my schooldays. Great Britain in the top left-hand corner; down and right to Europe; down again to Africa; across to India, bottom right-hand corner Australia and the two dots of New Zealand, remote and distant. The lifeguard was a better teacher.

The Wimbledon fortnight certainly provides me with the best seats in the house. For the first week, with so many matches scheduled, I usually sit in our small studio under the stand, surrounded by cards and charts and results, linking as directed to whichever court is providing the interest or the excitement. Since we started our Wimbledon coverage in its present format it has also given me great pleasure to interview so many of the celebrities who come to the tournament each year. I remember Charlton Heston, a very good tennis player himself, saying how much he would give to play just once on the celebrated centre court. 'But I'm not in that league,' he said. 'Would you find it harder', I said, 'than some of the spectacular chariot racing scenes we've seen you in in some of your films?'. 'Listen,' he said, 'in chariot racing you have a stand-in, on the centre court you don't.'

I remember Tommy Steele, on his first visit to Wimbledon, remarking upon how small the centre court was, compared to the wide-angled image portrayed by the television screen. 'Just like the Palladium', he said. 'It looks big on the screen, but it's really quite small and intimate. That's why I like playing at the Palladium, you can feel the audience all around you. They are part of you. Just like the centre court.'

There was Peter Ustinov with his brilliant mimicry, describing in a dozen different voices how national temperament produces different types of tennis stars. So Ilie

Nastase (and Mr Ustinov sounded just like Nastase at that moment) is different from Rod Laver in his approach; Bjorn Borg different from John McEnroe.

Then there was the lovely Joyce Grenfell deliciously describing taking tea as a guest in the Royal Box with dry but gentle humour, until the tears ran down our cheeks. And Ginger Rogers – still looking a star – telling of the hours of hard work and training (just like tennis players, she said) before she and Fred Astaire produced their brilliant musical shows, which all looked so effortless.

In the second week of the fortnight I usually link the programme from one of the two show courts, culminating in the women's and men's singles finals from the centre court commentary box. Then you know exactly what Tommy Steele means. There is no better seat in a sporting arena in the world. You are on the court. You fume at McEnroe's tantrums and then are dazzled by his genius. You cannot believe that Borg is only human after all. You die a little when Virginia Wade falters for a moment and the crowd groans. It's great stuff. A great fortnight.

Conversation piece. Umpire Pat Smyth of Kent discusses the meaning of life with John McEnroe at Wimbledon. Jimmy Connors (back to camera) is among the eavesdroppers.

Away from the sporting arena I have been fortunate enough to broadcast from some of the loveliest cathedrals in England, from the House of Lords, from the Royal Albert Hall and from the Guildhall in the City of London. But for the first of the two Royal Weddings we have covered in my time my seat was not in St Paul's Cathedral where Prince Charles and Princess Diana were married, but on a balcony of a small, very well-known pub at the lower end of Fleet Street. We had a team of commentators stationed along the route from Buckingham Palace to St Paul's. My job was to pick up from Rolf Harris, who was at Australia House, and describe the Royal procession coming down Fleet Street, across Ludgate Circus to Ludgate Hill, before handing on to Brian Johnston at St Paul's. Working with me on that pub balcony was the effervescent Lorraine Chase who, as the guard of honour cantered down Fleet Street, all dignity and pride, their horses gleaming in the sunshine, came out with the immortal cockney line: 'Cor, look at them geezers in red coats. Don't they look smashing!' They did too.

But for the second Royal Wedding – the marriage of the Duke and Duchess of York – my seat was perfect. High up over the choir stalls looking down the length of Westminster Abbey to the great West Door. The music, the singing, the architectural splendour of that great place, the obvious happiness of the bride and bridegroom, the total joy of the occasion made it a day to remember.

I have covered two Royal tours – one to Northern Ireland, the other to Italy, where Her Majesty the Queen and the Duke of Edinburgh had an audience with the Pope in the Vatican. In Belfast and Coleraine the sight of hundreds of smiling young faces and arms holding out bunches of spring flowers to greet Her Majesty gave you hope for the future of a troubled country. On the Italian tour we were privileged to be shown some of the artistic treasures inside the Vatican before the arrival of Her Majesty and the Duke of Edinburgh. Later that week my seat was indeed regal. We were invited on board the Royal yacht Britannia for a day's cruise. She is a beautiful ship, gleaming from bow to stern. Steaming slowly out of Naples harbour on a hot, blue Italian morning was a memorable experience.

Each year I derive enormous satisfaction from our Royal Maundy service broadcast. The form of the service has scarcely changed down the centuries, but each year as Her Majesty distributes the much-prized Maundy money to the recipients as part of that service, the setting of the Cathedral adds its own dimension to the occasion. My first Maundy was in 1978 in Carlisle Cathedral. An imposing, solid structure of rose red stone. My only problem was that my commentary position high up over the organ loft was so precarious that I needed a safety harness in order to lean out and watch the arrival of the Royal party. There was the glorious singing of the choir in Winchester in 1979; the following year the delicate tracery inside Worcester Cathedral. In 1982 the venue was the smaller Cathedral of St David's, overlooking a wild Welsh sea; the soft greenery of the West Country at Exeter in 1983, the stronger outline of Southwell in 1984; and in 1985 Chicester in Sussex – the only English cathedral spire that can be seen from the sea.

Finally to London, and three seats I have been using now for some years. First the Royal Albert Hall and the Royal Festival of Remembrance which we broadcast each year, an evening of remembering those who died for their country's cause and for freedom. But while there are solemn moments, there is joy, too, and community singing and displays by young men of the fighting forces and the famous muster parade, always ending with representatives of the Chelsea Pensioners. It is an emotional and uplifting evening.

Then there is the Guildhall in the City of London, a place of much history and architectural splendour, where we cover the Lord Mayor's Banquet each year. On this occasion the new Lord Mayor outlines his plans for his year in office and then proposes the health of Her Majesty's Ministers. The Prime Minister then replies. Our commentary position is in one of the galleries overlooking the top table and from there we look down on a splendid scene, lit by candles on each table and the soft light of candelabra overhead. Gleaming silverware and flowers are everywhere; the ladies in many coloured gowns; tiaras winking in the candlelight. It's one of the few occasions when I have to wear black tie for the broadcast – it couldn't be otherwise.

But for absolute splendour I think our most imposing position is in the House of Lords where I sit to describe the Opening of Parliament. We are in a sound-proof box that overlooks the scarlet and gold of the chamber, at one end the gold throne from which Her Majesty the Queen reads the speech outlining her Government's plans for the new session of Parliament. The ancient ceremony as Black Rod walks along the long tiled corridor to rap on the closed door of the House of Commons to order members of the Government and the Opposition to attend the Sovereign in the other place is a highly satisfying challenge to a commentator – provided, that is, that the sound of Black Rod's footsteps and the knocking on the door synchronise with what you are saying!

I cannot end without mentioning the name of one craggy Scotsman who started it all, the man who created radio sport – Angus Mackay. Angus changed the course of my life when he hired me as a sports assistant back in October 1965. I owe everything to him. Since then I have worked with a number of Heads of Department who have made their own individual and creative mark. I am grateful to them all for providing me with the best seats in the house all over the world. I cannot wait for the next curtain to go up.

Conversation

Sir Neville Cardus
and Alistair Cooke

Sir Neville Cardus and Alistair Cooke were introduced to each other not long before Sir Neville's death in 1975. It was a moment of high worth because both were distinguished members of the old *Manchester Guardian* school of journalism, each had become pre-eminent in his field (Sir Neville on cricket and music, Cooke on America) and yet, although they had been professional colleagues for much of their lives, they had never met before . . . and never met again. They were interviewed by Bryon Butler – and their conversation was heard first on *Sports Report.*

The formal introduction between these eminent journalists took place in Sir Neville's little basement flat just a step away from the infinite buzz of London's Baker Street. It was a cluttered place of worn browns and greens; books, newspapers, signed photographs and a grand piano.

Sir Neville, whose writing gave cricket a new dimension, was wearing a rumpled suit and carpet slippers, a gnome of a man whose eyes twinkled behind glasses that seemed as big as window panes, a Lancastrian to all the corners of his soul. Cooke, the Englishman whose *Letter from America* broadcasts explain America even to the Americans, was tall, straight and silver-haired, a mid-Atlantic man who wore a red silk neckerchief, a blue blazer and a mahogany tan.

Cooke began theatrically by revealing that they had spoken together before – just once. 'When I was a boy in the early 'twenties I asked Neville (or 'Cricketer' of the *Manchester Guardian* as he was then) for his autograph at the Blackpool festival. I caught up with him by one of the sight-screens, and he was clearly a great man because he was wearing a velour hat with the brim turned down. He had a pipe and was making notes.

I tapped him nervously on the elbow and asked him for his autograph. He said "My goodness" – and that was our dialogue. We haven't met again until now'.

B.B.:

Cricket and music have been the pillars of your life, Sir Neville. What's the connection between the two?

Cardus:

I don't know except that I like them both. Why people should imagine a man can't be interested in cricket because he listens to Mahler or Beethoven I can't imagine. Mozart played billiards but people don't say my goodness, how could a man who played billiards compose such music? The best remark ever made of my dual occupation was in a letter I once got from Sir Thomas Beecham. He wrote: 'In the winter I'm a great admirer of your writing on music, and in the summer I turn with great relief to your writing on cricket'.

Cooke:

I never saw any conflict between intellectual interests and playing games, yet I've heard about readers of the *Guardian* who have been absolutely shocked that I love golf. This is the attraction of the 18th Century to me. A man like Benjamin Franklin, for example, had no hierarchy of values. He didn't see why a man who travelled into the furthest reaches of philosophy shouldn't also float down a river on water-wings, play every known game and wonder how you run a post office or start a fire brigade. It's the very opposite of highbrow.

B.B.:

Sir Neville, didn't you once confess that all the wise and funny things you've attributed to cricketers, from Macartney to Emmott Robinson, weren't always said by them, which you then justified by adding that if they didn't say them they should have done, and that you were, in a way, serving a higher truth?

Cardus:

Oh, I couldn't have invented these characters. They *were* wise and funny. I couldn't write about modern players in the same way. They are simply very good technicians in a technological age. The climate is different because of the pressure on them. But I'm not a man who says cricket now isn't as good as it used to be. Some of the colonial cricketers, for example Viv Richards, Barry Richards, Clive Lloyd, Kanhai, Sobers, Engineer, would fit into any side I've ever seen, from Victor Trumper onwards. I do think, though, that cricket writers today are too concerned with facts. I'm astonished that Alistair should say I was making notes when he first met me. I was probably writing a love letter during a rather boring bit of cricket. I never took notes.

Cooke:

I think all journalists make up quotes. People you want to quote, whether they're cricketers or politicians, don't have the rhythm, the feel of cadence that, say, Neville Cardus has, and so they usually say things wrong. I admit shamelessly that I'm always saying 'somebody once said, and wisely . . .', and then I quote something I've just made up. Nobody ever changes anything if it's in quotes, but if you say something on your own account they may mess it up in the office. A higher truth? A higher truth is what goes under your by-line.

B.B.:

You both seem agreed that sport as a whole has changed. What's caused the change?

Cardus:

When I first watched cricket there was no such thing as television, and there wasn't a great deal of space for cricket in the newspapers. People who watched were different, there was more of an amateur attitude and you rarely saw any women there. It was a simpler world. Television has made people more sophisticated. Even when I used to go round with the Lancashire side, when they won the Championship three years

in succession, we didn't want to win so much that we couldn't enjoy ourselves – with the exception, that is, of the match against Yorkshire, which we wanted to win by hook or by crook.

Cooke:

I used to tell Americans coming to England that it was all a little lower-key here. 'Don't be impatient' I used to say. 'Get to know a bit about cricket. Their rugby is very simple to watch, and don't be surprised if a man gets killed and they don't send on a substitute. And when a man scores a goal in the Cup final they'll be very restrained. They'll just touch hands.' But now! Mind you, what we must realise when they kiss now is that it's simply because the goal that has just been scored is worth a few hundred pounds to every player. The money thing is vital, and I think it goes to the head.

B.B.:

Some people, I'm sure, believe that you both do your writing at a high altar with a peacock quill in your hand and soft music in the background. How and when and where do you write?

Cooke:

I'm shattered. I simply bang out my stuff as fast as possible. Usually I'm unable to write anything except a cheque. I always put things straight on to a typewriter, and I've always carried about a little 1926 machine which folds over and is the lightest portable there is. I always bang it out. I've really no time to polish.

Cardus:

I never use a typewriter – and I can write anywhere. When I was music critic of the *Sydney Morning Herald* I wrote all my pieces at the post office. I remember an article I wrote about Tom Richardson, who used to bowl for hours at Old Trafford. I wrote it standing up against a wall because I'd suddenly had my idea.

Cooke:

I think you've made a mistake. You're not in the presence of two journalists, but two reporters. A journalist is a man who bums drinks from reporters!

Cardus:

I don't like writing to order. That is why I don't like that book of mine *Full Score*. It was written to order and with a deadline. I had to write it in a given time and I hated it. Some people liked it, but I don't.

Cooke:

I really have to have a deadline. I'm not lazy but I am a terrific procrastinator. I need the fact that it has to be done in the next hour.

B.B.:

Sir Neville, what sort of man and what sort of achievement do you admire most in cricket?

Cardus:

My ideal cricketer? Very difficult. I'd have to name about three. Denis Compton is one because he summed up the youth of cricket, a great improviser who always played like a boy. When I

Denis Compton – 'a great improviser', said Sir Neville Cardus, 'who summed up the youth of cricket. They all wanted to play like him.' He was at his matchless best in 1947 when he scored 3,816 runs (average 90.85) including 18 centuries.

came back to England from Australia in 1947, and everyone was still suffering the wounds of war, there was Compton at Lord's with this pale-faced crowd of 20,000 or 30,000 cheering him on and running every run with him. He symbolised every boy in that crowd. They all wanted to play like him. But if I was asked which player I would have walked 50 miles to watch bat it wouldn't be an Englishman. It would be Ranjitsinhji. I only saw him when I was quite a boy. Ranji came into the English game when it was as English as it ever could be. No googly bowling and no jazz and W. G. going forward to a good length ball. And Ranji made such strokes. Such strokes! Ted Wainwright of Yorkshire and England was my principal coach at Shrewsbury and I asked him what he thought of Ranji. 'Ranji' he said 'never made a Christian stroke in his life'. I would add just one other player, Victor Trumper, who was the most gracious, most gallant batsman you ever saw. Tremendous panache!

(Sir Neville was talking with such enthusiasm at this point that he somehow managed to edge his chair so far forward that the microphone finished behind him.)

Cooke:

There's just one man for me, a golfer, and it is one of the great, great disappointments of my life that I never saw him play. Bobby Jones. But I've seen a lot of him on film and no one will manage what he did. He helps explain what we've been talking about. He was an amateur and he retired at the age of 28 having won everything in sight. It'll never happen again. Good amateurs these days can see a million dollars coming at them so they turn professional very quickly. But there was more to Jones than that. I have, you see, an absolutely imbedded English love of grace and style – and Bobby summed up that to perfection. Bernard Darwin said that Jones' swing was a reminder of the drowsy beauty of an English summer's day. Today's golf swing reminds you of the drowsy beauty of a hydraulic drill. Bobby Jones was also a very great human being.

Cardus:

One more thing. If you were to ask me about the ideal man in my own profession – if whatever gods there be asked me what journalist I'd like to be in my next reincarnation – I'd say Alistair Cooke.

It was the first day of a new cricket season. MCC were playing at Lord's and Sir Neville had been there in the morning to see 12 runs scored in an hour. 'By the Lord', he said, eyes twinkling, 'I've been away three hours. They'll have managed another 50 by now. I must go.'

And he went: and now he's gone. But – 'By the Lord' – those eyes will still be twinkling.

40 Years of Rugby Union

Ian Robertson

BBC Radio's Rugby Union correspondent and a former *Sunday Times* Rugby Union correspondent, Ian Robertson was a Scottish International (1967 – 70, 8 caps) who played for Watsonians, London Scottish and the Barbarians. He is a Cambridge Blue who read English History, Dandy and Beano; and he has also owned a 12th share of a large number of slow horses.

Mike Gibson, described by Ian Robertson as 'the most complete footballer I have been privileged to watch', in action against Wales in 1977.

When the Five Nations Championship got underway in 1948 – as part of the celebrations, presumably, to mark the birth of *Sports Report* – I was preparing to blow out three candles on my birthday cake. It was all a matter of priorities.

As a teenager, however, I realised I would one day have to write about post-War rugby for a book celebrating the 40th birthday of *Sports Report* so, sensibly, I read history at University. This taught me that history repeats itself, a thought which has been essential succour and consolation to my fellow Scots for an interminably long time. Patience, though, sometimes runs thin. Scotland won the Grand Slam in 1925 and the Triple Crown in 1938 and – for year after year after year – the tartan faithful wondered just how long history was going to take to repeat itself; and if there was, by any chance, a catalyst which might hurry the process along a bit. The perpetual claim that perfection cannot be rushed was beginning to sound a little hollow.

It was, along the way, hugely encouraging for despairing Scots to find that the Irish had managed to orchestrate the lightning, which had struck immediately after the War, to strike again, equally favourably, in the mid 'eighties. It was also jointly discovered by the Scots and Irish that the only secret involved is a very good fifteen.

The Irish certainly had exceptionally gifted players in the late 'forties. They won the Championship outright in 1948, 1949 and 1951 – collecting, en route, the Triple Crown in those first two triumphs and their only Grand Slam in 1948. Apart from one brief visit to the winner's enclosure in 1974, their next flurry of success came when they headed the Five Nations Championship in 1982, 1983 and 1985, enjoying the added kudos of a Triple Crown in 1982 and 1985.

The similarities between these two successful Irish sides are interesting. Both were captained by their hookers, Karl Mullen from 1948 to 1951 and Ciaran Fitzgerald from 1982 to 1985. Each side had a formidable set of loose forwards: Jim McCarthy, Des O'Brien and Bill McKay in the early days; Fergus Slattery, Willie Duggan and John O'Driscoll in this decade. Each had a match-winner at fly-half: Jackie Kyle in the 'forties; Ollie Campbell in the 'eighties. And between their two ascents of Everest they produced a host of great players, among them the most-capped player in history and the most complete footballer I have been privileged to watch, Mike Gibson. He won 69 caps for Ireland and played in 12 Tests for the British Lions on his five Lions tours.

Yet Ireland also produced another equally brilliant player, Tony O'Reilly, who later, in a career that was both flamboyant and meteoric, became president of Heinz. He was the man who, after winning 28 caps between 1955 and 1963, was brought back for one game against England in 1970. More than a shade overweight he looked every considerable inch a business tycoon, and he was heard on the eve of the match to admit that his opposite number, Keith Fielding, the fastest wing in the world at that time, might well have the speed to go round him – but, he added, he seriously questioned whether he would also have the stamina.

Known for his quicksilver wit and repartee, Tony O'Reilly entered the annals of BBC folklore when he flew in his private jet to London from his new home in Pittsburgh shortly after being made president of Heinz. A keen young radio reporter conducted an excellent, entertaining and informative interview at Heathrow, but fell down on the last question. It had been reported in the newspapers in Britain that week that the average annual earnings in this country were £3,000. It was imagined that the president of Heinz would be one of the highest-paid executives in America, and our intrepid reporter, on informing President O'Reilly that the average wage in Britain was £3,000, wondered if she might be so bold as to ask if he earned that sort of money as the head of the Heinz conglomerate. Without pausing for breath, Tony O'Reilly replied that it was a very difficult question . . . 'On some days, yes, on other days, no'.

In 1955 O'Reilly was just as quick on his feet and after a dazzling first season with Ireland he went on the 1955 British Lions tour of South Africa. He courted spectacular success from start to finish, scoring a record 16 tries, despite the fact that he was only 18 years old at the outset. The British Lions, inspired by the brilliant Cliff Morgan at fly-half, played some breathtaking rugby and consistently made the best of a threequarter line which had Jeff Butterfield and Phil Davies in the centre, O'Reilly on one wing and Cecil Pedlow and Gareth Griffiths sharing the limelight on the other. This team produced some of the greatest rugby of the post-War years, and they enjoyed the best record of any major touring team to South Africa this century up to that time. They shared the four-match Test Series and scored 418 points in winning 18 of their 24 matches. They were, in the opinion of that much respected and much travelled rugby scribe, J. B. G. Thomas, the third best Lions side ever to leave our shores, and they were arguably the most exciting.

'J. B. G.' placed the 1959 Lions side, who toured New Zealand, fourth in order of merit; and after following their fortunes for six months, he felt they were desperately unlucky not to have at least shared the Test Series. They scored four tries in the First Test, only to lose 18−17 to six penalty goals from the boot of Don Clarke. What other sport would frame its Laws to permit such a travesty? It will strike the modern reader as strange, too, that in those far-off Corinthian days all four Tests were refereed by a New Zealander. The All Blacks were fortunate to squeeze home by 11−8 in the Second Test, and all the heroics of the Lions in winning the Fourth Test counted for very little in the final analysis.

Nevertheless, a team liberally sprinkled with rare talent then remained unbeaten in six matches in Australia, including both Internationals, and, apart from the Test Series, they lost only two other matches out of 25 in New Zealand. They rattled up a record 756 points in Australia while conceding only 336, and the future president of Heinz entered the record books. His name, to this day, is indelibly etched at the top of the list of try-scorers on a Lions tour. Tony O'Reilly scored 17 tries in New Zealand, three in Australia and another three in Canada on the way home. I doubt if this formidable achievement will ever be beaten.

If British rugby was outstanding in the 'fifties, I am sorry to report that it plumbed the depths in the 'sixties and the 'eighties. But the great thing about floundering around in a sea of mediocrity is the delight which follows when Britannia does rule the waves. The British Lions were on top in 1971 and again in 1974. These were the best Lions sides this century, winning a series in New Zealand for the very first time in 1971 by two Tests to one with one drawn, and remaining unbeaten in South Africa in 1974, winning 21 games including the first three Tests. They rattled up 1,384 points on the two tours while conceding only 411 − a thundering good record against the two most powerful rugby nations in the world.

Maybe even two swallows do not make a summer, but when an elusive dream becomes reality we surely have the right to inflate our lungs, rev up our vocal chords and, at full throttle, let rip our delight. So it was in 1971 when a uniquely talented band of gifted individuals were moulded into a dynamic team by Carwyn James, the best British coach I am ever likely to encounter. An inspirational figure of rare vision, imagination and understanding, he masterminded the 1971 Lions' success. And what quality putty this ingenious man had at his disposal! Barry John and Gareth Edwards at half-back, Mike Gibson and John Dawes in the centre, Gerald Davies and David Duckham on the wings, and J. P. R. Williams at full-back. I doubt we will see their like again − seven stars all at their peak at the same time.

The forwards were formidable too. Ian McLauchlan, John Pullin and Sean Lynch played all four Tests in the front row. Willie John McBride, Gordon Brown and Delme Thomas shared the duties at lock, and John Taylor, Mervyn Davies and Peter Dixon made a superb back row.

It was hard to believe that such a magnificent side would ever be matched, but to the undisguised pleasure of British supporters, the 1974 Lions team managed to surpass even the exploits of Carwyn's men. Several players made both those tours, and played in the Tests, including J. P. R. Williams, Edwards, McLauchlan, Brown, McBride and Mervyn Davies. The backs were boosted by the inclusion of J. J. Williams, Ian McGeechan, Andy Irvine and Phil Bennett. The forwards were actually improved with the selection of Bobby Windsor and Fran Cotton in the front row, and Fergus Slattery and Roger Uttley on the flanks. I was present in the BBC commentary box for the runaway victories in the Second and Third Tests in Pretoria (28−9) and Port Elizabeth (26−9), and never have I been so proud to be British. They were stunning performances, producing a try count in the two Tests of 8−0 in the Lions' favour. It was a veritable thrashing. I remember leaving the stadium at Ellis Park in Johannesburg, after the Fourth Test had ended in a 13−13 draw, feeling a little frustrated because the Lions should have won; but, nevertheless, I was prepared to accept J. B. G. Thomas's view that this was the greatest Lions team ever.

It was a happy successful tour, full of great players and great characters. The only moment of internal strife in nearly four months in South Africa arose when the manager of the Lions, Alun Thomas, called the whole party of 30 players to an emergency team meeting because the host Union were upset by the large telephone bills the Lions had run up in the opening weeks of the tour. Thomas announced that from that moment on it would be forbidden for any player to make any long-distance call to Britain, and the next caught doing this would automatically be sent home on the first available 'plane. Two days later, Alun Thomas looked decidedly grave when he summoned the players to the team room in the hotel. He was clutching in his hand a telephone bill for £87 which had been charged to his room. He was not amused. 'All right, lads,' he said, 'has anyone got the decency to own up to this appalling deceit?' Silence. 'For the second and final time, will the culprit do the decent thing and own up to his crime?' Silence. 'That being the case,' continued Thomas with a disturbing air of confidence, 'I must expose the culprit myself. I have checked with the international operator and the calls were made to Newport 684210.' At this point, an

enraged Bobby Windsor leaped to his feet. 'OK, that's it', screamed Windsor. 'Which one of you bastards has been 'phoning my wife?' The entire gathering collapsed with laughter, and Thomas, totally disarmed, did the only decent thing − he paid the bill himself.

That was the only tiny cloud to appear on a memorable tour. Unfortunately, from this unaccustomed position, perched precariously on top of the world, British rugby had only one way to go. It has, in the past dozen years, as if turbo-charged, rocketed downhill. British rugby, humiliated and whitewashed by the All Blacks in New Zealand in 1983, and by the Australians here in Britain in 1984, has since been much of a muchness − or rather less of a lessness. But if, in global terms, we are struggling to match even remotely the three southern hemisphere super-powers − New Zealand, South Africa and Australia − at least there is always the glimpse of a Triple Crown to maintain domestic interest.

After Ireland's brief domination up to 1951, the next 12 years belonged largely to England and France who won (outright or shared) the Championship six times each. The English backs were peppered with great players at this time, including such notable personalities as Butterfield and Davies in the centre, Rickie Bartlett, Richard Sharp and Dickie Jeeps at half-back, and Peter Jackson on the wing. They had a host of outstanding forwards during this purple patch, spearheaded by players like Eric Evans, Ron Jacobs, David Marques and John Currie, Peter Robins and Budge Rogers.

No one would have believed when England beat Wales 13−6 on 19 January 1963 that they would not win another International at Cardiff in the next quarter of a century. Even worse, England have won only one Championship since 1963. However, on that splendid occasion, they did take the trouble to tie up all the loose ends by winning the Triple Crown and the

Bill Beaumont on the break for England against Ireland at Twickenham in 1980. Beaumont played at lock forward 34 times for England, 22 as captain, and in 1980 led England to the Triple Crown, International Championship and Grand Slam.

Grand Slam as well. The year was 1980. Captained by the redoubtable Bill Beaumont, England stormed past Ireland, edged past France, 'annihilated' (Beaumont's word) Wales 9 – 8 and crushed Scotland.

Beaumont was a giant in every sense. He commanded respect: if he said it was Tuesday, it was Tuesday. He was raised when meat was cheap, and his large frame was always to be seen leading from the front in the thick of the action. He and Maurice Colclough won more than their share of line-out ball, and Uttley, Scott and Neary gobbled up all the loose ball like frenzied predators. Cotton, Wheeler and Blakeway made up the best front row in Europe. They struck the fear of God into opponents.

Fran Cotton – that wonderful Desperate Dan lookalike – would usually enquire of his opponent at the first scrum 'Do you like hospital food, then?'.

Behind these men of steel, Steve Smith and John Horton controlled the destiny of each match, never afraid to introduce the bludgeoning power of Paul Dodge, the rapier thrust of Clive Woodward in the centre, and the blistering speed and skill of John Carleton and Mike Slemen on the wing. Full-back Dusty Hare kicked every goal that mattered, seemingly quite impervious to pressure.

Bill Beaumont might well have led England on to many more triumphs, but after just one more season of international rugby, he suffered a bad head injury and was obliged to retire. A great player and exceptional captain, he remains immensely popular in all circles, the very embodiment of a national sporting hero. His temperament was such that he did not mind sharing the pitch in his final International at Twickenham against Australia in January

1982 with the first rugby streaker, the voluptuous Erika Roe. When she ran on to the pitch, Bill, facing his team, had his back to her and he quickly appreciated he did not have the undivided attention of his colleagues. Despite the noise of the crowd, he steadfastly refused to turn round until, eventually, one of his players, Peter Wheeler, confided in him. 'You'd better look round because someone is trying to take the mickey out of you, Bill. A bloke has just run on to the pitch with your backside stuck on his chest.'

When he recovered from the shock, Bill told his team if they wanted a closer look, they would have to camp down on the Australian line for the whole second half. They followed his instructions, and won 15 – 11.

Wales won or shared the Championship ten times between 1947 and 1969, but their period of unparalleled pre-eminence came in the 'seventies. There was a quintuple tie in 1973, and the 1972 Championship was declared void because some matches were not played, but in the other eight years of this decade Wales finished top dogs six times. Furthermore, they played a thrilling brand of open rugby that delighted spectators and bewildered opponents. Their prime genius was Barry John, who was virtually untouchable as he ghosted and glided past despairing and desperate defences to score or set up so many spectacular tries. I always remember that marvellous Scottish rugby writer Norman Mair describing his first meeting with the magical Barry John, whom he admired enormously. It took place in a crowded hotel room. When Barry decided it was time to go he left by the door; and somehow, Norman felt just a trifle cheated. The door was, after all, the obvious way out of the room, and from the legendary Barry John he had expected something a little more eccentric or dramatic.

I doubt if I will ever see again a collection of such sensational backs as Wales mustered right through the 'seventies. I can only be grateful that I had the pleasure to watch and, indeed, play against the likes of Barry John, Phil Bennett, Gareth Edwards, J. P. R. Williams, J. J. Williams, Gerald Davies, Ray Gravell and John Dawes. But the yellow brick road does not go on for ever. Throughout the 'eighties Wales have suffered indignity after indignity. They have managed no Triple Crown, no Grand Slam, no Five Nations Championship or even a share of that title. They have not even come close. They know now how Scotland must have felt in their twilight zone between 1938 and 1984.

The Scots, like the English in 1980, won everything in 1984. One drop of water in a drought is welcome; and the 1984 Grand Slam was all things to all Scots. And to one young 88-year-old lady, too. Nan Drysdale, sister of Dan who was capped 26 times for Scotland in the 'twenties, had seen every home Scottish International between 1919 and 1984 with just three exceptions. Over the years she had admired stars like Andy Irvine, Ken Scotland, Arthur Smith, Sandy Carmichael, Ian McLauchlan, Gordon Brown and Hughie McLeod, but she told our listeners in an animated BBC Radio interview that she wanted to witness one more Triple Crown before she died to add to those she had seen in 1925 and 1938. The Scottish boys duly obliged and made her day with a signed programme and a magnificent bouquet of flowers which they delivered to their most loyal and long-suffering supporter.

Colin Deans, the captain, earned his place in the history books with a succession of rousing performances. Iain Milne was the cornerstone of the pack, and David Leslie, Iain Paxton and Jim Calder were the best set of loose forwards in the Championship. The world's most-capped half-backs, John Rutherford and Roy Laidlaw, were in complete command. In scoring the most tries that season (ten) and by scoring 86 points to 36 in the four matches, they

thoroughly deserved their long overdue success. For good measure, they shared the title with France in 1986 to prove, if proof were necessary, that 1984 was no flash in the pan.

The world of political intrigue has meant that South Africa have not toured here since 1970. In recent years New Zealand have swept aside almost all opposition. In 1963, Wilson Whineray's All Blacks lost only one of their 30 matches, and in 1967, Brian Lochore's side were unbeaten, winning all four Internationals and beating the Barbarians. Graham Mourie led New Zealand to four Test victories against the Home Unions in 1978, and for the first time ever Australia emulated this achievement in 1984. The architect of the Australian Grand Slam was the fly-half, Mark Ella. He was the playmaker supreme, aided and motivated by the current top coach in the world, Alan Jones. Ella, a thick-set, dark-skinned Aborigine takes real delight in recalling his first cap, and how he, as the only Aborigine in the side was immediately welcomed into the team.

'I turned up at the team hotel on the Thursday and met the rest of the side. The coach came into the room and told us we were going straight to the ground to train for the match against New Zealand on the Saturday. He stressed we were going as one united team — the Greens. [The Wallabies wear green shorts, and are known as the Greens.] He emphasised that we were all one happy family — the Greens — and that everyone had a part to play and everyone would be treated equally. On the short walk to the bus I thanked him for his welcome and told him I was very grateful. As we got on the bus I heard his next command: "Sit anywhere you like — except I would like the light greens at the front of the bus and

Police cover-up. Erika Roe, soon to be a household name, is invited to move along during England's Rugby Union International against Australia at Twickenham in 1982. England won 15–11.

the dark greens at the back". Everyone burst out laughing — I was now one of the lads. Two days later we beat New Zealand 13–9.'

If Australia and New Zealand are top dogs at present, the most encouraging development in the last ten years has been the explosion of interest in the game in over 100 emerging rugby nations. Nowhere is this better illustrated than in the Cathay Pacific Sevens each spring. I have covered this tournament for the BBC for the past seven years, and have watched it mushroom into the most exotic, spectacular rugby extravaganza, now attracting 24 countries annually with another 24 clamouring to be invited. It was the forerunner of the new World Cup, and in many ways dwarfs it.

I shall always remember my first trek to the Hong Kong Sevens which took place in a tiny, green oasis called Happy Valley, sunk in the midst of the most densely-populated concrete jungle in the world. Under the shadow of the Wong Nei Chong Gap, nestling between Mount Butler and Mount Nicholson, and surrounded by 1,000 skyscrapers which stretch upwards like giant stalagmites, lies the island's solitary pitch which is the incongruous stage where the world's top players meet the game's less celebrated, but equally fanatical, participants. For countries like Papua New Guinea, Thailand, Sri Lanka, Singapore, the Solomon Islands and Malaysia, the Sevens in Hong Kong are the focal point of the entire sporting year, and they relish every second of their week in Chinatown. The camaraderie and exchange of cultures is an integral part of the whole exciting exercise. Occidental faces Oriental, and good sportsmanship and fun dominate all else.

Teams from the four Home Unions, France, New Zealand and Australia, intermingle with sides from Western Samoa, Korea, America, Canada, Argentina, Japan, Fiji and the like. It is a glorious cross-fertilisation of ideas and philosophies. The players from the emerging countries return home with the latest techniques and coaching pamphlets to spread the gospel. I recall with pleasure an irrepressible Neanderthal man, four feet nine inches and nine stones in his bare feet – and he used to play in his bare feet – called Lucas Senar, who accosted me in the lavish Hilton Hotel at the end of the 1982 tournament. He regaled me with stories of how next year Papua New Guinea would beat the mighty Australians with the Ella brothers, Campese, Moon et alia. How, I wondered, would he stop the all-conquering Wallabies? From out of the depths of a jet-black face, a bright twinkle in his eyes gave way to his secret.

'With Papua New Guinea's very latest weapons – bows and arrows.' This same man plucked a newspaper cutting from the *Port Moresby Chronicle*, reporting on the previous year's tournament. It showed photographs of Senar tackling Andy Irvine of Scotland and the British Lions in one match, and Mark Ella of Australia in another. He was bursting with pride. From his humble background in Port Moresby he had not only met, but tackled, some of the world's greatest players. The grass roots of the game were being encouraged. William Webb-Ellis would have purred with approval and satisfaction in that great changing-room in the sky. However, I should add that for all the fun and friendship the actual matches are played in deadly earnest.

I shall take to my grave a memory of a match between Japan and America a couple of years ago in Hong Kong. America, who had played superb rugby in the early rounds, were a formidable team of huge, fit, strapping, athletic hulks; seven all-American Sylvester Stallone lookalikes. Their super-confident, scarcely reticent coach clearly expected his boys to crush the tiny Japanese side. It was the Brobdingnagians against the Lilliputians. America kicked off; the Japanese caught the ball, and a dozen quicksilver passes later they scored between the posts. The Yankee coach stood up in front of me and shouted encouragement to his team. They kicked off again, the Japanese repeated their Far Eastern, mystical sleight-of-hand to score again, and once more the coach leaped to his feet to scream encouragement to his bemused and confused American side. For the third time in as many minutes the Americans kicked off only to watch Japan score again to make it 18 – 0.

At this point, the deflated American coach sank to his knees, threw his head in his hands and was heard to cry out plaintively: 'Pearl Harbour I can forgive, but not this.'

Later that evening, the Japanese and American players were locked arm-in-arm in an hilarious sing-song which lasted into the early hours of the morning. Rugby brings nations together, and breeds a universal warmth and friendship in a way, perhaps, no professional sport can. Rugby is the last of the great amateur sports.

If I had to pick out just one highlight from the last 40 years it would be the Scotland-Ireland match at Murrayfield in 1973. Scotland led 16 – 14 near the end of the game. The Scottish scrum-half, Dougie Morgan, tried a long drop at goal which seemed to dip under the crossbar at the last moment. The referee, 40 yards away, and the 70,000 crowd were as sure as they could be that Morgan had narrowly failed to clinch the match. Only one person knew for certain what had happened – the Irish full-back and captain, Tom Kiernan. As he caught the ball, instead of opening out to launch a counter-attack, he raised his hand high in the air to signal the three points for Scotland. It was a remarkable gesture from a true sportsman in the heat of a furiously contested rugby International. It was like a batsman giving himself out lbw in a Test Match, or John McEnroe informing the umpire that the linesman was wrong, his opponent's shot was actually in, and insisting on his opponent being awarded the point.

Kiernan knew his gesture guaranteed Ireland defeat, but it was an instinctive manoeuvre. It symbolises the whole spirit and ethos of rugby over the past 40 years, and I've every reason to hope it will be the same for the next 40 years and the 40 after that.

The fact is that, like everything in life, you win some and you lose some, and rugby players the world over have long since learned to take the rough with the smooth. No one has summed up the vagaries of sport better than the current Australian rugby coach, Alan Jones. In one phrase he encapsulated it all: 'One day you're a rooster, the next day a feather duster'.

'But he hasn't given it'

Brian Moore

ITV's popular main football commentator, Brian Moore was BBC Radio's first football correspondent (1963–68). A former *Times* man and an ex-director of Gillingham FC, he has also introduced *Sports Report* and a wide variety of television programmes. His books include *The Big Match*.

'Stiles with a long ball through to Ball . . . and Ball will run for all he's worth after this one . . . and he turns it in . . . can Hurst get a shot in? There's a chance for Geoff Hurst [voice begins to go through the commentary box roof] and he's hit the bar! It must be a goal − I would have thought that went in. But he hasn't given it.'

They are words that have followed me for 20 years and more, thanks to a BBC gramophone record, as it would then have been called, capturing every precious moment of England's triumph in the World Cup final of 1966. That July day, I remember, I shared one of those heavy-duty radio microphones − they used to wrap themselves around your jaws like a cross between a dog muzzle and something you

Did the ball cross the line? The 1966 World Cup final is 100 minutes old and Geoff Hurst (right, arms raised) is convinced he has scored England's third goal. Alan Ball (number seven) is already having a quiet word with Tofic Bakhramov, the Russian linesman, and the West German protests are led by goalkeeper Hans Tilkowski. Referee Gottfried Dienst consulted Bakhramov and the goal was given, but the argument lives on.

would expect to find in a war-time Lancaster over Berlin − with Alan Clarke of the fruity voice and northern authority and Maurice Edelston, renowned for his scholarly summaries.

We took it in turn to do 15-minute bursts of commentary that afternoon, and I was addressing the eccentrics who had not found their way to a television screen when Hurst scored that crucial and much-debated third goal. 'I thought that hit the bar and went in. Maurice Edelston?' 'I'm not certain', added Maurice cautiously − and then 'Yes, it's given, it's given . . . England are in the lead.' Rarely, if ever, has a football moment been so carved open, dissected more clinically or argued about more passionately, notwithstanding that little matter of an Argentine handball in Mexico 20 years later.

Years of practice now enable me to spot an earnest and disgruntled German football supporter at 50 yards; and a much-used body-swerve usually does the trick. However, to this day, if you are unlucky enough to bump into a German in any bar in the world he'll be prepared to argue, at

tedious and futile length, with photographic and filmed evidence thrown in for good measure, that the ball did not cross Tilkowski's line, that England got away with the most glaring piece of sunlit robbery and that Swiss referees and Russian linesmen were never to be trusted anyway.

But I know differently, and that gramophone record proves it for one. I can close my eyes to this day and see the ball hit the bar and, most important of all, see the sliver of green as it bounces down and beyond the line. Yes, a goal. No argument. But what is infuriating is that when I close my eyes again I can see little else from that most famous of English footballing days that falls into the same sharp focus. I have dredged my memory in vain. It is a bit like that frustrating moment of waking when last night's dream, so vivid at the time and surely so well worth repeating at the breakfast table, remains shadowy and tantalisingly beyond recall.

Why does so much of it remain no more than a summery haze in my mind? Taking the microphone on World Cup final day should remain the high point of a commentator's career. And not just any old World Cup final – the one that ended in glorious victory for England, for Heaven's sake.

However, I do recall slipping into Broadcasting House on my way to Wembley that day to pick up some bits and pieces and finding a single postcard on my sports room desk. My impact on the listening public was some way from causing headaches for the BBC post room! It was simply addressed: Moore, BBC, London. And the message was simple too: 'You'll never be as good as Raymond Glendenning as long as you live'. A splendid shot in the arm you must admit for any young commentator on his way to his most important assignment!

The point is that I would not disagree with that view – Raymond was, after all, my broadcasting idol. But that slight really

hurt, and still does, right through all the years of commentary. 'What is your greatest commentating moment?' they ask. 'It must be that 1966 World Cup' they say. 'No,' I reply, 'it was a pretty insignificant Second Division match of the early 'sixties – Portsmouth against Bolton. It was the greatest day of my commentating life because it was the only day I ever shared a commentary box with the illustrious Raymond Glendenning.'

I treasure still that long-gone afternoon at Fratton Park when I sat beside this large, jovial man with the most famous handlebar moustache of the time. And a man who had by far the best commentating voice before or since, with a priceless ability to generate excitement and a sense of thrilling expectancy which made the hairs stand out on the back of any true sports-lover's neck. His was the style of a bygone age with its frequent 'By Jove', 'I say' or 'My word', and only a favoured few, like Stanley Matthews, could expect to be referred to by their Christian names. Not for him a Nobby or a Greavsie!

And here was I, sitting beside the great man whose voice had crackled through to my boyhood bedroom on big boxing nights from the Harringay Arena; or to the back of the cricket pavilion on so many Cup final days; from the Epsom Derby; from Aintree. I'm only surprised that I was able to utter anything at all that afternoon in the presence of such a man. It was as though some Neopolitan urchin had suddenly found himself lining up alongside Maradona.

There remain no end of broadcasting stories about Raymond, most too good to run the risk of a check on their authenticity. One of the best concerned an FA Cup final at Wembley when, with the match in full swing, Raymond decided it was time for another of the Churchillian cigars that he loved so much. He kept his commentary going while he pulled out his cigar-cutter and his matches and was actually in the act of lighting up when, such inconvenience, a goal was scored and the crowd roared. Now he was never one to spoil a good cigar so he continued to pull gently on it. Unflurried, he let the goal go by unannounced. But a few minutes later, with the cigar now drawing splendidly, there was a near miss on the field. Again the crowd roared. And that is when Raymond popped in the goal with the sort of graphic detail that only he could produce. A cool customer indeed.

That afternoon at Portsmouth would have been one of Raymond's last commentaries and by the time 1966 came around our radio team had changed. Alan Clarke, like Raymond, had a splendid broadcasting voice. And he was a real pro. I remember one occasion – I think in Milan – when the taxi taking him to the match was involved in a really unpleasant accident. Alan was badly bruised and heavily shaken, but he promptly grabbed another taxi, performed to his usual high standards and the story only emerged after he had returned safely to London the following day.

Maurice Edelston was a players' commentator, as befitted a man who played inside forward for Reading as well as for the England amateur team. He was kindly, authoritative and loved the game. Deep into his fifties he was still playing, I recall, in the Reading Shopkeepers' League on Thursday afternoons.

Then there was our producer, Bert Kingdon, one of the old school at Broadcasting House. Having come up through the ranks he was a real stickler for what was right and what was best for the BBC. Early in my career he slapped me hard across the knuckles after a commentary at West Ham. I had been filling in at half-time on a bitterly cold day and merely conjectured how pleasant it must be to go into the warm directors' room at Upton Park during the interval to have a cup of tea, and how agreeable it would be if a cup were to find its way to the commentary position.

It is curious how those little remarks catch the ear of an audience and for the next week I was bombarded by everyone from colleagues to taxi drivers: 'Getcha cuppa, Brian?'. As it happened I didn't but, more important, none of this impressed Bert. 'Never do that again', he frothed. 'We must never let people think that the BBC get anything other than the best treatment.'

Bert was in the commentary box with us that day in 1966, when iced water would have made a more appropriate refreshment. We were over the Royal Box – Her Majesty was dressed in an eye-catching but neutral yellow, England playing in unfamiliar red and West Germany in white. And it is the colour of the day that now sticks in my mind. Uppermost the red, black and gold of the German flags, far outnumbering the Union Jacks, thrust with a mixture of confidence and arrogance into the Wembley air. And alongside them the German banners. These were new to the English scene: 'Erfurt grusst Deutschland' and 'Mannheim grusst Deutschland' and so on. These, and the klaxons, wrong-footed England's fans. They were still whirling those old-fashioned rattles that had been cranked vigorously on our terraces for decades: it took a few more years for a 'Norman Bites Yer Legs' banner to appear.

The goals that day we know by heart. Germany ahead, a moment that full-back Ray Wilson will take to his grave. As he said recently: 'It was a Third Division ball played in by the Germans and a marshmallow header by me'. It fell to Haller who beat Banks with ease. England were quickly level, Bobby Moore's free kick rifled home by Geoff Hurst's head. I have always thought that was the major turning-point in the game, simply because it killed off the Germans' growing confidence and set up the winning events that followed. Incidentally, when that lunatic decision to take the Horse of the Year Show to Wembley Stadium in 1968 led to the whole pitch being dug up (it took another 20 years

for it to recover) I plundered that square yard of turf where Bobby placed the ball, and transplanted it on to my lawn in Bromley, Kent. I have since moved on, but one unsuspecting suburban gardener still tends to this day a small stretch of grass on which football history was made.

Then England went ahead for the first time with the short-range goal by Martin Peters. Have you ever stopped to consider that had not Weber scored that cruel, last-minute equaliser for the Germans, Peters would have been our World Cup-winner, not Hurst? And how much that might have changed his whole career, perhaps his whole life? But Weber did score after a free kick had been given harshly against England. Then came that controversial third England goal which was added to thunderously in the dying seconds by the last goal of Hurst's hat-trick. I don't remember how we radio commentators described it; but I know we could never have matched the words of Kenneth Wolstenholme on television.

As Hurst made his approach down the left-hand side a few spectators, imagining they had heard the final whistle, started to run on to the pitch. 'They think it is all over' said Ken into his microphone as Geoff Hurst now rammed in a truly majestic goal. 'It is now!' As long as football is covered by television or radio, and commentators continue to strap themselves into another 90 minutes of flying by the seat of their pants, none will find better words than these.

The final score was 4 – 2: our work was done. Now it was the turn of the reporters down in that dark, dark Wembley tunnel outside the dressing-room to confront Alf Ramsey. The England manager scarcely disguised his contempt for the Press. There were two golden rules: never put yourself in

the front row at Ramsey Press conferences and always wait for someone with a stronger heart to ask the questions. Alf had the habit of answering every question with a half-cough – a mixture of annoyance and scorn. And he had the habit of referring to the Press corps as 'you people'. It did not go down well but few stood their ground.

I remember Ken Wolstenholme once asking him for his views on the way Nobby Stiles had dealt with Portugal's Eusebio. 'Dealt with?' said Alf. 'What do you mean dealt with? I don't think [half-cough] that is the way I would describe it. I don't know what that means. Stiles marked Eusebio well.' Subject closed. Poor Ken. It was a path so many of us had trodden before.

Alf was in a less tetchy mood after the final, as you would expect, but he remained just about the calmest man in the stadium. The story goes that when the game ended at last, trainers, coaches and reserves all leaped from the England touchline bench. Only Alf remained seated. 'Sit down you silly blighters' were his words of celebration.

Yet he remains England's most successful and, many agree, best manager. And even those of us who so often felt the sharp edge of his tongue believe it a travesty that he was later dismissed by the FA and allowed slowly to drift from the game. Is our football so rich that it can afford to turn its back on such a man? In later years Alf – now Sir Alf – mellowed. I recall having a very relaxed lunch with him three or four years back and we got to talking of the 1950 World Cup in Brazil and that infamous defeat of England by the United States in Belo Horizonte. I could not remember whether Alf was in the England side that numbing day. 'Did you play in that match, Alf?' I asked. He thought for a moment. 'Most certainly. I was the only one who did', he replied, with a smile full of mischief that in 1966 would have been a collector's item.

World Cup celebrations after the final swung westwards to the Royal Garden

Hotel. As I recall radio's plans did not include any such shenanigans; we were off the air soon after the final whistle and that was that. But the television cameras were there and I watched it all from home. Everywhere the cameras turned that night they picked out people who looked as though they had all won the pools. A nation was united as it had not been since 1945, and 11 young men, in the course of a single day, had become national heroes. Their lives would never be the same again.

It was great to be English and our football surely would never turn back. Nobody gave

The jubilant winners of the 1966 World Cup. England captain Bobby Moore holds aloft the Jules Rimet Cup as he is chaired by his team-mates following their 4–2 victory over West Germany.

a passing thought to the Germans. Yet within eight years they had beaten us in Mexico and won the World Cup in front of their own people; Sir Alf had been sacked; and those euphoric hordes who had chorused 'Eng-land, Eng-land' so joyously and triumphantly during that glorious July were to be replaced by vile and violent hooligans who came close to bringing this greatest of games to its knees.

Watching, recently, an excellent television documentary of those World Cup days called *The Boys of '66* I was struck by the words of Alan Ball, who had telephoned his father on the morning of the final. 'Take everything in about today', said Ball senior, 'It will be over in a flash.' I didn't; it was. But it has been lovely trying to slip back through to those wonderful days.

40 Years of Boxing

Harry Carpenter

Harry Carpenter is BBC Television's highly respected boxing commentator and tennis and golf presenter. He is a former boxing correspondent of the *Daily Mail*, an author and a contributor to *Sports Report*. He was once introduced as 'Your carpenter, Harry Commentator'.

Forty years ago I hadn't quite made my move into televison. Who had, apart from Muffin the Mule? In those days my work entailed writing one article a week on boxing and little more. It sounds like Heaven and it was. I spent almost every day hanging around Jack Solomon's gym in Great Windmill Street, just off Piccadilly Circus.

Across the road, chaps in mackintoshes with battered trilbies tugged furtively over their eyes queued impatiently for the mid-day opening of the Windmill Theatre ('we never closed') and the latest edition of Revudeville with its peek-a-boo fan dance. Somebody once told me about it. Having overcome the temptation to tag on to the queue, you stepped through this grubby entrance next to Carroll's Salt Beef Bar and climbed the 39 steps, quickly past the smelly dustbins on the landing of the first floor (where the wide boys played snooker before it became popular), on and up to Jack Solomons' gymnasium on the floor above.

Jack's office was on the right as you went in. Grubby walls were plastered with fight pictures and posters and the great man lorded it behind the leather-topped desk.

Yes, he did actually smoke those big cigars all the time. Perched on the desk, like as not, would be Clifford Webb of the *Herald* or Desmond Hackett of the *Express*. Out would come the whiskey bottle. Solomons would lift the 'phone and get through to Terry Donner, his amazing Girl Friday in the adjoining office: 'Get me Lew Burston in New York'. Burston was his American agent. You'd sit and listen while another bum heavyweight from the States was signed up for Harringay or White City.

To be fair, they weren't all bums. Lee Savold, past his best, came over and made a right mess of Bruce Woodcock, the Doncaster heavyweight, one of Jack's post-War trump cards. Another trump was fighting Freddie Mills, wonderful, irrepressible Freddie, a caveman with a mop of unruly black hair, who started out as a milkman in Bournemouth, fighting in the booths, and wound up light heavyweight champion of the world by beating Gus Lesnevich of America at White City in 1948. Freddie would come into Jack's office and sing his own version of a current hit: 'There's No Business like Fight Business'.

Outside, in the gym, unsung fighters who would never make the big-time paid their

Freddie Mills versus Gus Lesnevich: they met in two epic world light heavyweight title fights just after World War Two. Lesnevich stopped Mills in the tenth round at Harringay in 1946, but two years later, at the White City, Mills dropped Lesnevich for two counts of nine in the tenth round and took the championship on points. Mills was a regular contributor to Sports Report.

half-crowns (12½ pence) and hammered away at the heavy bag suspended from the ceiling. As the years went by the gold lettering on the bag was punched away, but even in the 'fifties you could still make out the inscription: 'Presented to Jack Solomons by Gus Lesnevich and Joe Vella'. Vella was Gus's manager and he'd coaxed just under £16,000 out of Solomons for putting up the title against Mills. It may not sound much today, but it was big bucks in 1948.

It is difficult now to explain the importance of Solomons' gym in British boxing life at the time. Jack was not just the king of boxing: he was Emperor and for years had no challengers. When Jack was tops, I was in my early twenties and so was Mickey Duff. Mickey, like Solomons, grew up in London's East End. After a brief career as a professional lightweight, he was projecting himself as 'the youngest licensed matchmaker in Britain'. Mickey was the most aggressively confident young hustler I had ever come across.

If you have read *What Makes Sammy Run?*, an American novel by Budd Schulberg about a young film producer whose ambition would not be thwarted – that was Mickey. He was running boxing shows on a ragged bomb-site just down the road from Mile End tube station, light years away from the Solomons ambience. But whenever Duff hit Jack's gym the place went into uproar. Mickey cussed at, argued with and yelled at everyone. Usually, he made his point and got his way, mostly with managers he was trying to beat down to their lowest prices. Through the flimsy walls of his office, Jack could hear Mickey in full spate. 'That Mickey Duff', he would say with a shrug. 'He only comes in here to make trouble.' Not so many years later, Solomons wasn't top man any more. Duff was.

No one has ever matched Solomons' flair for showmanship. He invented the dramatic trumpet fanfare and the finger of light tracing champion and challenger to ringside.

His shows throbbed with atmosphere, notably the open-air extravaganzas at the old White City, now so sadly demolished. The best seats cost 20 guineas (£21) and film stars and politicians fell over themselves to be in them. At ringside evening dress was *de rigeur*, and ladies smothered themselves in fur and diamonds. And in case they should get bored while waiting for the fights to start, Jack hired Joe Loss, his neighbour from the posh side of Regent's Park, to bring his band along and play from the ring. Sometimes the fights didn't live up to the preamble. When they did, it was a night to remember. Solomons always boasted that his famous luck would ensure it did not rain on the night. It never did – well, hardly ever.

The greatest night of Solomons' life, however, was indoors at Earl's Court on 10 July 1951, when Sugar Ray Robinson, middleweight champion of the world, boxing's most glittering star, came from Harlem to defend his crown against Britain's Randolph Turpin. With Robinson came the renowned entourage: his barber, masseur, golf pro, even a dwarf who played court jester, and, of course, a chauffeur for the lilac Cadillac which was Sugar Ray's state carriage.

Robinson was 30. A professional fighter for 11 years, he had won both welterweight and middleweight world titles; in 133 fights, only one had been lost, to Jake La Motta, the 'Raging Bull'. Such was the man Solomons was throwing against Turpin, our 23-year-old champion from Leamington Spa, whose reputation was built on the 'lightning strike'. Turpin, a formidable physical specimen, could destroy lesser men with a single punch from either hand, but most of us were convinced Solomons was mad to put him in with Robinson. The American came to England straight from a tour of Europe where he had fought six times in six weeks. There were rumours that much of his training had been done on a soft mattress, not unaccompanied.

At the end of that night in Earl's Court, 18,000 people were on their feet chanting 'For He's a Jolly Good Fellow'. After 15 rounds, Turpin's arm was raised. Hardened critics wept with emotion. And yet, in all truth, it was no great fight. The magnificent Sugar Ray did little more than cover and clutch. Try as he might, Turpin couldn't find him with a clean shot. Victory was enough, however, to establish Turpin as British boxing's hero. Unhappily, the fame quickly dissolved into disaster, which is not something I shall debate here. The memories are still painful.

Five years later, in that same Earl's Court arena, Solomons' luck ran out. His heavyweight stars of that time, Don Cockell and Jack Gardner, came to grief in separate fights, both in the second round: Cockell KO'd by the Tongan, Kitione Lave, and Gardner stopped by Jamaican Joe Bygraves. Neither man ever fought again and from that dismal point in 1956 Solomons' grip on the fight game was prised loose. I remember the old rascal with affection.

Which leads me to another genial old rascal: the late Jim Wicks, manager of Henry Cooper. They don't make them like Jim any more. He was know as 'The Bishop' because he was bald and benign and his low-key rumblings on behalf of his clients had an episcopal quality about them. The nickname had its irony. Jim was famed for his affable relationship with one or two gentlemen who had brushed with the law, such as Albert Dimes. A quiet fish lunch in Soho with Jim could well be interrupted by Albert. When he sat down and joined in cheerfully with the boxing chat, it was difficult not to recall that Albert had once stuck a knife into Jack Spot in the greengrocer's shop just up the road. The saving grace was that in those days villains generally only duffed up other villains.

For a time I was bothered by a punter who resented something I had said in a commentary. He got hold of my 'phone number and innumerable calls came threatening death or worse, until finally the police were called in and I went ex-directory. I was telling Jim the story one night after *Sports Report*, leaning on the bar in the BBC Club. Jim mulled it over, then rumbled genially: 'You should 'ave let me know. I'd have sent one of the boys round to sort 'im out'.

Henry Cooper will be the first to proclaim that no one could have taken better care of him than Jim Wicks. For a start he kept Henry well away from Sonny Liston ('We don't want 'im; 'e's too ugly for us') and got him two fights with Muhammad Ali, in one of which Henry dumped The Man on the seat of his pants with the famous left hook, an achievement which only has to be mentioned at any occasion today, nearly a quarter of a century on, for Henry to draw the ovation of the night. Rightly so. Henry was the longest-reigning British heavyweight champion and will remain the only man to win three Lonsdale Belts. Arguably, he is the most popular ex-sportsman in the country, loved by millions, and enjoys fame, fortune and a happy home life, a credit to his parents and dear old Jim Wicks, who taught him that you can spend a bob or two eating Dover sole at Sheekey's or roast beef at Simpson's and still keep your feet firmly on the ground. It helped, of course, that Henry shrewdly picked the right girl to marry, the lovely Albina, who will hit me over the head for mentioning her.

People sometimes ask me to name the finest performance I have seen from any British boxer. I wish they wouldn't. The question is impossible to answer. A judgement in favour of one merely insults a dozen others. So many moments are indelibly imprinted on the mind, like Frank Bruno's recent gallant efforts against Tim Witherspoon; or the night in Madison Square Garden in 1971 when Scotland's Ken Buchanan defended his world lightweight title against Ismael Laguna of Panama. Half-blinded by a cut and swollen

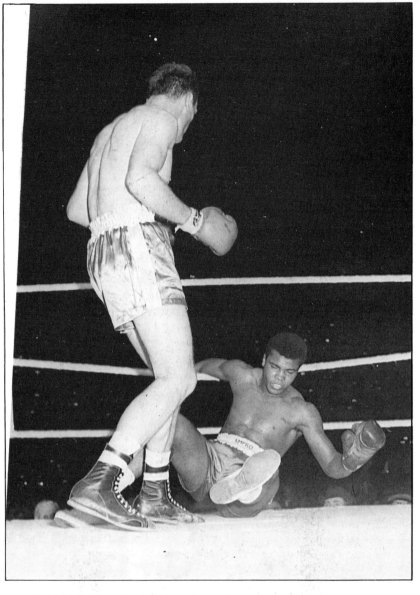

eye, Buchanan poured pure boxing skill and aggression into Laguna to win a convincing decision. That night I heard New Yorkers wildly applauding Ken's old-fashioned straight left, a punch which had long since been dropped from the repertoire of American world champions.

I could quote you Howard Winstone's three magnificent fights with tough Mexican Vicente Saldivar, or Barry McGuigan's superb night of triumph against Eusebio Pedroza. In the 'forties and 'fifties it was rare for Britain to have a world boxing champion, except in the lightest weights.

Recently we have had them at many weights: Terry Downes, John H. Stracey, Maurice Hope, Jim Watt, Cornelius Boza-Edwards, Alan Minter, Charlie Magri, Dennis Andries, Lloyd Honeyghan and Terry Marsh. One of my great disappointments was the premature downfall of John Conteh, a talented box-fighter with a shining personality. His hold on the light heavyweight crown was ridiculously brief.

Barry McGuigan outpointing Eusebio Pedroza for the world featherweight title in Queen's Park Rangers football ground, June 1985.

128

Ignoring professional advice, he gave up his world title on a dubious point of principle, and never regained it, a wanton waste of talent. John hit a fearful low point and I admire the way he has restored his place in life.

Sweeping changes have come over the sport in the past 40 years, one at least for the better: constant assault from the medical profession has tightened regulations and made the sport much more humane than when I first covered it, although I still occasionally see fights which horrify me, when a referee is slow to call a halt. The vigilance must never cease, or boxing will. It has powerful enemies, but I believe a majority of people in Britain would vote against its abolition. When an audience of some 20 million can be gathered for an outstanding fight on television, it cannot be offending too many.

My conscience in not entirely clear and never will be. I understand the danger, which is enough to make you question the value of the sport. But I also see the good it can do, principally in re-routing young men from possible delinquency into decent citizenship. No one becomes a proficient boxer without immense self-discipline. It cannot have escaped your notice that boxers are better behaved in their arena than are, say, soccer players or tennis stars in theirs. If I may point once again to Henry Cooper: here is the prime example of a man whose role in life has been enriched by his association with boxing. Not that Henry was ever delinquent or likely to be so: his education for life began at home. But he could not have attained his status today without the background of boxing. His experience is repeated a thousandfold and in cases that are not publicised. When I weigh the advantages of boxing against the dangers, I must come down firmly in support of it.

Like most professional sports, boxing today wallows in obscenely huge amounts of money, available only to the privileged few who are courted by television. Comparisons with past days are easy to assess. Rocky Marciano, the outstanding heavyweight of his time and a huge draw at the box office, had 49 professional fights, all of which he won, from 1947 – 1955. The total receipts from those 49 fights – not Marciano's share – amounted to $4,150,000, which today would not be enough to compensate Larry Holmes for just one title fight. Marciano's actual payment for seven world title fights was $1,460,000. He was the last of the 'poor' champions.

By the time his successor, Floyd Patterson, came along, satellite and cable television were flourishing and now fights could be relayed into cinemas across the States and around the world. The 'megabuck' era had arrived. Good luck to the handful of boxers who command five million-dollar purses, but one is entitled to ask whether they give five million-dollar value every time they climb into the ring?

There never has been a single world governing body for professional boxing, and the situation has never been as tawdry as it is today. We now have no fewer than three self-proclaimed governing organisations: the World Boxing Council, the World Boxing Association and the International Boxing Federation. The WBC insists on 12-round title fights, the other two on 15 rounds. Britain at one time recognised only the WBC (which it helped to found), but the WBA titles were dangled before British boxers, and the attitude was relaxed. Then in 1986 an IBF fight was staged on British soil, with a British boxer and Board approval.

Once upon a time there were merely eight weights, from fly to heavy. As I write, there are 16 divisions, separated in some cases by only three pounds. And at most of these weights, there are three 'world' champions. In 1986 only two men were recognised as undisputed champions: America's Marvin Hagler (middle) and Britain's Lloyd Honeyghan (welter). As I write, I can count

40 men all claiming 'world' titles of one sort of another. The coinage has been debased – and that's putting it mildly. I sigh, quite uselessly, for the days when the man in the street unerringly named the heavyweight champion of the world. That has not happened since the retirement of Muhammad Ali.

Nat Fleischer, the American ring historian and publisher, marked my card about Cassius Clay before the 1960 Olympic Games in Rome: 'The guy's a dancer, not a fighter'. Not even Nat, who had watched John L. Sullivan fight, foresaw the impact Clay would make on the game. Just like Nat said, Clay fancy-footed his way round the Olympic ring to win the gold medal, but if you looked closely you noticed the hands were also doing a bit, like gouging the face of Pietrzykowski, the best light heavyweight in Europe, into little pieces.

However, that did not make him a future heavyweight champion of the world, let alone the most charismatic figure the sport had ever seen. A story doing the rounds in Rome told how he had spent a lot of time chasing America's gold medal sprinter, Wilma Rudolph, but that she had too much speed, even for him. For a time after Rome I forgot about Cassius Clay.

And then, early in 1961 in London, I picked up a copy of the American magazine, *Saturday Evening Post*. Writer Dick Schaap contributed a big feature on Clay, telling how he had worn his gold medal night and day on his return to the States, how in New York he had gone into a penny arcade and had a mock newspaper headline set up. A picture showed Clay holding the paper up for his family to read. The headline blared: 'CASSIUS SIGNS FOR PATTERSON FIGHT!' At this time he had taken part in precisely five professional fights, but he knew exactly where he was going. I quote from Schaap's article: 'From the time he was 12 years old, when he first discovered that his fists and footwork were "real good", Clay has believed he would get on

top – "I dream about what it's gonna be like. I'll have a hundred thousand dollar home and a beautiful wife. I'll own two Cadillacs, and then I'll have a Ford for just getting around in . . ." '.

And so it went on: how Sugar Ray Robinson was his idol, how the name of Clay would one day be just as famous. Curiously there was no mention anywhere of the rhyming predictions for which he later became world famous (and which proved uncannily accurate), but slap in the middle of the piece the *Saturday Evening Post* editors had placed a comic verse by one Hal Chadwick, which they presumably thought would put the young braggart in his place:

'It seems the modern youngster
 Is quite correct in banking
 On getting all he asks for . . .
 Except, of course, a spanking.'

The view that Clay would get his come-uppance long before he ever got his hands on the world title was commonplace. Very few took him seriously.

Two years go by, and now I am at the top of the Empire State Building in New York interviewing Cassius Clay, and he is telling me he is The Greatest and that when he starts to jive, Henry Cooper will fall in five. My first interview with him, and I'd got it by ringing him up and suggesting that if he really was The Greatest, it was time he met The Highest, i.e. the Empire State Building (yes, I know it isn't The Highest now, but it was in 1963). Never had I been exposed to such an amazing outpouring of gibes and gibberish. No boxer had ever talked like this. Come to that, no heavyweight had ever fought like him. It was fashionable then to say he was too flashy to be great – 'how can the guy throw a big punch dancing around like that? He's got no platform to work from'.

The first big test had come in 1962 when he was matched with one of boxing's legendary figures: ancient Archie Moore, ex-light heavyweight champion of the world, now almost at the end of a 30-year career. Poetry prediction was already part of the act with Clay: 'I knew I had to have a publicity gimmick to get my name in the newspapers. I thought, I'm going to liven up the fight game. There's not enough talking. The game's dying. I had to find a word that rhymed with Moore. So I said: "Archie Moore, if you don't fall in four, I won't fight no more" '.

Moore fell in four. And Cooper went in five, albeit with a cut eye. Then, the unbelievable. Sonny Liston, who had upended Floyd Patterson twice inside a round and was the most menacing character around since King Kong, handed Clay the title by quitting on his stool after six rounds, only moments after Clay had himself tried to retire from the fight, complaining of burning stuff in his eyes. Bizarre – but Clay was Champion of the World.

These were the days when he upstaged the all-conquering Beatles on their trip to the States. They paid him a visit in his Miami gym and they wound up being photographed stretched out on the floor, all four of them, with Clay upright, towering over them, his fist raised in victory. These were also the days when he dropped the name of Cassius Clay and acquired his Islamic title of Muhammad Ali. I remember calling his Miami bungalow from a 'phone box. His brother answered. 'Is that Rudolph Valentino Clay?' I asked. The reply was surly, 'No, it ain't. This is Rahman Ali.' I asked to speak to Cassius. The reply was even surlier. 'There ain't nobody here by that name. Do you wish to speak with Muhammad Ali?' I never called him Cassius again.

As he went on, out-thinking, out-boxing and out-punching every challenger in sight, we slowly realised that here was the most exceptional champion of all time. When the USA stripped him of his title for refusing to take the oath of allegiance for National Service ('I ain't got no quarrel with them Viet Cong') he won the world's sympathy. The first city to offer him a fight after his three and a half year suspension was Atlanta, Georgia, the setting for *Gone with the Wind* and a former hotbed of slavery. The governor of Georgia at the time was the future President, Jimmy Carter. This was another bizarre night. Ali dealt with Jerry Quarry, a white Californian, in three rounds before an audience predominantly black and blatantly rich: the so-called 'Beautiful People', the women svelte and sleek in black dresses lit by diamonds, the men swirling silk-lined capes and sporting floppy velour hats. While they sat and rapturously applauded the return of Ali, a gang of robbers raided their homes. The rapture dissolved into anger.

But the most amazing night of all was the Second Coming of Muhammad Ali in Zaire, where he destroyed the formidable George Foreman to recapture his heavyweight crown at the age of 32. The fight took place in a ramshackle soccer stadium on the outskirts of the capital, Kinshasa, an arena on the very edge of the jungle. Here Foreman and Ali were to share the $10,000,000 it had cost to bring the fight to Zaire, the former Belgian Congo. The expenditure was authorised by the nation's President, Mobuto Sese Seko Kuku Ngbendu Wa Za Banga, in a bid to promote Zaire as a good pull-up for tourists. My own feelings about that were confirmed one lunchtime in my Kinshasa hotel when I watched two waiters chase a rat across the floor of the dining-room. The rat won.

Ali won in the eighth round of yet another curious fight. True to his belief that you should never fight the way the other guy expects you to, he let Foreman take him to the ropes and unload punch after punch. Ali dodged some and took some. He made no other move for seven rounds. In the eighth, as he lay on the ropes and his arms dropped, I ventured the opinion in my television commentary: 'Ali seems to be getting tired'.

The words were scarcely out of my mouth when the great man heaved himself off the ropes and swung the right that sent Foreman crashing on his back, floundering in the dark mists of concussion while ten was counted over him. The African night was split by the triumphant screams of Ali's handlers. Straw-skirted native warriors bearing spears stamped out a dance of celebration on the jungle earth. It was close to three o'clock in the morning (so as to catch prime time on US television). As we made the journey back to the city, the heavens opened with a vast tropical storm. Lightning flashed, thunder roared and Kinshasa almost disappeared beneath the flood waters. At five o'clock in the morning, back at the hotel, Bob Duncan, my producer, had to break the news to me that my father had died in London earlier that day.

The Wit of Sport

David Lacey

The *Guardian*'s lucid football correspondent, and a contributor to *Sports Report*, David Lacey has covered six World Cups. He began his career with the *Brighton Argus* and his passions include cricket, music, photography and westerns.

Professional sport has become a grim business. Study the faces on the bench at a football match, or the expression of a Wimbledon finalist awaiting serve, or the intensity with which a top golfer lines up a putt or a Test batsman awaits his first delivery. Not much room for laughs there.

Group a large number of sportsmen and women together and ask them to walk across London Bridge at about 8.45 on a January morning and they would be indistinguishable from the glum hordes hurrying to the City. The only difference would be that they were making more money more quickly and had even less time to spare for the odd joke. Yet without humour sport would be a barren occupation since, by definition, it is 'fun or diversion'. Fortunately, there will always be those either playing games or watching them who will see the funny side of the grimmest situation.

In the quarter-finals of the 1964–65 European Cup, Liverpool were due to play Cologne at Anfield but the pitch was icebound and the game was always in doubt. Still, the fans turned up and hung around patiently while officials prodded the frozen surface and wondered whether or not the game should go on. After a while one or two Kop supporters strolled out and began an impromptu 'skating' session to keep warm. They were joined by others and, in next to no time, the scene resembled a winterscape. Right on cue, a group of fans picked up the numbers used for the half-time scores and held them up as if they were judges at a World Ice Dancing Championship. Even by Liverpool standards it was a rare moment of spontaneous wit.

When you talk about humour in soccer it so often comes back to Liverpool and when you mention Liverpool the conversation soon turns to Bill Shankly. Tales of Shanklyisms are legend: like the time visitors to Anfield were invited 'to walk around' Ron Yeats; or his description of the young Phil Thompson – 'he tossed a sparrow for knees and lost'; or his dismissal of the aerially talented but slow-moving Tony Hateley as 'football's Douglas Bader'. What many people do not realise is that to Shankly these were not jokes. He was being deadly serious, which of course makes his sayings all the funnier.

In the early 'seventies Liverpool had arrived in Munich to play Bayern in the West German club's old stadium. There had been a heavy fall of snow followed by a rapid thaw which had flooded the pitch. Bayern said they were very sorry but they could not see how the match could be played next day. It would have to be postponed for 24 hours. Shankly was furious. Liverpool always timed their European trips to perfection; arriving as late as the rules allowed, leaving immediately after the game – 'and who are we playing on Saturday?'

He could not argue with the weather but the Bayern officials were not going to get away with it lightly. After an hour or so of heated discussion at the team's hotel Shankly finally turned on two large Bavarians and glared up at them. 'It's always the same here', he growled, pointing at each in turn. 'It goes from Hitler to Goebbels.' Exit two respectable West Germans muttering bemusedly: 'Hitler? Goebbels?' Only Shanks did not see the funny side.

At one time the wit of the Kop was second only in footballing fame to the Liverpool team itself. When Inter-Milan visited Anfield for the 1965 European Cup semi-finals the Kop warmed up by chanting 'Ee-aye-addio – Mussolini's dead'. The Milanese VIPs in the directors' box were not amused. They were even less amused when, as Liverpool won 3–1, the Kop switched to singing 'Go back to Italy' to the strains of 'Santa Lucia'. Yet Inter had the last laugh, winning the second leg 3–0.

Some of the best remarks from the stands or terraces are made at those times when, for no reason at all, the crowd falls silent. Liverpool were playing at Highbury one afternoon and carrying out their usual function for an away match of denying the opposition the ball and waiting for something to turn up. Tommy Smith was being particularly tiresome so far as Arsenal were concerned. He would keep taking the ball off their players and, what is more, he was doing it legally. Came a second or two's silence. From the back of the main stand at Highbury came a stentorian North London bellow: 'Smiff – you're a poof!' The lack of logic of this remark did not rob the moment of its humour.

Jack Charlton's reaction to Gary Sprake's famous 'own goal' when Leeds United played at Anfield comes into a similar category. A Liverpool attack had been broken up and, as Sprake prepared to clear the ball upfield, Charlton turned his back on the goalkeeper and began to trot back towards the halfway line. Suddenly there was a roar from the crowd and Charlton turned round to see Sprake sheepishly collecting the ball from the back of the net. He asked the referee, Jim Finney, what had happened. Finney explained that Sprake had been about to throw the ball out to Johnny Giles but, seeing that he was marked, had changed his mind and in the confusion had hurled it back over the line. 'Surely', exclaimed the outraged Charlton, 'you're not going to give a goal for that!'

When it comes to writing about football the best lines are those that come easily to mind. For instance, only Hugh McIlvanney could have described a goal scored by Petras of Czechoslovakia against Brazil in the 1970 World Cup thus: 'Scorning both delay and elaboration, he lashed the ball with his left foot in the direction of his run and it hurtled high behind Felix's right shoulder. Petras veered away, fell on his knees and crossed himself before being buried in rowdy congratulations. Among other things, he had just ensured that Glasgow Rangers would not bid for him'.

That is a marvellous piece of irony but the danger with irony is that sometimes readers miss the point. John Macadam, a wonderfully witty writer in the pre-War and immediate post-War period, describes in his autobiography, *The Macadam Road*, how, as a joke, he set out to describe a match between Wolves and Bolton Wanderers as an old-time reporter might have written it. A rare collector's item it remains. All the dusty phrases are there: the 'homesters' captain and pivot' who was 'a tower of strength' in a defence 'that held the visiting quintet'. At one point 'dubious tactics crept into the play' but eventually a goal was scored 'with a rasping shot which the home custodian was powerless to save'. And so it went on: 'Stung by this reverse, the homesters crowded on all sail' and 'towards the close of the initial moiety the boys sporting the black and gold drew on level terms'. Wolves scored with a penalty or to put it another way 'the official had no hesitation with a right-foot drive that suspended the spheroid in the rigging well out of the custodian's reach'. The game ended in a draw and 'a division of the spoils was a worthy culmination'.

Macadam recalled that the report caused so much amusement on the sports desk that it was decided to let *Daily Express* readers in on the joke. However, most of the letters that followed tended to say: 'Thank God there's somebody who knows how to write about sport'.

Even Macadam would have found it hard to parody a soccer report that appeared in *The Times* in 1911, an extract of which was published by Tony Mason in his absorbing study of Association Football and English Society from 1863 to 1915. The journalist wrote about Newcastle United and compared them with the 'regiment of German condottieri who were in the pay of the Polish Commonwealth during the long struggle with the Cossacks of the Ukraine and were caught and surrounded by a vastly superior force led by Honelnetzi the Cossack hutman'.

Olga Korbut of the Soviet Union, just 4 feet 11 inches tall but the most original and charismatic gymnast of all. Her winks and smiles made her a pin-up on the way to Olympic gold in Munich in 1972 and Montreal in 1976.

Try getting that past a sub-editor on a tight night. One of Macadam's best lines never appeared in newsprint. He began a report of a particularly tedious goal-less draw by referring to 'Much ado about nothing-nothing'. It appeared in the paper as 'Much ado about nil-nil'. All a matter of style, old boy!

Perhaps modern sport might have appealed to the Cossack hutman. After all, the mercenaries are better rewarded these days and the coaches are always going on about battles, bullets and bayonets. 'Conflict and Art', was J. B. Priestley's famous description of a game of football. The same applies to boxing, only more literally. Here you need a touch of trench humour not merely to break the tension but to ease the pain.

The loneliness of the ring gives boxers a quiet dignity not found in other sports. A. J. Liebling summed up the profession better than most in *The Sweet Science*. 'A boxer, like a writer, must stand alone. If he loses he cannot call an executive conference and throw off on a vice-president or the assistant sales manager. He is consequently resented by fractional characters who cannot live outside an organisation. A fighter's hostilities are not turned inward, like a

Sunday tennis player's or a lady MP's. They come out naturally with his sweat, and when his job is done he feels good because he has expressed himself. Chain-of-command types, to whom this is intolerable, try to rationalise their envy by proclaiming solicitude for the fighter's health. If a boxer, for example, ever went as batty as Nijinsky, all the wowsers in the world would be screaming "Punch-drunk". Well, who hit Nijinsky? And why isn't there a campaign against ballet? It gives girls thick legs.'

Whether or not you agree with this traditional view of boxing it would be hard to find anyone who has put forward a wittier argument in its favour. Tommy Farr, who took Joe Louis the distance and, in the opinion of many, won on points, was a marvellous advertisement for professional boxing and became a regular correspondent for one of the Sunday newspapers. Liebling met him on an Aer Lingus flight to Dublin and asked him how his new career was going. 'I love writing', said Farr in his deliberate Welsh way. 'I give it to them straight. No split affinitives, you know, or other Oxfer stoof. Oh, of coorse I split an affinative now and then, to show I know 'ow, but I don't believe in it.'

You will not find many split infinitives in cricket, that most reflective and literate of sports. Here is the richest source of sporting humour, with the works of Robertson-Glasgow, Peebles, Cardus and others timeless in their wit and imagery. Take this gem from a Cardus report in the *Manchester Guardian* of a county game between Lancashire and Surrey at Old Trafford, three days before the outbreak of the Second World War. 'In the pavilion the old gentlemen watched philosophically, and now and again they discussed Hitler, but always with a reservation that the talk could at once be directed to matters of the moment, such as the bowling of a good ball, the performance of a good stroke, a swift piece of fielding, or the general condition of one's lumbago.'

Cricket tends to bring out the best in readers as well as writers. One S. A. Nicholas wrote thus to the *Guardian* from Gloucester: 'Sir, on Friday I watched J. M. Brearley directing his fieldsmen very carefully. He then looked up at the sun and made a gesture which seemed to indicate that it should move a little squarer. Who is this man?'.

Cricket spectators develop a wit of their own and nowhere more so than in Yorkshire and Lancashire. During a 1950 Roses match the *Manchester Guardian* printed a recollection from an elderly reader who remembered being taken to the famous fixture in the 1890s. A statistical argument developed between supporters of the opposing counties which grew quite heated. Eventually the Yorkshireman produced irrefutable facts to support his case. The Lancashire man fell silent for a few seconds then retorted: 'I sh'd laike to knaw what thee knows about cricket. Or any other so-and-so as 'as 'is pudden afore 'is meat'.

Cricket anecdotes enliven many an after-dinner speech; some are even true. From a personal point of view one of the best lines of unintended humour came from an umpire of a game in southern India during a club tour there. Stomach upsets and the lure of a superb beach had reduced the tourists to three regular bowlers, one of whom had operated throughout most of the afternoon session. The innings continued after tea and the same bowler carried on where he had left off. But as he sent down the first delivery the umpire cried: 'No ball!' The captain was close enough to see that his foot had been well behind the line and politely queried the shout. The umpire explained that he had not been informed of a change in the bowling. 'But', said the bewildered skipper, 'this is the same chap who has been bowling all afternoon.' 'So sorry,' said the umpire, unabashed, 'you all look alike to me.'

The very fundamentals of golf make it a subject ripe for humour. Somebody once described golf as 'a good walk spoiled'. All that fuss to knock a small white ball into a hole using a maximum of 14 sticks. 'What's so special about the number 14 anyway?' asked Peter Dobereiner in an article for *Golf Digest* which was reproduced in his anthology *For the Love of Golf*. 'In demonology the number seven was significant for its evil properties and 14, presumably, would be doubly so. It is certainly a hellish number in golf, either as a score for one hole or as the number of clubs in the bag.' Dobereiner favoured ten.

Even this number would probably complicate life for Michael Green's Coarse Golfer, whom he defines as 'one who, when playing alone, is regularly overtaken by women's foursomes', 'one who normally goes from tee to green without touching the fairway', and 'one who has to shout "Fore" when he putts'. To this must be added another, strictly personal, definition: 'One whose first tee shot strikes the red marker on the ladies' tee and rebounds 30 yards behind him.'

But, of course, golf at any level is surely a social activity, a game of manners, a chance to make friends. Not if you read *The Art of Coarse Golf* where, according to Green, 'one of the common fallacies is that golf breeds wonderful friendships and sportsmanship. One has only to watch the face of a man missing a two-foot putt in the Open on television to see how far that is from the truth. Indeed, as far as making friends goes, golf is the finest game in the world for making enemies. Oddly enough, while it isn't difficult to make friends in this world, it's extraordinarily difficult to make a good enemy. But, by George, you can do it through golf. The game's capacity for arousing hatred is greatly underestimated'.

Not that anyone could make an enemy of Lee Trevino, surely the best example of a professional sportsperson who has never let the tension of winning − or losing − overcome a sense of humour. Yet when Dobereiner first encountered him 'he was scowling as he walked into headquarters. Everything about him was belligerent'.

That was the beginning of a piece Dobereiner wrote for *Golf World* in 1973 entitled 'Will the Real Lee Trevino Please Stand Up?' He argued that there were three Trevinos: the sullen Mexican orphan with a chip on his shoulder and the cheerful extrovert, at his best in a crowd. 'He may be as shallow as a dirty limerick, we told ourselves, but he is a lovable guy and terrific company away from the course'. Later there emerged a third Trevino, 'a profound thinker about the techniques of golf' who had worked out his own style and 'totally rejected most of the concepts of good swings and bad swings'. Dobereiner's description of the man is at the same time witty and masterful: 'He was like a boxer without any coach or trainer, or fancy gymnasium to practise his moves in. He was straight into the fairground booth, knowing that he had to win to eat'. According to Trevino: 'When you're playing for five bucks and you've got two bucks in your pocket, that's pressure. Where's the pressure when you've got a five-footer for the Open? Hole it or miss it, you'll still end up with a pocket full of dollars'.

Well, that was the mercenary talking. In truth the McEnroes, the Nicklauses, the Bothams and the Navratilovas of sport play to win longer than they need to win. This has made them what they are. None is noted for humour on stage. Oh, of course, there is Gordon Hill, ex-Millwall, Manchester United, Derby County and QPR winger, who remains the undisputed champion of imaginary lawn tennis. Confused? You ought to be, unless, that is, you have read Eamon Dunphy's *Only A Game? The Diary of a Professional Footballer*.

Millwall had gone to Bournemouth for a pre-season break. 'Orient went to the Bahamas; even Hendon went to Spain; and we come to Bournemouth!' writes Dunphy. Anyway, late one night in the team's hotel the players asked Hill, who had been boasting about his tennis prowess, to play an imaginary game in the lobby with the settees pulled across as a net but no balls or rackets, just mime. 'Finally we persuaded him. So they line up the settees. 30-love. 40-love, 40 − 15, 40 − 30. Out!' 'That wasn't out.' He was really getting in a state now. Protesting violently. Eventually the Millwall manager came in and the gag ended. But did Hill ever catch on? Later, on an England tour, he revealed an unexpected ability for impersonating Norman Wisdom. Funny? Well it all depended on your sense of humour.

In sport the sharpest wit is the wit of skill. Surprise is a basic part of comedy and so when Maradona sends the English defence all ways with his second goal for Argentina in the Aztec Stadium the natural inclination is to applaud and laugh − not at England but at the sheer impudence of the moment. As John Macadam wrote: 'Fewer and fewer of them [footballers] on the field of play do things with a flair that makes spectators laugh − not so much from an appreciation of the comic, but rather from surprise at the sheer brilliant effrontery of it.'

Macadam approached Alex James, the great Arsenal and Scotland inside forward, after a match with the words 'That was funny, the way you left that big fellow standing. The crowd loved it'. 'I'm a fitba' player,' growled James, 'no' a comedian.' Macadam concluded that 'he had no awareness that his gadfly changes of pace and direction that had opponents running all the wrong ways were magnificently comic. To him, they were intensely serious tactical moves and he was too much the innate gentlemen to get a laugh at another fellow's expense'.

But, as Dryden wrote: 'Wit will shine through the harsh cadence of a rugged line'. He could have been describing one of Platini's free kicks.

40 Years of Racing

Peter Bromley

BBC Radio's racing correspondent, Peter Bromley, has commentated with model precision on races big and small for more than a quarter of a century. A former amateur rider, assistant trainer and owner, he is an authority on British breeding and the author of *The Price of Success*.

When *Sports Report* opened its eyes in 1948 it did not see much racing because of the big races only the St Leger was run on a Saturday. The Derby, then as now, stuck to its traditional Wednesday; and all the major betting events, too, like the Spring Double – the Lincolnshire Handicap and the Grand National – avoided the weekend. Imagine, then, the problems faced by the editor of a Saturday sports programme. The prestige races were either run or just in front of him. It meant *Sports Report*'s racing content was a very mixed bag.

Sometimes they played a recording of a Raymond Glendenning commentary, or there would be a short review of the week's racing, compiled by Peter O'Sullevan but read by Peter Dimmock. John Hislop, the amateur rider, would also pop into the studio to look ahead to big races, and also to marvel at Angus Mackay's near apoplectic fits when a contributor outside London failed to respond to a cue.

One difficulty facing all broadcasters at this time was the BBC's inflexible rule about gambling. The Board of Governors decreed there was to be no mention of betting, nor any semblance of a tip, lest the BBC should be accused of encouraging the public to have a flutter. It was not until 1958 when Independent Television began to cover horse racing with betting shows and starting prices that the BBC was allowed to compete on equal terms. At this time Angus's main contributor on racing was Tom Cosgrove of the *Star* who, when that paper closed, joined Tom Webster on the *Evening News*. Tom Webster was for years Raymond Glendenning's 'race-reader' and accompanied him on just about every big race broadcast. How Tom Cosgrove ever managed to look ahead to the Spring Double, without actual reference to the ante-post market, I shall never know; but he succeeded in satisfying Angus without putting the Governors on 'red alert'.

I found my early days as BBC racing correspondent extremely difficult. I alternated between radio and television but found considerable opposition from the editor of *Sports Report* who preferred his Fleet Street journalists. Eventually, after pressure from above, he called on me for all the previews and reports on racing. By 1960 the radio coverage of racing had increased to 50 races. Although I nearly always previewed the big Saturday races on *Sports Parade* earlier in the day, I rarely got a look in on *Sports Report*, which seemed to be dominated by football and boxing.

Angus Mackay, that acerbic Scot, demanded the highest standard of reporting from his contributors and no programme mirrored the character of its editor more than *Sports Report*. We had several brushes. One day at the Cheltenham National Hunt Festival I was commissioned to do a one and a half minute piece looking forward to the Gold Cup. However, the race on the Wednesday, the Champion Hurdle, provided what my producer, Tony Preston, and I thought was a first-class news story. The race was won by a one-eyed horse called Winning Fair ridden by Mr Alan Lillingstone, the first amateur to win it since 1938. I, therefore, began my report with a 20-second mention of this before dealing with the Gold Cup.

The next day I was admonished for departing from my brief. The following correspondence resulted:

Memo to: Angus Mackay
From: Peter Bromley
I acknowledge that I departed from my brief and spoke for 0'20" on the Champion Hurdle and apologise if it spoilt the impact of the piece about the Gold Cup.
However, I would like to point out that:-
1. I was convinced that there was a news story in the Champion Hurdle.
2. I suggested the 20 seconds on the Champion Hurdle to the producer before the programme, who accepted it.
3. I did not over-run.
4. I *did* tip the winner of the Gold Cup.

Memo from: Sports Editor, Angus Mackay
To: Peter Bromley
1. We weren't.
2. He didn't
3. You're not expected to.
4. You are expected to.

That exchange is one of my most precious documents in nearly 30 years with the BBC. I also recall that whenever I produced a racing story that beat everyone, Angus always wrote a personal note of thanks. For all his fire and brimstone I regard Angus Mackay as the true architect of this fast-moving programme that has become the envy of the world.

Among the many racing stories I reported on for the programme over the years were the rash of doping scandals in the 'sixties, now happily a thing of the past. Then there were the numerous inquiries after the 1964 Schweppes Gold Trophy involving Rosyth and Captain Ryan Price's subsequent disqualification; the Jockey Club inquiry into alleged doping after Relko had won the 1963 Derby; the Hill House affair in 1967; the introduction of starting stalls and, more recently, the theft of Shergar, the Dickinson-Sangster row and Sunday racing.

The Relko inquiry was a strange business. The Jockey Club headquarters were then in Cavendish Square, conveniently close to the BBC Club. On the pavement outside, photographers and journalists camped out and lay in wait for those attending the inquiry. Photographers fared best because owners, trainers and jockeys were usually tight-lipped as they came and went. Sometimes they even managed to elude the waiting mob by slipping out of the back door.

It was a sensation when it was revealed that the French-trained colt Relko had failed a routine dope test. The inquiry, attended by Relko's owner Madame Dupré and trainer Francois Mathet, went on for over five hours and that evening the result was inconclusive. It was not until the following day, when the findings were published in the Jockey Club's official organ *The Racing Calendar*, that it was revealed that the expert veterinary and scientific witnesses had disagreed. The charge of doping was removed and Relko was confirmed as the winner. Jockey Club inquiries were always a hazard before the days of legal representation. The Jockey Club made no statement and, unless the subject of the inquiry was prepared to talk, the vigil on the pavement was wasted effort.

In the 40 years of *Sports Report*, racing has undergone more changes than at any time in the sport's 200-year history. It has grown from a sport run mainly for the benefit of owner-breeders, trainers and the Jockey Club to a huge entertainment, breeding and gambling industry. Now every section of the racing industry has its own representative body and the Horserace Advisory Council (HAC) represents their views in regular meetings with the Jockey Club. Racing continues to intrigue and seduce gamblers. It is far and away the most popular betting medium, attracting an annual turnover of over £3,000,000,000. The public are now properly catered for, better informed and, having been to most racing countries, I consider that the sport here at the major courses is the best in the world.

Racing's movement towards the 21st Century gathered pace in 1960 when off-course betting was legalised and betting shops, the new outlet for gambling, appeared in every High Street. The Horserace Betting Levy Board was formed to administer the levy on bookmakers and to distribute a percentage of the profits back into racing. Without this annual sum, currently running at £23,000,000, racing would be in dire straits. The lion's share of the Levy Board's income comes from the bookmakers and over 45 per cent of this income goes towards prize-money. In my time as the BBC racing correspondent I have seen the introduction of starting stalls, the camera patrol and photo finish extended to all courses. Now there are rigorous stable security and anti-doping measures, and the routine testing of winners. Running commentaries on the public address are now standard and many courses have closed circuit television in bars and private boxes. All of this, provided by Racecourse Technical Services, is paid for by the Levy Board, to the tune of £3,250,000 a year. The Levy Board has also helped to finance major rebuilding programmes on many of our racecourses and to assist in the new attitude to fire and safety following the Bradford Football Club disaster.

The most significant change in the racing programme came about with the setting up of the Pattern Race Committee following the Norfolk Report in 1965. The status of about 130 races in the calendar was recognised and incorporated into what became known as the 'Pattern'. This was later further classified into Group races consisting of Groups One, Two and Three. The Group races are the backbone of British racing and the calibre of a winner of these races is recognised throughout the world. In 1987 the Levy Board allocated almost £1,000,000 towards prize-money for Pattern races.

In 1972 a new trend emerged when De Beers Consolidated Mines sponsored the King George and Queen Elizabeth Stakes at Ascot. The inclusion of the word 'Diamond' opened the floodgates and now all the Classics and most of the Pattern are sponsored. Another development which arrived on the racing scene was the televising of races first by the BBC and later by the ITV companies. With television came sponsorship which now accounts for about 20 per cent of prize-money.

Even though the cost of maintaining a horse in training has risen steeply over the years, at the height of the summer there are over 14,000 horses in training. Few individuals can afford to deal with a monthly training bill of about £700 and that

accounts for the growth in partnership horses, in syndication and in company-owned horses. Racing continues to get remarkably good coverage in the Press. Race programmes are printed for practically every race and, thanks to the system of overnight declarations, are 100 per cent accurate, unlike in the bad old days when sometimes there were more non-runners than runners and the occasional additional runner was slipped in by an unscrupulous trainer to put away the off-course backers.

Since 1984 racing has observed the Arab invasion. The oil-rich sheikhs have gradually taken over racing at the highest level. The Maktoum family, which has horses spread around Europe, is numerically the strongest, but Prince Khaled Abdullah from Saudi Arabia has been notably successful, particularly with Dancing Brave. The personal involvement of these super-rich Arab families is very deep and has brought considerable benefit to those who produce yearlings at the highest level. The Arabs are clearly here to stay for they have invested in the finest collection of brood mares and studs that money can buy and so are now producing their own stock to race. The Arab involvement in European racing has brought nothing but good to the sport. Not only are they fiercely competitive, they believe in testing their stock and they have resisted substantial offers to sell their best racing stock to America. They stand their stallions here in Britain. The only drawback to Arab ownership is the fact that I must now get my tongue around some very difficult Arab names.

Most of the famous names in racing have been on *Sports Report* at some time or other including Sir Gordon Richards, a peerless champion jockey and truly wonderful ambassador for the sport; and Scobie Breasley, whom I once interviewed for the

At the races. (Above) Raymond Glendenning at Ascot 1949, and (below) Peter Bromley at Aintree 1987 – with German binoculars that date back to the Second World War.

programme in the ladies' loo at Manchester Racecourse after he had won the Jockeys' Championship in 1963, finishing one winning ride ahead of Lester Piggott. Lester himself was a reluctant interviewee and we missed him on a vital occasion at Doncaster in 1985 when he won a record number of Classics. The Racecourse Manager, Don Cox, had unlocked the back door of the weighing-room so that Lester could slip out of the reach of the waiting Press men.

National Hunt champions such as Fred Winter, Josh Gifford, Terry Biddlecombe

Red Rum, ridden by Brian Fletcher, takes the last fence in the 1974 Grand National. Red Rum was the first horse to win the National three times and in five runs (1973 – 77) his record was 1,1,2,2,1.

and lately John Francome have always been a pleasure to interview but probably the most popular, the most respected and loved personality in racing since Sir Gordon Richards has been Jonjo O'Neill. 'Jonjo is Magic' ran the headlines after he had won the most moving Tote Gold Cup on Dawn Run in 1986. Whenever he came anywhere near a microphone this quiet and modest man was magic to me and, I suspect, to the majority of our listeners.

I look forward to being involved with the next 40 years of *Sports Report* – or some of them at least! – and to being able to continue to talk to the members of that rich vein of personalities which makes racing one of the most glamorous and exciting sports.

Words: With and Without Pictures

Desmond Lynam

Desmond Lynam is the only man to have regularly presented the BBC's two flagship sports programmes: television's *Grandstand* (more than 300 editions) and radio's *Sports Report* and *Sport on Two*. He presents major sporting occasions, among them the World Cup and the Olympic Games, and has commentated on boxing for BBC Radio. He spent his early days with Radio Brighton and in *Who's Who* he lists his club(s) as Brighton and Hove Albion.

'We have nothing against him, but think he lacks background, experience and personality.' That was how one of BBC Radio's senior management figures reacted to a proposal that I should be the new presenter of *Sports Report.*

Nothing against me! Mr Angus Mackay disagreed, won the day and so, 18 years on, I can proudly claim to be the only man to have been at the helm of both *Sports Report* and *Grandstand* for any length of time. I can't imagine what I would have been doing for all those hundreds of Saturdays in the meantime if that original critic had had his way. Mind you, after my very first *Sports Report*, the great Mr Mackay himself was wondering why on earth he had put up such a valiant fight so that this incompetent could very nearly ruin the programme made famous by Eamonn Andrews.

During a nerve-wracking ordeal I had managed to fluff my way through the opening headlines, to speak on the air to someone who had given me a direction over my headphones and to end the programme an interminable number of seconds early, creating one of those heavy and nasty silences between my closing remarks and the start of that famous old signature tune 'Out of the Blue'. Limited in experience though I was, I had actually dealt with all those problems before in both local and network radio. It was just that this was the 'Big One'. Mr Mackay was present and my nerve went. I could almost hear the 'senior management figure' laughing up his sleeve. Things, it must be said, got better. Soon I held the chair on a regular basis and spent many happy years doing so. Eventually, television beckoned me towards another nerve-wracking and unimpressive debut.

Stangely enough, there is no real training for being a television sports presenter. They tend to throw you in at the deep end. And then a judgement is made – either you can do it, they say, or you cannot. There is no school where you go to present hundreds of 'pilot' shows and learn technique. In

comparison to my first months with *Sports Report,* when I received much advice and positive criticism from Mr Mackay and his then number two, Bob Burrows, the reaction to my early television performances was deafening in its silence. When I think of the little tricks of technique I had to pick up the hard way, I often reflect how someone could have saved me a lot of heartache by offering some early advice. My advice to myself at the time was 'pack it in'. I was uncomfortable and it showed. I had felt completely comfortable in front of the sound microphone and I thought: 'Enough of this. I'll go back if they'll have me'.

I don't subscribe to the notion that television is a progression from radio – for the performer anyway. There are plenty of good broadcasters who have moved from television 'up' to radio. It's horses for courses, it's what suits you. My ego was not at stake, but at the time I didn't want to let certain people down, and so I persevered. *Grandstand* is, of course, the flagship of BBC Television sport. It began in 1958, only ten short years after *Sports Report* began on radio. I have often felt it's a shame that television was developed so successfully so soon after the sound medium. Radio, and particularly sport on the radio, was only really getting into its stride when it had to start competing for audiences with the magic 'box'. How splendid it might have been if *Sports Report* had had, say, a whole quarter of a century in which to influence the nation's sportsmen and women before a large proportion of them turned to television.

No other country in the world can boast a more famous or longer-running radio sports programme than *Sports Report.* In television terms the same can be said of *Grandstand.* In many ways the programmes are the same. They run for around five hours on a Saturday afternoon. (*Sports Report,* remember, is now the final hour of *Sport on Two.*) Each programme deals with the sporting news, views and live action; but, of course, while *Grandstand* can show you what is going on, *Sports Report* has just the one dimension − words. On television, words are secondary to the pictures. On radio, the words have to be spectacularly good, or else everyone goes nicely off to sleep.

Radio has to be more inventive. Unless the occasion is an important one, live commentary does not work. Radio sport, however, and *Sports Report* in particular, has shown much inventiveness down the years. The Wimbledon Championships, for example, work wonderfully well on radio, but it was not always the case. Tennis is a particularly difficult sport for a commentator to describe. Imagine a women's doubles between Martina Navratilova and Pam Shriver on one side of the net and say Mrs Mochizuki and Miss Yanaga of Japan on the other. Any of their names plus the description of the shot they play takes a lot longer to 'say' than to 'do'. The result can be chaotic, with a distressed commentator three shots behind the action, his overworked larynx desperately trying to catch up.

Once upon a time tennis on radio was covered like this, but now a more reflective style is used with lots of opinions, discussions, interviews and interjections. In television, the exact opposite applies. The match itself is self-sufficient. It needs little more embroidery than a suitable remark from Dan Maskell and his pals after the point is played.

Although I have commentated on several sports for radio and television, the only sport I have done for both is championship boxing. In radio you are the listeners' 'eyes'. Your job is to describe exactly what is going on in the ring or outside it if that is of any interest. The television viewer can, of course, see for himself precisely what is happening; so here, the commentator's job should be more one of explanation. The viewer wants to learn something from him that he cannot see for himself. Most radio commentators who switch to television suffer one major problem: they talk too much!

Presenting sport on radio and television − being the 'link man' as we say in the trade − is basically the same job. Many of the skills required are identical. You must know your subject; you must be articulate; you must be able to interview anyone from any sport without making a complete idiot of yourself. After that, though, the techniques begin to differ. *Sports Report*, for example, is basically a 'scripted' show while *Grandstand* is largely unwritten. Clearly, a presenter cannot have his head down reading from a script in front of a camera, so he has to be able to 'ad lib'. Some sports programmes and all news programmes, though, use a device called 'autocue' which allows the presenter to read his script while looking straight down the lens. This is not used for a show like *Grandstand* which is fast-moving and very changeable. It would mean lots of re-writes throughout the day, and is not worth the bother.

As a result, the *Sports Report* presenter can appear to be a cleverer 'wordsmith' than his *Grandstand* counterpart. The television man makes his remarks simpler because he has to remember them. No point in going down some clever avenue of thought which turns into a verbal cul-de-sac. If you are embarrassed on television, it shows. Radio is easier on the presenter. If he's scrambling about trying to find some scrap of paper with notes on it, no listener knows. If he hasn't bothered to shave or comb his hair, no listener cares. His voice and the quality of what he has to say are all that matter. The television presenter has, of course, to take some care with his appearance. Regular viewers will quite often make known their preference for a certain colour tie. Some like you to smile all the time; others accuse you of grinning foolishly if you do. I have even had a letter from a Major-General demanding: 'How dare you speak to me with your hand in your pocket! Lord Reith would have sacked you on the spot'. And there was I thinking I looked nonchalant!

It is interesting to learn of the visual images people have of you. When I eventually appeared on television I received a number of letters from people who had listened to me regularly on *Sports Report* and almost all said they imagined me to be short and fat with glasses. In fact, I am tall and fairly slim with eyesight that, so far anyway, has worked well unaided. Clearly, I must be a tall slim man with a short fat man's voice.

There is a great danger in being the 'presenter' in our business. If you are not careful you end up being twice removed from the reality of your subject. This was acknowledged by Mr Mackay and his team in my early broadcasting years. He would insist that I didn't present *Sports Report* all year round. He wanted me to get out and deal with the sports and the personalities involved. This experience was invaluable when subsequently I had to chair a discussion or deal with a contentious issue back in the studio. It was felt imperative that knowledge wasn't 'second-hand'. This holds good for me today. Even though I am quite often studio-bound in Television Centre in London I take care to keep in touch with as much live sport and as many sports people as possible. I like to form my opinions 'first-hand'.

It has certainly helped me as 'link man' to have been asked to commentate on such varied events as Wimbledon, four Olympic Games and Commonwealth Games and Soccer's World and European

Carl Lewis, the hero of Los Angeles in 1984. No thought of failure occurred to him and he won gold in the 100 metres, 200 metres, long jump and 4 x 100 metres relay.

Championship Cups, not to mention many sundry minor sports. But boxing has always been my favourite. The sport has been a special interest of mine since I had a go as a kid, and found it one of the most effective laxatives known to man. I have never stopped admiring the courage of those willing and able to go to battle, man to man, in that loneliest of sporting arenas – the ring. Footballers and cricketers have their team-mates to help them along but when the fighter goes to business he is on his own. For whom the bell tolls!

My years of covering boxing for BBC Radio were dominated by Muhammad Ali. Not so long ago, I received a telephone call at the *Grandstand* office from a gentleman in the Midlands. 'I have Muhammad Ali on the line for you', said an unfamiliar voice. I knew it could be possible because Ali, now retired, was making a visit to Britain. When the great man came to the 'phone I could just decipher that he wanted to come on the programme the following day. He wanted to show British people, he said, that he was fit and well. At the time, the newspapers were full of stories about Ali's ill-health. The punches had finally caught up with him, they were saying.

Arrangements were duly made for the great man to come in and as he walked through the television studio the crew, cameramen, sub-editors, floor managers and tea-girls all stood to their feet to give him a spontaneous round of applause. I have never seen that happen before or since in a business where the technocrats are often wrapped up in their own task and somewhat blasé about the presence of the famous. The great old fighter raised his arm in acknowledgement and the famous smile that captivated the world lit up his face. We went through the motions of an interview that once would have been the highspot of television's week.

But Ali was no longer floating like a butterfly or stinging like a bee. His world had become a slower, more sombre place,

and this broadcaster was so upset by the changes that a five-minute 'breather' was necessary during the videotape. I have so many visions of Ali in his prime. He provided me with some great radio 'coups' over the years. He even recorded the opening of *Sports Report* for me once from Kuala Lumpur, the capital of Malaysia, where he subsequently toyed with Joe Bugner for 15 rounds. 'Welcome to *Sports Report*. This is Muhammad Ali in Malysia. I like your class and I like your style – but your pay is so cheap I won't be back for a while. Now the classified football results'.

Unforgettable – the Ali 'staged' hyperbole – yet absolutely perfect for our programme. A feather for the Lynam cap.

Then there was Zaire. What the hell was I doing in the President's bungalow in Kinshasa in the middle of Africa? Well, of course, it was there that they staged the 'Rumble in the Jungle', Ali's attempt to win back the championship from George Foreman which, against all the odds, turned out to be successful.

There I was in President Mobutu's bungalow, which he had given over to Ali, listening to the great man describing how he would win back the title – and, in company with two British Press men, not believing a word of it. As Ali's forecast of the fight got more descriptive, he shot out the most famous and certainly the fastest heavyweight jab in the history of the sport: 'Bop, bop, bop – Round Four. Bop, bop, bop – Round Eleven. Bop, bop, bop . . .'. The bop-bop-bops were full-arm jabs stopping about a millimetre from the Lynam nose. I had seen him pull this stunt before with the recipient flinching and withdrawing his head from each punch. I decided I would neither blink nor move. If he actually connected, it would make a great story after I woke up. Of course, the man's timing and judgement were perfect. He kept my hooter that millimetre away all the time but at the end of his tirade he acknowledged I had put on my own little performance in a way. He winked and out came the familiar 'You're not as dumb as you look'.

One of the main hazards of interviewing Ali in those rare years was putting up with his so-called 'mentor', Bundini Brown. It was Brown who coined the phrase 'Float like a butterfly . . .'. He was Ali's confidant, witch doctor, whipping-boy and 'gofer'. Ali fired him most weeks and re-hired him the next. I personally couldn't stand him. I thought he was an absolute fake and largely responsible for Ali boxing on too long. Every time he saw me coming with my tape recorder to talk to Ali, wherever we were in the world, he would want to put his two penn'orth in. I have recorded many 'Bundi' rantings which usually descended into the worst kind of racist meanderings. None of them ever made the airwaves. However, there was one occasion when Bundini was the only one doing the talking. Before Ali's defence against Leon Spinks in 1978, the champion hit on a new gimmick. He decided to stop talking. The famous Louisville Lip was sealed. Of course, newspapers could write about it and television could show Ali with a sticking-plaster across the most famous mouth in sporting history, but it was a disaster for radio. No one believes me when I say I am probably the only reporter who ever pleaded with Muhammad to talk; but I did and eventually he gave *Sports Report* listeners about ten minutes on why he wasn't talking. It was, as always, sheer delight.

The 'sharp end' away from the studio is, of course, fraught with difficulties from time to time. I once arrived in the United States for one of Ali's fights and, after a long exhausting flight, found to my horror that not only had my bags been lost (with all my commentary notes) but the hotel had no record of my booking. Needless to say they were full up. While I was standing in the lobby trying to work out what on earth to do, a receptionist called my name. At last, I thought, they have found me a room. Not a bit of it. It was *Sports Report* on the other end of the line with a harassed producer screaming at me 'Where the hell have you been? You're on live in two minutes'. And the first question from the presenter at the other end was 'Just how is Ali looking in training?' There are lies, damned lies − and pieces from reporters in difficult situations abroad.

Happy days! I wouldn't trade my present job on *Grandstand* for anything, but *Sports Report* was where it all started for me and the love affair goes on. Oh, and by the way, I am still working on the old 'background, experience and personality'.

40 Years of Tennis

Gerald Williams

BBC Television's tennis expert and, before that, BBC Radio's first tennis correspondent, Gerald Williams is a former tennis and football writer for the *Daily Mail*. He is a disarming interviewer, and the author of *A Whole New Ball Game* (Christians in Sport).

The first BBC tennis commentator I ever saw in my life was playing inside right for Reading. It's a funny game, life. Who would have thought that, one day far off, Maurice Edelston, of Reading Football Club and England, would have been together in the *Sports Report* team of reporters and commentators at Broadcasting House with the little evacuee standing with his nose pressed against the railings of Elm Park?

That was me, the little evacuee. I probably carried my gas mask in a small, brown cardboard box slung over my shoulder by a long cord. And I was probably with my pal Keith, who lived only a couple of Johnny Mapson's long goal-kicks away from the Reading ground. (Today that same Keith is a venerable cleric in the Church of Wales, and he's chaplain to Newport County Football Club; but it's still Reading's result he wants to hear first when Radio Two plays the famous signature tune at five o'clock on Saturday afternoon.)

Come to think of it, the first tennis star I ever saw in my life was a bit of a prodigy at my cricket club in South Norwood. He was only about 15, and he used to score runs very quickly indeed. He also used to play centre forward in the Sunday team I graced at left back (noisy and non-tackling). And he used to drive a golf ball so far that we took him along to let Harry Weetman see him, and even he was impressed. His greatest flair, though, was on the tennis courts near the cricket pitch, and whenever the rather crabby ladies who seemed to make up interminable fours waddled off to the clubhouse for a cup of tea, Roger Becker (for that was his name) would borrow a tennis racket and wallop the grubby balls with the aggression that was to help him into the British Davis Cup team a few years later.

How, with the benefit of hindsight, we view these extraordinary twists and turns that our lives take depends, I suppose, on whether we think there is a destiny that shapes our ends or believe, simply, that we're the result of an accident of chemistry. In my own case, there were pointers, signposts along the way, from almost the very beginning, though I certainly never recognised them. For example, the house where I was born backed on to this large sports club. More precisely, it backed on to the tennis courts, courts where, already, two British Davis Cup players had emerged long before Roger Becker bustled into view. They were 'Bunny' Austin and C. M. Jones.

And it was C. M. Jones who first prompted me (by now a cub reporter on the local newspaper) to organise my first tennis tournament. It was for juniors in our neighbourhood, and the untouchably famous Geoffrey Paish used to come along every summer and play an exhibition on our junior finals day. It was hardly the sort of occasion that the BBC would have bothered with. In fact, not even the Lawn Tennis Association bothered with us until our little promotion had been going a few years. Then, at last, recognition came. A letter arrived from the LTA headquarters remonstrating with me because we had not sought their sanction! That letter, I am sure, lit a flame of resentment against that authority which has burned in me until, just a few years ago, a Government inquiry and a critical Press stirred the LTA to put their house in order.

Tennis, in those faraway days of the mid 'forties, was just taking off its flak jacket and tin helmet and blinking into a free tomorrow. Wimbledon, the game's true heart, had been very much part of the War effort. They had grown vegetables in one of the car parks at the All England Club, and the main concourse had been a parade ground for detachments of the London Welsh and London Irish regiments.

Many of the buildings were occupied by the ARP and the Civic Defence services. No fewer than 16 German bombs fell on the All England grounds during the War, one on a corner of the centre court, near the competitors' stand. By 1946, after a five-year interruption, it was possible to get the Wimbledon show on the road again. Twenty-three nations sent their best players and, though a Frenchman, Yvon Petra, was the men's winner of the first post-War singles championship, it was the Americans who dominated the international game. In the first decade after the War, seven American men won one each and five American women won all ten singles titles at Wimbledon.

It was the era of Kramer and Falkenburg, Louise Brough and Margaret du Pont, of the handsome Budge Patty and the courageous Doris Hart. And I, a fledgling journalist learning his trade in Leicester and Cardiff and Manchester, used to thrill to the wireless reports of their excellence, never for once even daring to think that this glittering world of international travel, hob-nobbing with celebrities in Palm Springs and Buenos Aires, Rome and Paris, doing radio commentaries from all these dreamlands, would ever be mine. I think I would have burst if I had known that, one day, Billie Jean King would stay in my home, and famous footballers like Joe Mercer and Raich Carter, too. Or that the fair-haired small boy I sometimes used to throw balls to in his parents' lounge in Ipswich would grow up to keep goal for England. He was Gary Bailey.

But which ever way I leaned, professionally, I always seemed to end up in the direction of tennis. I drove miles in the summer, often on the way to write about county cricket matches for the *Daily Mail*, with my imagination honed in on some epic tennis match described by Max Robertson with a display of verbal gymnastics that held me in awe then and continued to do so when, as our careers unfolded, we were paired up in the BBC Radio commentary boxes. Paish versus Cucelli in a Davis Cup tie at Eastbourne! Didn't I actually see it? No, I didn't. I listened to it on the radio.

And I never actually saw Pietrangeli and Santana in their glorious final on the clay court at Roland Garros, though I can picture these two artists and friends with their arms round each other after the final point as if I did. I heard it on the BBC. And I heard on the BBC about Little Mo Connolly, and then about the new Australians, Frank Sedgman, then Hoad and Rosewall. I had finally made my breakthrough into the Wimbledon Press box by the time Rod Laver and Angela Mortimer were winning.

Laver, judged on all surfaces, was the best player I ever saw, although I think John McEnroe would have served too well for him on grass. Laver, however, could beat the best on clay as well, as he had to do to achieve his Grand Slam not just once but twice. Mind you, it was close the time he did it in 1962, because my pal Martin Mulligan had held a match point against him that summer on the centre court during the French Championships.

Fully to understand what happened that oppressive, thundery day at Roland Garros you need to appreciate that the French Championships – and indeed all international tennis – have changed almost beyond belief in the last 20 years or so, since Open tennis, in fact. And before the game exploded, sometimes almost out of control, into a major global industry, there was a relaxed camaraderie between the people who played the game and those of us who wrote and broadcast about it. Of course, you were always liable to get the occasional ruffled temper: living and working together in so highly pressured a world, seeing incidents sometimes from different perspectives, plus the odd act of insensitivity of thoughtlessness, sometimes worse, you were bound to get confrontation from time to time. This was usually settled amicably enough over a few raised voices and then a few raised glasses. By and large, though, as I say, there was a chummy atmosphere away from the courts.

Players and Press tended to fly together, to eat together, even, occasionally, to share hotel rooms to save money, because this was in the days before the millionaires. Martin Mulligan and I, in fact, had shared a modest hotel bedroom in Rome (where he almost always seemed to win at that time) because we were both saving to get married. So we were good friends.

There was a Wagnerian heaviness about that afternoon he played Laver, and we all sat in the Press area watching the drama unfold − all, that is except one of the writers from Fleet Street, who had gone to the races instead, and had asked us to keep notes for him until he turned up at the tennis. Well, Mulligan had his match point, and Laver saved it. The air crackled with electricity. Mulligan was taut and edgy at losing his chance. Then he had what the players termed a 'bad call'. Suddenly, utterly out of character, he hit a loose ball in his hand as hard as he could in the direction of the linesman who gave the call. The linesman ducked, and the ball was travelling so fast that it knocked over a high chair immediately behind him. For a moment that seemed to last for ever, the official walked a few steps on court, his face a mask of rage, and looked as if he was going to strike Mulligan. Martin raised his racket. Then they both saw sense and calmed down.

A few minutes later Laver had won this quarter-final 6−2 in the fifth set, and the two little Australians walked off to the locker-room. One of us said in the Press room, 'Unless Mulligan's careful he'll get suspended for that'. (It was long before the days of penalty points and automatic fines.) We agreed that he should be advised to say emphatically that he had no intention whatso-ever of aiming a ball at the linesman: that it was done on the spur of the moment, and that he hadn't realised the linesman might be in danger.

As Mulligan's closest friend there among the reporters, I was deputed to go and tell him that. I hurried off to the dressing-room.

There, amid the linament, the bandages, the rackets, the discarded shirts and shorts, Martin sat on his own, in deep shock. 'Look', I said earnestly, 'Whatever you do you must say you didn't mean it, or you'll be in terrible trouble. We're going to quote you as saying that. OK?'

I wasn't sure whether he had taken it in, but I returned to the Press room, where the journalists were scribbling their day's reports, and we all agreed on a quote from Mulligan. While we were intent on making our deadlines in strode the English colleague who had been at the races, dog-end of a cigar in his lips, tatty raceguide in his jacket pocket. 'What happened today, lads?' he inquired. One of us, abstractedly, told him of the incident in the Laver-Mulligan match, and, because telephones were by now ringing from London offices, forgot to tell him the quote we had agreed we should attribute to Mulligan.

So our colleague, like the good professional he was, went in search of Martin and found him having a glass of beer. Martin assumed that this news man, too, was in on the act and spoke to him quite unguardedly. 'I'd have killed the guy', he said animatedly. 'Honestly, I'd have killed him. The guy was asleep, or blind or something.' Our colleague, innocently enough, went away and filed a highly-coloured account of a match he had not seen, adding the outraged quote from Mulligan. His story, the next morning, was far more sensational than all of ours, and I was reprimanded by my own sports editor for having sent an inferior article.

These days, such a thing almost could not happen. There are such huge, usually capacity crowds at the Grand Slam Championships, especially, that the reporters and commentators have to be carefully segregated and only get to see each other at the news conferences that follow important matches. The champions, in fact, arrive at the courts in their chauffeur-driven cars, accompanied by minders, girl-friends,

agents, and even trainers, and they are hustled through the scrum of autograph-hunters and well-wishers into the competitors' private rooms. We only see them on court, playing their matches, or in formal interviews. There are also far fewer friendships between the leading players and the Press. In fact, there has been a good deal of antagonism, particularly surrounding John McEnroe, for which both sides have to take the blame.

To give you an example of this change, which in some ways is unavoidable though much to be regretted, I could count on one hand the number of times I have socialised with the present world champion of women's tennis, Martina Navratilova, though we are on friendly, first-name terms and have met in many corners of the world. On the other hand, Billie Jean King and I were good friends on a personal level, as she was with some others of my trade. In fact, with a young British player of that era, Richard Avory, I gave Billie Jean her first look at the famous centre court that was to become the stage for her greatest achievements. Richard and I took Billie Jean and her travelling companion, Carole Caldwell, to the All England a week or so before the Championships, and I held my hands over her eyes until we were standing right inside the court. 'Now look', I said.

The coming of Open tennis in 1968 changed it all, for better or for worse. My own judgement is that, except in one or two areas, the change has been outstandingly for the betterment of the game. Until 1968, because the game was still called 'amateur' by its legislators, the cream of the champions was annually scooped off by Jack Kramer's professional circus, who, as honest and open professionals, were excluded from the established world circuit. Not only did

Roger Taylor, the only British player to reach the semi-finals of the Men's Singles since Wimbledon went open in 1968 – and he managed it twice, in 1970 and 1973.

this mean that the traditional events like Wimbledon, Paris, Forest Hills and the Australian were no longer authentic world championships (because all the best players were no longer competing), but it also meant that the simmering deceit of under-the-counter payments was allowed to grow unchecked among the 'amateurs'.

The prime movers to clean up tennis were the All England Club. The rest of the world, including Britain's own LTA, clung to their positions of power, not always for the wrong reasons. In July 1960, as the clamour grew to throw the game open so that all could compete together and all could honestly earn the money that their skill and effort merited, it looked as if the wind of change would finally blow away the dishonesty, because the annual meeting of the International Federation (the world governing body) seemed set to change their rules. Instead, the Open lobby failed by five votes. They failed, what is more, because three of the delegates who would have voted in favour were out of the hall at the time, one of them arranging a seating plan for the dinner to be held that evening.

The outcome was that, from 1960 to 1968, when the nations did at last bring in Open competition, the scandal of bogus payments grew, and entrepreneurs began to line up to move in on a game of enormous commercial potential, whose administrators obstinately held on to a code that was outdated and, anyway, quite impossible to police. By the time the 1968 vote was carried (after Wimbledon had almost threatened to go it alone) tennis was in disarray.

Mercifully, not all those tycoons who now sought to commercialise the game were men without integrity or respect for sport; and one of these was certainly Lamar Hunt, who contributed astute business sense as well as much needed artistic showmanship at a time when tennis threatened to be rudderless in the big seas.

The lesson that other sports should learn from the agonies of tennis, as it entered its brave new world, is surely this: the critical issue is not so much whether competitors should be paid but that the elected governing bodies should themselves expertly control the events they promote, i.e. *expertly* negotiate radio and television and sponsorship contracts so that the vast sums generated by the game can be wisely shared among those players who deserve fair reward and the balance ploughed back into development. For all the birth pangs of Open tennis, its adolescence has been vigorous. Tennis, as a pastime and sport, is today played almost everywhere in the world. Standards of play have risen enormously, even if standards of discipline, as in all walks of life, have declined. In most countries, the game is now run by skilled professional people.

Nowhere is this more obvious than at the three major Grand Slam Championships: Wimbledon, the US Open and the French. In the mid 'seventies, as tennis approached the Borg era, the US Open and the French Championships, in particular, made spectacular advances. Until then, Wimbledon had been pre-eminent, virtually unchallenged, as the world's major championship, but the growth of the game in America was making the dollar the most telling currency, and the United States Association had encouraged ambitious and visionary men to graduate to the top of their organisation.

The US Open had become cramped at the elegant but rather old-fashioned West Side Tennis Club in Forest Hills, New York, and club members had been reluctant to commit themselves to drastic redevelopment under the terms suggested by their national association. The president of that association at the time, a bluff, hearty man named 'Slew' Hester, set in motion plans to move the US Open from Forest Hills a few miles across the teeming New York suburbs to Flushing Meadow Park, site of two World Fairs. It was an audacious gamble of the kind that Americans, especially, seem

more willing to make. Guillermo Vilas won the 1977 US Open against Jimmy Connors at Forest Hills, and 12 months later the Americans opened their brand new National Tennis Centre at Flushing Meadow, with its massive 19,000-seater centre court stadium, for the 1978 Championships. You wouldn't have believed it possible.

But 'Hester's Folly', as the project had been called, was no folly at all, if you could forget the thunderous noise of the planes taking off from La Guardia Airport just a mile or so away and flying, almost every two minutes, right over the centre court. It was the most significant new venue for world tennis since the All England moved to their present site in 1922 and Stade Roland Garros was opened by the French in 1928. The reward for typical American business enterprise was an immediate leap in attendances, which began to rival Wimbledon's, and prime network televising of the finals.

The French, meanwhile, were being inspired by the dynamic leadership of Philippe Chatrier, the outstanding administrator in post-Open world tennis. Chatrier's new team, installed after a state-prompted coup of the old guard, brilliantly engineered a spectacular growth in the popularity of tennis in France until it became their second most popular sport. In 1979, the French increased the capacity of the centre court stadium at Roland Garros to 17,000 seats as part of a major renovation that included the opening of a stylish new second show court the following year and still more refurbishment later. It was another dramatic transformation. Where, in my first years covering the French Championships, you would have expected to find seven men and a dog on the early days of the Championship fortnight, now the place was packed. Twelve of the tournament's 14 days were sold out in that significant year of 1979. Tennis was the fashionable sport in France and Wimbledon was beginning to be rivalled.

Significantly, one or two important players began to voice their resentment of what they saw as the British toffee-nosed attitude towards them. Some of these players were millionaires by now: they had become accustomed to being fêted, even spoiled. And 'player power' had demonstrated itself as a potent influence with the formation of the two players' associations, the men's and the women's. The men's boycott of Wimbledon in 1973, however you viewed the rights and wrongs, had bound the players into a cohesive force and demonstrated to themselves, as well as to the governing bodies, that they had the clout to demand a say in the running of the game.

Consequently, the separate men's and women's International Professional Tennis Councils were set up to represent the three major strands of the modern game: the International Tennis Federation (the traditional world body), the players and the tournament directors. In this climate Wimbledon had to change. It did.

In style, it changed almost imperceptibly to the outside world, but the overseas players detected a more professional and, in some ways, a softer, more conciliatory approach. Mark Cox and Virginia Wade were brought on to the Championships Committee, which became altogether more modern and enlightened in its approach. Elegant new restaurants and lounges were built for the players. Wimbledon had reasserted its position, and without forfeiting its dignity.

The result is that, today, tennis has three outstanding championships, each with its own style and personality: Wimbledon, regal and traditional but subtly modernised and generating vast income from commercial enterprises so that the Lawn Tennis Association's own revolution could be funded (last year by £6,000,000); the US Open, a huge concrete park, noisy and bustling with modern catering and jazz bands, tennis for the common man and his

family; Roland Garros, as French as croissants and the *vin rouge* they bottle specially for it each year, where the famous champions of yesterday are given some of the best seats in the president's tribune. One championship on grass, for the dash and daring and reflex shots of power players; one on a sort of polished cement, a middle-paced court where the base-liner can survive if he has finishing shots as well but power can still conquer if it is harnessed by intelligence; and one on Continental clay, where the skills of control, guile, patience and mental endurance reap their rewards.

Now in 1988 the Australian Open will surely begin to re-establish itself as a genuine fourth Grand Slam event. It will do so with the opening of the Australian Assocation's new National Tennis Centre at Flinders Park, near the famous Melbourne Cricket Ground. The surface will be synthetic, instead of grass; the centre court stadium, covered by a sliding roof, will accommodate 15,000 spectators, with room for another 15,000 round the outside courts. What is more, with their new January date, the Australians now begin, instead of end, the Grand Slam sequence, so that any champion bidding to do the Grand Slam of the four major titles in one year must start in Melbourne. In recent years, unless they already had the French, Wimbledon and US Open titles safely in their pocket, they sometimes stayed away and relaxed over Christmas at home.

The modern tennis industry seems to be emerging from its noisy revolution. Who would have dared to think that a game for vicarage lawns and flannelled gentlefolk would grow into such a giant? Certainly not the winner of the very first Wimbledon men's singles championship, an Old Harrovian called Spencer W. Gore, who won his final before a crowd of 200. Spencer Gore's assessment of tennis was off-handedly dismissive. 'It lacks variety', he said at the time. 'I seriously doubt if anyone who's really played well at cricket, Real

Tennis or even racquets would ever seriously give his attention to Lawn Tennis. Compared to them, the sheer monotony would choke him off.' Today, Messrs Spencer W. Gore and Brian Redhead are in a decided minority!

The 1986 record attendance for the Wimbledon fortnight was 400,032. The Championship was watched by television viewers around the world, and Wimbledon simply cannot accommodate the mushrooming number of radio stations from all corners of the globe who these days ask to send their reporters and commentators

Tennis has become a market for high finance, too. When BBC Radio first broadcast tennis commentaries, prize-money was unknown, and what fairly meagre (by today's standards) payments did take place had to be carefully made in secret. At the first Open Wimbledon Championships the men's winner, Rod Laver, received a cheque for £2,000 and the women's champion, Billie Jean King, won £750. Boris Becker, the 1986 men's champion (one of four singles finalists that year all born in Europe, incidentally) made £140,000. Martina Navratilova's seventh Wimbledon singles triumph (in 1987 she equalled Moody's record eight) banked her £126,000.

That is the kind of income, from prize-money alone, the leading players are consistently making these days. When you add to their prize-money their earnings from other sources, such as exhibitions, endorsement of rackets, sportswear, motor cars, drinks etc. etc., you realise we are talking of the plutocracy. We commentators blither away about these millionaires from our cushioned, air-conditioned, sound-proofed commentary boxes . . . well, *sometimes* in such comfort but by no means always. Next time you switch on *Sports Report* to be informed of the very latest in the current Grand Slam final being played, in charity consider that all may not be quite so luxurious for the Beeb's man there.

I mean, there was the year − not so very long ago, either − when five minutes before I was due to begin reports and commentary from the French Championships at Stade Roland Garros for *Sport on Two*, the only thing in a totally bare *cabine* was a disconnected wire poking through a hole in the floor! Hours of watching and gleaning information, all the morning's preparation of biographical details, the heightened sense of excitement you always experience before a broadcast − and this total shambles! It was enough to induce paranoia. Me, all alone for the BBC, with the most rudimentary French that hardly extended beyond *Trente-quarante* or *Deux glace chocolat* and one unconnected wire. I mean what do you do? 'Je m'excuse, Monsieur. Je suis from the BBC . . .'.

Then there was the time we nearly broke even Dan Maskell's heart for tennis in the desert of Palm Springs, in California. It was 1978, and Britain, led by Buster Mottram and John Lloyd, had reached the final of the Davis Cup. Because BBC Television were not covering it, radio borrowed Dan Maskell for the week, and Dan was to join the BBC Radio commentary team of Max Robertson, Jim MacManua (USA) and me for the occasion. It sounded terrific in prospect: drinks by the poolside, Californian sunshine, luxurious new club in the desert at Rancho Mirage, down Frank Sinatra Drive . . . The reality was a little different. The Americans had never really experienced live ball-by-ball radio commentary the way we were going to do it for hours on end, and they naively thought a temporary perch on the roof of the clubhouse, overlooking the court, would suffice. No cover whatever; nothing to muffle our voices (Max and me when we got excited!). Worse still, when we came to begin our programme there was a serious fault on the line to London, which made it imperative that we kept our voices up.

On McEnroe's very first service point, he tossed up the ball, caught it in his hand and

asked the umpire to 'tell the English commentators to be quiet'. In our headphones our producer from Broadcasting House was shouting: 'Don't drop your voices!'. In that long, long day it never got better, only worse. We were warned repeatedly by the umpire; screamed at by our London producer. The crowd became restive. Voices were raised. We kept going. Once, in mid-flow, our radio line became so indistinct that, in between two points, I was handed first a microphone, then a telephone, then the microphone again. A scribbled note was pushed in front of me by the shaking hand of Geoff Dobson: 'Keep Going'!

By late afternoon we were into the second single, Mottram against Brian Gottfried, and suddenly the desert heat gave way to an icy freeze. A compassionate wife sent some rugs and whiskey up to our beleaguered, maligned, demented commentary team. Dan said (off air): 'I've never seen anything quite like it, old boy. I really haven't'. Well, we made it that day. So did good old Buster. But at the end of our desert nightmare, as we sat drained and ashen, I could not help thinking that, back home, someone was sitting in his lounge in Maidenhead, or somewhere, a gin and tonic by his side, and he was probably saying: 'Don't think much of these commentator chappies these days. Not a patch on Freddie Grisewood'!

Even in England, where radio sports coverage has become so sophisticated, no one is immune to the daftest, most unexpected crisis, like the time at the Royal Albert Hall just a few years ago, when I was doing live commentary on Radio Two on the Wightman Cup. The first match of the evening had just ended, and our producer told me, in my earphone, to leave the commentary box and hurry to the interview area near the courtside to talk to the winner on air. I was to cue across to Peter Jones, and Peter would keep talking until I got to the interview point.

There was one minor difficulty. The door of the commentary box had somehow locked itself and couldn't be opened from the inside. We needed someone to come and unlock it from the outside. The other problem was that we had a technical breakdown which meant that I could not speak to my producer without the listeners hearing. At times like these you suffer a kind of death. I had only one way to solve the impasse, and I did it. I told the listeners that we were locked in the commentary box and needed someone to come to our aid!

The truth is that nowhere in the world does any radio station provide tennis coverage even approaching the quality of the BBC's. Its daily programmes from Wimbledon through the fortnight are regarded by other broadcasters as a marvel. Many producers and technicians whose names you seldom hear have played their part in the development of this unique service. I think, particularly, though, of Bob Burrows, under whose direction the BBC Radio coverage of Wimbledon was transformed. And at least two distinguished BBC Television personalities, Desmond Lynam and John Motson, look back with pride to our days with radio sport. I would wager that, next to the memories of his Wimbledon titles and his great affection for his family, the great Fred Perry himself has in recent years got most enjoyment from his involvement as a part of that team of broadcasters. Long may they all continue to provide their unrivalled best.

It's a Small World

Paddy Feeny

Paddy Feeny presents the BBC World Service's *Saturday Special* and is known to millions of listeners all over the globe. He also hosts *Top of the Form* on radio and television and *Young Scientists of the Year*. A former film projectionist, scene shifter, electrician and repertory stage manager, he is a cricket crank: an expert watcher but self-confessed dud player.

In 1974 the Saturday afternoon sports programme on the World Service held a competition asking listeners to forecast who would win soccer's World Cup and by what score in the final. Entries poured in from well over 100 countries and island states which proved that people were tuning into the programme all round the world and all round the clock.

When it's tea-time on a winter afternoon in London it's almost breakfast-time on a summer morning in New Zealand where John Mullen, who works for the Otago Harbour Board, listens to what he refers to as 'the best sports coverage anywhere in the English-speaking world' over his first cup of coffee of the day. At the same time it's the middle of Saturday morning in California where Jimmy Jordan is also listening to London; and it's late on Saturday night in Nepal where Suresh Thapa is waiting to hear how Liverpool have done. So there are listeners who have just woken up, listeners who are about to go to bed, listeners at every hour and in every season. They are in Asia and Australasia, in Africa and Europe, on the islands of the Caribbean and the South Pacific and in North and South America.

Some of them were born in the United Kingdom but are now overseas either permanently or temporarily. Every winter thousands of refugees flee from the cold and damp at home to the sunshine of southern Spain and Majorca. They still, though, want the results from Ibrox or White Hart Lane or Sandown and the voices of Peter Bromley, Peter Jones, Ian Darke and Larry Canning boom out from the bars of Benidorm and Palma Nova.

By way of contrast, Father Joe Cain sits on his own at Malindi Mission praying that no one will knock on his door during the report on Manchester City's game. Father Joe must be the farthest-flung priest of the Manchester diocese. Malindi Mission is in a remote part of Kenya, near the Ugandan border and about 5,000 miles away from Maine Road. For a while on a Saturday afternoon, though, in spirit he is back on the terraces, cheering on the Blues as he used to do in person many years ago, before his Bishop told him of the need in Africa.

Dick Howe in Sun City, Arizona, left England even longer ago – back in the 'twenties. He lived for quite a while in California in the days when radio transmitters and receivers weren't as efficient as they are today. So he would pick up the scores from London through the static and 'phone them on to ten friends of his, each of whom was charged with passing them on to a further ten. And so the ripples spread. There was a fashion for English fish-and-chip shops in California at the time and on a Saturday they would chalk up 'Arsenal 2, Chelsea 2' on their blackboards, instead of 'Scampi and French Fries.'

People do go to amazing lengths to get the sports news. Radio officers on merchant vessels from the China Seas to the South Atlantic are badgered to note down the scores and Chris Stevens even managed to keep up to date with Gillingham while working in a submersible off the coast of Penang in Malaysia, burying 'phone cables on the ocean bed so that they wouldn't be damaged by trawl nets or stray anchors. It's also commonplace for sports enthusiasts with unsympathetic families to have to listen surreptitiously, like resistance fighters during the Second World War. For instance, Phil Davies' family in Middelburg, Transvaal, want pop music from their local station so he goes out to his car and listens to London and thinks of his father who is doing the same in his greenhouse in Prenton, Birkenhead. Graham Turner, working as Terry Venables' interpreter at Barcelona Football Club, was luckier. His wife, Molly, would relay the news to him at the ground so that Mr Venables would get the results from his former clubs as soon as he came off the pitch.

But most of the listeners are not expatriate or exiled Britons. They are natives of their countries who have never been to the United Kingdom in their lives and are never likely to. They are people like Wojtek Kaminski in Poland, T. H. Gho in Singapore, or the group of Wollofs who meet outside a garage in the middle of Banjul, in the Gambia, every Sunday morning to discuss what they've heard Mike Ingham, Bryon Butler and Jimmy Armfield talking about the previous day. During a brief visit to Banjul in 1984 I was asked if I would go and talk to an elderly Wollof who was in hospital awaiting an operation and who wanted to chat about football. I found him sitting in his bed in thick flannel pyjamas, despite an ambient temperature that must have been at least in the eighties, with a bright red Manchester United scarf around his neck and a bright red Manchester United woolly hat, complete with bobble, on his head. The surgeon who was going to operate on him was a Sierra Leonian who supported Chelsea.

The relationship between listeners, however, isn't always so amicable or therapeutic. During the War in the Indian sub-continent that resulted in the creation of Bangladesh I heard regularly from the commander of a squadron of tanks on one side and the commander of an anti-tank battery on the other. I don't know if they ever faced each other in battle but it struck me as ironic that two such bitter opponents could be listening to the same programme and could share a love of sport.

On reflection, though, it's not all that surprising because, hackneyed as it may sound, sport is a universal language, a shared experience. There can't be many people who've never played some sort of game and, in fact, it's through play that babies start to learn. Studies have shown that infants deprived of toys and games develop mentally far more slowly than others. So sport is a fundamental activity which transcends barriers of race, colour, religion, caste or wealth. On the one hand there's a regular Saturday listener in Indonesia who is very well off indeed; on

the other there's F. W. H. Jackson, who wrote from Hilton, Natal, on behalf of the 64 lads who belong to the Umgeniz Football Club: 'The purpose of this club is to give the children of the area of the Natal Midlands the opportunity to play soccer. All the boys come from a very poor area and have never had the chance before to be coached in the game. The money for this project has been raised by donations, and coaching is done by professionals free of charge. On Saturdays all the boys listen to the BBC sports programme'.

If further proof was needed of the importance of sport to the listener, it came in letters from a blind boy in Mombasa who said that it helped him to 'see'; and from a Sheffield Wednesday supporter in Sweden who wrote to say that he'd just been told he was dying of cancer and that one of his main regrets was that he wouldn't live long enough to see Wednesday return to the First Division.

There was a time when I used to wonder why people hundreds or thousands of miles away bothered to tune in to London when they often have excellent local radio stations. In some cases the answer is that they don't tune into London, or at least not consciously. Several local stations themselves are relaying the World Service, just as the World Service is, in part, relaying material from other networks within the United Kingdom. Quite a number of Commonwealth broadcasting organisations take chunks of sports output from London and either broadcast it live or record it for use in news and magazine programmes the next day.

But there are a lot of direct listeners too, and their reasons vary for seeking out London among the welter of voices in the ionosphere. For Britons temporarily abroad it's a straightforward case of keeping up to date with what's happening until they return home. So 'D.T.' and Gwynn, working for the Chipperfield's Circus on a tour of the Far East, write in to ask for as many reports as possible on the programme of Everton and Birmingham City.

For the permanent expatriate, though, there's a bit more to it. Sport is often just part of a more general nostalgia for what has been left behind. Don Roatstone on Vancouver Island, British Columbia, has been listening to the Saturday afternoon show on the World Service 'each and every day over many years for a touch of the old country'. Raymond Glendenning's cousin, Bert Glendenning, now a naturalised Canadian, reminisces in his letter about the days of Elisha Scott and Dixie Dean and he's not alone in harking back to a previous generation of heroes whose behaviour was more acceptable to our listeners than some of today's. For better or worse, most expatriates retain a picture of Britain as it was when they left it. Hobbs and Donoghue and Herbert Chapman are fresh in their minds, as if trapped in Baltic amber. If they ever return to their original homeland, the reality can be distressing to them. But radio is one step removed from reality and serves to keep the happy memories green.

As to the appeal for the other listeners – the ones with no memories of the United Kingdom – the Commonwealth connection and the fact that, largely thanks to the Americans, English is the international language of communication both help. But the largest single factor is probably that so much sport originated in this country and they still think of it as a kind of Founding Father and a repository for ideals of justice, impartiality and fair play.

Certainly in the 17th, 18th and 19th Centuries Britain was the cradle for an impressive number of sports and games. Horseracing, boxing, cricket, soccer, Rugby Union and Rugby League, golf, badminton, squash, tennis and many more first developed in their modern forms here, with the result that British sport holds a very special place in the affections of millions around the world. Wimbledon isn't the richest tennis tournament any more; the St Leger isn't the richest horse race; and the Open isn't the richest golf championship. But history has given them a patina that can't be rivalled and a store of goodwill that even hooliganism cannot expend.

The same is true of football clubs. The longest-standing Manchester United Supporters' Club is not in Manchester but in Malta, and grown men wept openly in the streets of Valetta when so many of Busby's Babes met premature death on a Munich runway. There's a Dundee United Supporters' Club in the Netherlands. And in Norway there are so many people interested in so many clubs that on 15 March 1986 they set up in Oslo an organisation called *'Supporterunionen for Britisk Fotball'* to cater for them. Before they knew what was happening they had 3,800 members with allegiances to Arsenal, Liverpool, Manchester United, Birmingham, Cardiff, Chelsea, Crewe, Derby, Everton, Manchester City, Norwich, Rochdale and Tottenham. Such is the legacy of history.

History has also given the BBC an edge over its international rivals, and rivalry is intense in worldwide broadcasting. Nobody in their senses would tune to London to hear about basketball, volleyball or handball because, although these are among the most popular games elsewhere, they are minority sports in the United Kingdom and what little radio coverage there is lacks conviction and expertise. Even the BBC's coverage of the 1986 Hockey World Cup, which was held in London, was – to be as charitable as possible – perfunctory. Having said that, it probably offers a wider range of other events for the listener than any other major broadcasting service, simply because the British play a wider range of sports at a reasonable level than any other major country. This may harm their prospects of excelling at any one of them, but it does at least mean that sports programmes have some variety.

Among overseas listeners, I would guess

that the men's singles final at Wimbledon, which is far more significant internationally than the FA Cup final at Wembley, has the biggest audience for an individual, annual event. Soccer, though, must be the most popular on a week-to-week basis, helped by the fact that most football pools in the world are based, from August to April, on the English and Scottish Leagues. There is, incidentally, one school of thought in West Africa that believes the results which are read out on a Saturday do not refer to games that have actually been played but are simply made up by the BBC so that its own staff can win a fortune on the Treble Chance. Hence some letters from Nigeria contain lists of advance results and ask for them to be announced the Saturday after next!

The pools are popular everywhere but in some regions betting on the horses runs them a close second. One visitor from Sri Lanka in the 'sixties told me that at home people timed their cocktail parties to finish just before the racing results came through on the World Service. But even Sri Lanka can't rival Radio Trinidad, which not only takes all the racing it can on a Saturday but also pays for satellite time to relay any British race commentaries during the week. Satellite time is not cheap but, with listeners tuning in not only in Trinidad and Tobago itself but also in Guyana and up as far as Barbados, they find that firms are falling over each other in their anxiety to sponsor the programmes. So you can lie on beautiful Maracas Beach, on the north coast of Trinidad, with the sun, the bright blue sea and the tropical rain forest rising steeply behind you, and you can hear a nearby tranny blasting out the 2.30 at Ascot.

The main sport in the Caribbean, as in the Indian sub-continent, is cricket and during a Test Match every car radio in the daily traffic jam in Bridgetown, Barbados, is tuned to the game. On the other side of the world, an airline pilot once said he could tell if the Kiwis were playing at Edgbaston or Headingley by the number of lights still burning in Auckland in the early hours of the morning. In Canada there's a demand for information about motor racing; in Rosewhite, Victoria, Australia, Adrian Johnstone struggles to stay awake until after 2.30 a.m. for news of motor cycling. There are indignant letters from Pakistan about the paucity of squash coverage and from South Africa if anything interrupts the Rugby Union reportage. Jamaicans want to know why we don't take more boxing and a tennis fan in Malaysia would like there to be details of every game in every set in every championship everywhere. The demand for sports news seems insatiable.

When I started introducing the World Service sports programme in 1959 it was all very different. In those days we would feature the British Racing Drivers' Clubs' annual event at Silverstone and the Oxford versus Cambridge athletics meeting, neither of which would command much airtime today. On the other hand, the Saturday afternoon show devoted less time to the 1960 Olympics than to a county cricket match, and even, in 1966 extra time in the World Cup final at Wembley between England and West Germany had to make way for a news bulletin. In retrospect our coverage then appears slightly ridiculous and very insular, but sport itself was insular at that time. Tennis players couldn't whisk around the world as they do now and, even if they had been able to, we would have had technical difficulties in trying to follow them.

A quarter of a century ago an England-Australia Test Match meant far more than now because it was so rare, and the Olympics were less important than they are today because fewer countries could get to them. Even the soccer World Cup was only starting to attract a mass audience. Until the late 'sixties sport was largely national rather than international. Countries were concerned with their own affairs and only occasionally ventured abroad.

Trevor Brooking (second left) is congratulated by Alan Devonshire, Paul Allen and Geoff Pike after scoring West Ham's winning goal against *Arsenal in the 1980 FA Cup final. Allen, later to join Tottenham, was 17 years 256 days old − the youngest player to appear in the FA Cup final.*

It was the explosion in transport and communications that transformed the picture. Wonder at hearing a voice from Australia, through the crackle and hisses, gave way to impatience at any delay in the news getting through and exasperation at anything but perfect quality. Everything suddenly became a great deal faster and more immediate. The voices of the broadcasters were more clipped, their delivery more staccato and the programmes more densely filled with information. *Sports Report*, which had always pioneered new techniques, was in the forefront of a revolution that brought Kinshasa almost as close to London as Kidderminster.

The effect overseas has been in some ways more dramatic even than in Britain. Great

runners from Africa have emerged and great boxers from Cuba have been able to live in style while remaining amateurs. More people know of Viv Richards than ever knew of Learie Constantine and Jahangir Khan has become more famous at squash than any other Khan before him. In radio terms, listeners are now frighteningly knowledgeable and their range of sporting interests inexhaustible. The BRDC meeting at Silverstone in 1959 seems now to belong to another planet.

Something which has not changed, though, is the relationship with the listener in the one-way conversations over hundreds or thousands of miles. Paradoxically, I've always felt closer to listeners far away than to those in this country. Perhaps it's because they reveal more of themselves in their letters. Perhaps it has something to do with the effort you know they have to make to listen to you. Perhaps it's because sport is obviously so important to them. Whatever the reason, I often feel I know more about Paddy N'Suh in Cameroon or John Zavodna in Czechoslovakia than I do about the family three doors down the street.

There are signs that the feeling is mutual, because Ian Robertson only has to miss the Calcutta Cup or Christopher Martin-Jenkins the Lord's Test for the letters to start coming in to ask how they are and when they will be back. When Maurice Edelston died, sadness at the loss of such a fine broadcaster stretched all the way from Mike Truran in Hong Kong to Scotty Aitken of Trail in the Canadian Rockies. That is the measure of the bond. That is what a distant voice can mean. Not just in times of sadness but week-in week-out throughout the year. Nil Idstrom of Gothenburg expressed how he and millions of others feel about their Saturday 'fix' of sport from London when he wrote: 'It makes my ears smile'.

40 Years of Golf

Renton Laidlaw

Renton Laidlaw has been golf correspondent of the *London Evening Standard* since 1973 and is a recent presenter of *Sports Report* and *Sport on Two*. He has worked for the *Edinburgh Evening News*, Grampian Television and BBC Radio and Television in Scotland. An indefatigable traveller (always with golf clubs) and a frustrated actor, his natural habitats are airports, fairways, studios and theatres.

I sometimes wonder how the late and great Bernard Darwin would cope with the frenetic lifestyle of the modern golf reporter and broadcaster. He operated in an era when there was still considerable style and grace around, when the amateur game still meant so much and was a golf reporter's main preoccupation.

Of course, there was the Open – there has been since 1860 – but the British professional circuit 30 years ago was skeletal compared to the programme our professionals face today in Europe and around the world. As recently as the early 'sixties the bulk of golf professionals in this country had club jobs. That is why tournaments finished on a Friday, allowing them to be at their club for weekend business. There was also another reason why tournaments were well spaced out: it was not easy to get from one end of the country to the other in the days before the M6 motorway! John Panton, the quietly-spoken former pro at Glenbervie near Stirling, often recalls the nightmare drives he had to make over Shap to keep his

golfing engagements, one of the greatest of which came late in his career when he beat Sam Snead for the World Senior title at Wallasey in 1967. Panton won by 3 and 2 in scorching sunshine and it was the only time a British player won! I still remember it well.

Yet I am jumping ahead of myself in this purely personal recollection of some of the great moments I have enjoyed in 40 years of following the game and almost 30 reporting it around the world. I cannot remember why I was not at Muirfield in 1948 to see the great Henry Cotton win the third of his Open Championships by five shots from the previous year's winner Fred Daly, but I suppose there were other far more

Henry Cotton drives at the fourth at Sandwich in 1934 on his way to winning the first of his three British Open Championships (1934, 1937 and 1948). Cotton, as player, club professional, coach, tournament organiser, course designer and television expert, probably did more than anyone to promote British golf, and for services on and off the course he was one of the few players elected an honorary member of the Royal and Ancient.

important things for a nine-year-old to do! I missed, then, the sight of King George VI walking the fairways and watching a supreme performance by a golfing stylist who curiously, at time of writing, has never received any official recognition for the huge part he played in revolutionising the game and giving professionals much-needed pride. For a long time after the War many clubhouses were still out of bounds to the pros. It is all different now. At Woburn, the pro, Alex Hay, is also the club director!

If there had been some chance of my making the 30-mile trip from my home in Edinburgh to Muirfield in 1948, there was no chance of being taken to Royal St George's, in the furthermost tip of south-east Kent, where in 1949 Bobby Locke, of the magic if somewhat unorthodox putting style, beat Harry Bradshaw for the title. It is, I suppose, ironic that a bottle (and not a Guinness one at that) should have played such a vital part in the jaunty Irishman's failure to win! You remember the story, of course. Bradshaw found his ball lodged in a bottle at the fifth on the second day and took a 6 — an incident far better documented than Bobby Locke's 7 at the 14th on the same day. That 7 which cost him the chance of beating Henry Cotton's record 65. Cotton's record, by the way, was to remain until 1985 when Christy O'Connor Junior shot 64 en route to what he hoped might be an Open success. Only Sandy Lyle had other ideas!

Locke won again in 1950, and in 1951 that man of many putters, the extrovert Max Faulkner, took the title at Royal Portrush. I remember reading somewhere that when in the 'twenties Walter Hagen used to ask on the first tee 'Who's gonna be second?' and would then win, it was impressive; but when some British professionals tried the same dodge and finished 15th the joke fell flat.

Well, it did not do so at the Open that year. Faulkner said he would win and did, and for the first time in broadcasting history

listeners to the BBC heard commentary on his doing so. Henry Longhurst, so closely involved latterly with television commentary (the job he admitted gave him the greatest delight of all) was invited to act as radio's golf host with the late Tom Scott and John Neill in a makeshift studio built on the clubhouse roof. Henry recalled, when I travelled on the overnight train once with him from Euston to Gleneagles, that that year the BBC had felt obliged to give him just four and a half minutes to describe all the last-day action in the Walker Cup. He had tried hard to do so but had experienced the humiliation of being faded out by a producer over-anxious to switch to a county cricket match.

Golf took a low priority nationally, but not in Northern Ireland. The local regions' executives and engineers there pulled out all the stops. They provided not only last-green commentary facilities but two broadcasting points out on the course which on the final day (if not on the first two days when Henry admitted closing scores were more important) enabled commentators to report closely on how the championship was shaping up! What a breakthrough. Now the radio coverage at the Open is more comprehensive than even television provides and it is not unknown for listeners to watch the pictures and tune into the BBC Radio commentary, with its ability to provide greater detail.

I am not sure what Radio Scotland provided for the commentators at Ben Hogan's Open at Carnoustie but that truly was one of the most memorable golfing occasions of many in the past 40 years. Hogan had won the US Masters and US Open, the latter from Sam Snead, and came to Carnoustie early to prepare. When he discovered that his hotel room did not have a private bathroom he considered jumping right back on the boat and sailing home but wiser counsels prevailed and he was fixed up in a house in Dundee, well away from the clamour of the Championship. Not that there was any of the razzmatazz off the course then that there is today! In 1953 all that mattered was the golf, and Hogan set about meticulously planning his campaign. He spent ten days getting to know every blade of grass on the famous championship course, making copious notes, and all this in the days before Jack Nicklaus made the yardage book a must for any budding champion.

Hogan opened with a 73, followed up with a 71, improved with a 70 and won the title with a closing record of 68. He could not complete a Grand Slam that year because the US PGA Championship came too quickly after the Open and he could not get back to America in time to play in it. Eye-witnesses recall the shot that sealed his Open success on his only visit. It happened at the fifth where, proving that even he was human, he had missed the green with his approach. The ball hung on a mixture of sand and grass 25 yards from the pin. The shot demanded the ultimate in skill and feel and courage – and he holed it! No wonder he got a ticker-tape welcome when he returned home.

A bad car accident that almost cost him his life shortened the career of one of golf's true greats who played his last public round – a practice round at Tulsa with Tony Jacklin – in 1970. Hogan was not well enough to tee up in the tournament proper the next day and called it a day. Now a very private person he still plays regularly at his club in Houston. When asked to share his thoughts in a recent BBC Television history of the game he politely but firmly declined which is, in some respects, sad. So many golfers today have seen so little of him in action. Film of America's World Cup success at Wentworth in 1956, in which Hogan took the individual title, is the only glimpse thousands have had of him playing. He played in Britain only twice and remains the only great golfer in history never to have walked over the Swilcan Bridge at St Andrews.

In 1952 and 1953 Australian Peter Thomson, another supreme stylist, had finished second in the Open. He won it three years in a row from 1954, then came second in 1957 when Reid Jack won the Amateur Championship (a fact emblazoned on my mind because he just happens to have been the last Scot to do so). Thomson, the Melbourne Tiger, collected the title again in 1958, a year before Gary Player arrived on the scene, resplendent in white suit.

Like Hogan six years earlier Player improved his score every round at Muirfield but then he had started with a 75. He thought he had blown his chance of winning as he waited for the others to finish but his closing 68 was good enough to give him the first of his three titles. I worked at that Open for quietly-spoken John Baker of the Exchange Telegraph agency. It was my job to send all the scores and keep John liberally supplied with sandwiches and cups of tea in the little tent that served as our headquarters. I say little because only about 30 Press men were present compared with 400 or so from around the world today. There was not a Japanese photographer in sight that year. Now they hunt in packs, wiring pictures back to Tokyo to a population so captivated by the game that it has become something of a religion.

The boom started there in 1956 when Torakichi Nakamura and Loichi Ono did the unthinkable – they won the World Cup. Today membership of a golf club in Japan is a business luxury. It is financially impossible for thousands of Japanese to afford the membership fees, even if they could get in, so they make do hitting balls at triple-tiered driving ranges in the city centre. Driving range golf has become so sophisticated that it is known for customers to drive up, change into their golfing gear in the car, hire a caddy and play a 'round' to varying targets set out in front and below them. A small green of artificial turf is provided for putting! Some of the range booths even have showers provided to simulate playing in the rain! It is little wonder that Japanese visitors to this country cannot believe their luck when they find it is possible to play a round over the famous Old Course at St Andrews, the home of the Royal and Ancient Golf Club and a golfing mecca for thousands each year.

It was to St Andrews that the Open went in 1960 when Arnold Palmer came needing a victory to maintain his Grand Slam hopes. He had won the US Masters and US Open but Australian Kel Nagle spoiled it all for him. The key to the ever-so-relaxed Nagle's success was his playing of the famous Road Hole – the 17th – which has proved a score-wrecker for so many golfers over the years. In the Centenary Open in 1960, Nagle played it in 2 under par and picked up vital shots on Arnie. Ironically, Palmer was to win in the following two years at Royal Birkdale and at Troon, the last time spectators were allowed to walk the fairways with the stars. Palmer that year coasted home by five shots and the closing scenes were reminiscent of the children's fairytale about the Pied Piper. It seemed everyone wanted to walk down the last with him. He loved it, of course, and in ensuing years did much to revitalise the Championship by encouraging younger Americans to try to win the oldest, most prestigious title in golf in conditions that would test their overall shot-making ability far more than the manicured American courses.

In our Open it has always been necessary to hit every type of shot well. Jack Nicklaus got it right when he stated unequivocably that until a player has won our title he cannot count himself a true world star. Incidentally, Nicklaus made his first appearance as a chubby, crew-cutted, frankly unattractive-looking youngster at Troon in 1962 and finished 29 shots behind Palmer, whom he was so soon to eclipse in the record books. In the next 18 years he won three times, was second eight times, third twice and fourth twice. His worst finish was twelfth.

By now television had become interested in the game, however, not without considerable persuasion from the Royal and Ancient. In 1957, the year Locke won the title at St Andrews despite replacing his ball on the wrong spot as he putted out on the last green, the chairman of R and A's Championship Committee, R.C. Selway, had asked BBC Television to cover at least the final day's play. There must have been few golfers on the BBC's executive floor in those days because they were reluctant to do so! At last, after lengthy talks, they did agree to limited coverage – the last hour – but only if the R and A would put the leaders out last in the final round. They did and a new tradition was created! Thirty years on BBC's hole-by-hole coverage of the Championship is beamed to over 30 countries around the world and the global audience is many millions. How times change!

Today the commentators headed by former Ryder Cup golfer Peter Alliss have the lastest computerised and electronic equipment to help them keep everyone bang up to date as they operate from their luxurious commentary box far removed from the little shed that was provided (if he was lucky) in the early days for Henry Longhurst. I can still see Henry clambering up the rickety scaffolding ladders at tournaments to his commentary position. Now proper staircases are provided – the result of Henry's insistence. Appropriately enough they are called the Longhurst ladders!

In 1963 I was at last on the road. I had given up taking down someone else's copy and was assigned to cover the Lytham Open by myself. Those were the days when the secretary of the Royal and Ancient Golf Club would, from time to time, pop round

Sandy Lyle recovers from sand at the 16th at Wentworth in 1982. Three years later he became Open champion at Sandwich – the first Briton to win the title since Tony Jacklin in 1969.

to the Press tent and chalk up a few more scores on the blackboard provided.

Life was so much more gentle in those days, although I do recall driving hastily back north with *The Scotsman* golf writer Frank Moran to be on site for the first day of the Scottish Amateur, won that year and the ensuing four years by the unbeatable Ronnie Shade, now sadly no longer with us. The rush was caused by a 36-hole play-off for the Open title between a jovial American, Phil Rodgers, and a stony-faced ex-bank clerk from New Zealand who played left-handed. Bob Charles was his name and he outputted Rodgers in the last of the marathon play-offs. Now if there is a tie after 72 holes of an Open the golfers stick around and play a few more just to get a result that day.

Not everyone agrees with this pandering to television, not least the United States Golf Association, which still insists on an 18-hole play-off the following day even if this sometimes backfires badly and the occasion is marred by husky scaffolders and insensitive tent-hirers noisily pulling down the canvas village as if trying to make the *Guinness Book of Records*. Those tented villages were the brainchild of an early promoter, Binnie Clark, who conceived the idea for his Senior Service tournament, a pace-setter of an event which for some obscure reason has been left out of the *Golfers' Handbook*'s list of prominent but now discontinued events. Binnie Clark could hardly have imagined what he was starting. Now the R and A have to control strictly the size of their tented village as more and more companies want to share with their clients the enjoyment of a sport which, thankfully, has not fallen victim to the professional foul or the hooligan.

If my memories of the early years have been more of Open Championships than anything else I do not apologise. They were the focal point of each season, packed with drama and pathos and showmanship. Take 1964, for instance, when a good-looking

American cheekily flew in the day before the Championship began and proceeded to win over the Old Course helped by a caddie fixed up for him by Arnold Palmer (who did not play that year). Tony Lema, who was to be killed in a 'plane crash just two years' later, had tremendous panache and a great belief in 'Tip' Anderson, Palmer's caddy, who knew every inch of the old course. Lema did exactly as he was told, took first prize (watched all week by as many fans as now watch one day's action) and then celebrated with Champagne.

His manager, the likeable Fred Corcoran, who had also looked after Sam Snead, was so excited about the possibility of his man winning that he couldn't bear to stay on at St Andrews for the final round. He fled the scene. He was heading for Gleneagles Hotel, his watering-hole during the Championship, when he could take the uncertainty no more. He stopped the car, knocked on the door of a roadside cottage and pleaded to be allowed to watch the closing stages on television. Like any good manager he had prepared well for victory. Even before Lema had signed the card, the Open's always immaculate Press officer, George Simms, had taken delivery of the bubbly for the celebrations.

There were celebrations, too, that year in Rome when Ronnie Shade, Michael Bonallack (who had won the first of his five Amateur titles in 1961 and the first of his five English Championships a year later), Rodney Foster and Michael Lunt, captained by Joe Carr, won the Eisenhower Trophy, the World Amateur Team Championship. It was a close match and Canada made us sweat at the end, but the anthem that was played by the brass band was ours and no one cared too much if the Italians, in their natural excitement, flew the Union Flag upside-down.

By being there that year I missed the start of something that has become an institution in golf, a tournament which was the brainchild of a man whose influence in the game has been considerable if at times controversial over the years. Mark McCormack, a Cleveland lawyer, who had written to Arnold Palmer in the early 'sixties suggesting he look after his affairs, and then had added Jack Nicklaus and Gary Player to his 'stable', had always felt the need for a world matchplay championship. With the help of the Piccadilly cigarette company he got it started at Wentworth in 1964, Palmer beating Neil Coles in the final. Two sponsors later, the event is still going strong and over the years has produced some memorable encounters: five-times winner Gary Player fighting back against Tony Lema; Tony Jacklin versus Lee Trevino; and more recently, a birdie battle between Sandy Lyle and Tsuneyuki Nakajima that was in the *Boys' Own* mould.

In 1963 I was in Paris for the World Cup at St-Nom-la-Bretèche when Palmer and Nicklaus won and Chi Chi Rodriguez entertained us in the fog to a wonderful clinic. Two years later the venue was Madrid and, as always, we were treated to one glittering function after another. We were returning from one of them in a bus and there was quite a sing-song in progress with Scotland's effervescent Eric Brown acting as master of ceremonies. Joan Fontaine, the beautiful actress, married at the time to the late Alfred Wright, the American golfing journalist, was sitting in front of me and tentatively suggested to the larger-than-life Eric that the bus sing 'Home on the Range' for her. 'The Bomber' (yes, that was Eric's nickname) thought about it for a time then gave his decision. As Joan sat down ready to join in patriotically with the chorus, she heard Eric announce that the next song would be 'I belong to Glasgow' and that that was that! It was all good-natured but Miss Fontaine was clearly taken by surprise.

Jack Nicklaus, always a great hero of mine, won the Open at Muirfield in 1966 the year the rough was so long that Doug Sanders wished he had had the hay

concession; and that year, too, Ronnie Shade failed to win the Amateur title at Carnoustie. Bobby Cole beat him over 18 holes but I've always been convinced that if fog had not disrupted play and the final had been a normal two-round affair 'Right Down the Bloody Middle' Shade would have won the title his dedication deserved.

If ever an international player, well loved by everyone, deserved to win an Open it was Roberto de Vincenzo, a gentleman in every sense! He had been taking part since 1948 and it all came right for him in 1967 in the last Open ever played at Hoylake (there just is not the room there for all the modern paraphernalia). So pleased was Roberto he even forgot to take the trophy! It was the only major he ever won although he might have earned himself a Masters green jacket a year later when, having gone to the turn in 31 in the final round and shot a 65 he expected, at least, to be in play-off with Bob Goalby. What Roberto, charged with emotion at the time, had not spotted was that Tommy Aaron, his playing partner, had marked him down for a 4 and not a 3 at the 17th. Roberto signed the card and as a result of the higher figure his score became 66 – one shot too many for a play-off.

Seldom does anyone remember who comes second but there are no prizes for remembering the runner-up in the 1970 Open at St Andrews. It was Doug Sanders, of the much-coloured wardrobe, who was left with a two and a half-foot downhill curling putt for the title everyone dreams of winning at least once in their careers. He knew he had missed it immediately he had hit it and the title went – after an 18-hole play-off the next day – to Jack Nicklaus, a giant in every sense.

The year 1970 was another golden year, too, for the lad from Scunthorpe, Tony Jacklin, who had given British golf such a boost with his stirring Open Championship victory at Lytham the year before. Cocky, confident, talented Jacklin was at his peak

Tony Jacklin, winner of the Open at Lytham in 1969 and the US Open at Hazeltine in 1970. He was the first Briton to win the Open for 18 years and the first to win the US Open for 50 years. He was also the non-playing captain of Europe's Ryder Cup team which beat the United States at the Belfry in 1985 – the Americans' first defeat for 28 years.

when he arrived at Hazeltine, a Bobby Jones-designed course, for the US Open. He had always been a streaky putter, curiously hitting devastating form for a few weeks and then mysteriously losing it again. He could not work out how or why it happened but that week at Hazeltine he 'murdered' the Americans. On the first day in a 40-mph wind only Jacklin, on 71, beat par. Palmer had 79, Player 80 and Nicklaus 81. Three more 70s and the title was Tony's. He was the first Englishman to win since Ted Ray in 1920 – 50 years earlier!

If he mastered the weather that week it was only fair because it mastered him at the Open which was played a few weeks later at

St Andrews. Out in 29, on the first day, he was heading for an Old Course record when a thunderstorm broke over the course. Jacklin hit into a bush at the 14th, play was suspended and the extra special magic had gone the following day.

It should always be remembered that Jacklin could quite easily have won four Opens instead of one because he was in contention in the next two years as well. He finished third behind Lee Trevino in 1971 at Royal Birkdale when Mr Lu, the jaunty Far Easterner with a natty line in pork pie hats, came and almost conquered. In the space of four weeks Trevino won the US Open, Canadian and British that year, but in some respects a romantic winner would have been Jack Nicklaus who, on the last hole two years earlier in the Ryder Cup, had conceded Tony Jacklin a nasty little two-footer. Had Jacklin missed it would have given America victory. American team captain Sam Snead was not too happy at Jack's magnanimous gesture but Nicklaus had earned the warm appreciation of golfers around the world. Tony has always wondered whether or not, had the roles been reversed, he would have done the same!

Anyway, Trevino took the title that year and the next to spoil Jack's Grand Slam bid. Nicklaus had won the first two majors, but finished second at Muirfield to Trevino, who holed from off the green four times, never more devastatingly than at the 71st on the drama-charged final day when he killed off our own Tony Jacklin's chance. It had looked as though Jacklin had another title win in his grasp. The pair were level but Trevino, bunkered off the tee, was through the green in 4; Jacklin was on in 3. Without appearing to take too much care about the shot, Lee chipped in for 5 and Jacklin three putted for 6. Tony never got the chance to get back into the game and it took weeks for him to reco- ver. Indeed, the incident at the 17th on that final sunny day at Muirfield virtually spelled the end of the greatest period in his career. He was uncertain about his future after that.

He enjoyed playing the American courses but hated the American way of life and the 'junk' food. He gave up his playing card and got it back, then let it go again as he came back to Europe to help build, with John Jacobs, what is now the highly-successful PGA European Tour. No one begrudged him his appearance money. He was a crowd-puller and, more importantly, sponsors were only too willing to increase the prize-money for everyone's benefit if they knew he was playing, just as Severiano Ballesteros and Greg Norman dominate the circuits of the world today.

In 1973 Tom Weiskopf came to a very wet Troon and won his only major; and at Oakmont Johnny Miller came from 6 behind with a closing record 63 to win the US Open. A year later he won tournaments back-to-back in Arizona with a combined total of 49 under par! Peter Oosterhuis, dominating the European circuit with his deadly short game (he was number one money-earner four years running), nearly won the Open in 1974 but Player took the title; and in 1975 it was a new boy, Tom Watson, who had had a reputation as something of a choker, who was successful. He won in a play-off against the Australian Jack Newton at Carnoustie. What made that Championship so poignant was that a few years later in a horrific accident which would have killed someone less strong, Newton had his right arm sliced off and lost the sight of an eye when he walked into a rotating blade of the small plane that was taking him home from a Sydney sports final. Courageously, Jack now plays one-handed and has become a respected golf commentator.

It was 1975, too, that provided what I used to believe was the greatest-ever finish to a Masters with Johnny Miller, Tom Weiskopf and Jack Nicklaus trading birdie for birdie right to the line before the Golden Bear clinched victory. I say 'used to' because Nicklaus upstaged that himself in 1986 when he came from behind to beat

Seve Ballesteros, Greg Norman and company to win a sixth Green Jacket at the age of 46! That performance – he covered the last ten holes in 7 under par – ranked with another great moment in golf which had me on my feet as I watched and broadcast with Desmond Lynam at St Andrews in 1978. I'll never forget the ovation Jack Nicklaus was given that year when he won his second Open at the home of golf. Fans were on housetops and hanging out of the windows cheering him home, and I suspect that there was a tear in the Bear's eye on that occasion just as there was at Augusta in 1986 when to add to the drama he had his eldest son caddying for him. What a family triumph that was!

Back in 1975 Miller had given his very best at Augusta and lost. So, too, did Weiskopf: 'I cannot play any better and yet I still came second', he said with deep emotion in his voice. He was a broken man that day in contrast to Miller who confidently predicted he would be back to win another year. He never did, but he did win the British Open in 1976, achieving a personal goal in the process. He had been brought up at the Olympic club in San Francisco where former Open champion Tony Lema had played years earlier. Miller had always had the burning desire to match Lema and did so during that scorching summer at Royal Birkdale when another young man grabbed many of the headlines and nearly the title.

Severiano Ballesteros did not speak English very well in those days but the magic was there for all to see. The farmer's boy from the quiet little village of Pedrena in northern Spain had a golfing talent that in the next ten years was to earn him two US Masters and two Opens, both emotional victories. At Lytham in 1979 when he became the first Spaniard to win the title he had been told by Roberto de Vicenzo to go out and play 'with his heart'. He did. He may well have sprayed his tee shots all over the place (even into the car park at the 16th)

but he won and the tears flowed as he hugged his brothers behind the green after it was over. He was just 22 years 103 days old, the fourth youngest winner of the title and the youngest of this century.

A year later he was also Masters champion, having built up a ten-shot lead with 9 to play! He hung another Masters green jacket in his wardrobe in 1983, clear indication surely of how much he loves the course which is a permanent memorial to Bobby Jones. Seve returned to St Andrews to win the Open again, this time 'for his mother' in 1984. That year he beat Bernhard Langer, the West German who courageously beat the 'yips', and Watson, who was trying to match Harry Vardon's record of six Open triumphs. It was desperately close with Ballesteros holing out brilliantly on the glassy greens. Appropriately he finished with a birdie and the ecstasy he showed on that huge last green had to be seen to be believed. The relief that it was all over and that he had finally made sure of the title again at St Andrews, where all the great players have come to do battle for 200 years, was quite apparent.

How I savoured that moment as I stood in our commentary box high above the 18th with colleague John Fenton and our analyst Peter Townsend. We have the greatest view of the finish of the greatest Championship each year, and I am proud to be part of a team that relays the greatest moments in sport to listeners in Britain and millions of others who tune in to BBC's World Service – a tremendous advertisement for the country and a service that enjoys a reputation for neutrality that is second to none.

Golf, too, abounds in funny stories – like the year a 26-year-old American invitee won the World Under-25 Championship. The embarrassed organisers tried to cover up by announcing that the entrants had needed to be 25 not on the day the Championship began or even when entries closed, but on the day before the eventual winner was 26!

Covering golf has taken me around the world. It is possible to be at a tournament every week of the year somewhere, and one season I was at 47 events, a marathon performance which took me to Australia, the Philippines, Hong Kong, South Africa, America and all round Europe. The boom in the popularity of the game continues unabated with the latest record-breaker, Greg Norman, winner at Turnberry of the Open in 1986, playing his part in the now multi-million dollar business that still manages to preserve the old standards and traditions. In 1986 Norman grossed over five million dollars from prize-money and contracts, and became the first man to win more than a million US dollars in a year. Where will it stop? Already the players earning the big money are thinking of ways in which they can divert some of their winnings to charity which, after all, is one of world golf's greatest winners.

I'm sorry I missed the golden era of Ben Hogan but I'm glad that I was around and reporting the exploits of Palmer, Nicklaus, Player, Watson, Ballesteros, Norman and the talented Sandy Lyle, who took the Open title at Sandwich in 1985 with such quiet modesty and who won the Tournament Players Championship at Sawgrass, the US Tour headquarters in 1987. If the next 40 years can provide as much excitement as the last 40 then no one will have cause for complaint.

My golden moment? Nicklaus at St Andrews in 1978? Seve in 1979 or 1984? Nicklaus winning a sixth Masters? All come high on the list, but pride of place must go to what happened one Sunday in September 1985 when European golf finally came of age and won the Ryder Cup at The Belfry.

The Americans, just as they had when we last won the Cup in 1957, complained about the partisan crowds but they were well beaten – and they knew it – by the new breed of European professionals. When Sam Torrance finally holed across the green to clinch victory and spark off a great Champagne celebration there was a lump in my throat – a lump that grew larger when Concorde flew over and dipped a victory wing. That was an unforgettable day and did much to boost the confidence of the Curtis Cup team when they went to Kansas in 1986 and became the first side, male or female, pro or amateur, ever to beat the Americans on home soil. Sadly, only a handful of reporters were there to see that triumph and no television station covered the match that made history! No radio reports were filed either. In 40 years there had to be one major slip-up, and that, surely, was it.

40 Years On

Ian Wooldridge

Ian Wooldridge is the greatly praised, bountifully awarded sports columnist of the *Daily Mail.* He has been the British Press Awards Sportswriter of the Year three times and the Sports Columnist of the Year twice. He previously worked for the *New Milton Advertiser,* the *News Chronicle* and the *Sunday Dispatch* and has presented a wealth of television documentaries. A contributor to *Sports Report,* his partialities include dry martinis, bad golf and falling around Australia.

The lyricist of Sir Winston Churchill's school song had none of the misgivings that confront me now as I set out to imagine what *Sports Report* will sound like 40 years from now. 'Forty years on', he asserted with unquestioning authority. 'this field will ring again and again with the tramp of the 22 men'.

Harrow, of course, was slightly more than a soccer school. It nurtured the builders of the empire on which the sun never set and the guardians of a social order impervious to criticism or threat. Coups and revolutions only happened in such unspeakable places as Bolivia. It is, therefore, significant that Harrow's most famous old boy, having just saved the nation from a nasty fate called Hitler, was democratically pitched out of power at the time – give or take a few months – that *Sports Report* first came on the air. Thus, apart from reporting sport, *Sports Report* has unconsciously reflected the astounding changes of the four most tumultuous decades in British social history.

An era that began with a genius like Stanley Matthews forelock-tugging in the presence of Football Association officials who had never travelled by aeroplane virtually ended with a soccer match in the Heysel Stadium, Brussels, at which the scum of the earth, with plenty of money to travel anywhere, were directly responsible for a human massacre that shook the world. That is a pretty big leap. Obviously sport has changed dramatically during those 40 years yet still at a snail's pace compared with the social structure of which it is only a part. It has been an accelerating process and still is, therefore my first inclination is to prophesy that *Sports Report*, 40 years from now, might open on a Tuesday evening with: '*Dobri vyetcher.* Arsenal *odeen,* Manchester United *dva. . .'*

I am assuming optimistically that Highbury and Old Trafford will still be standing and suggesting that we may all be speaking Russian by then. The pessimism about playing the matches on Tuesdays while the peasants are toiling on factory floors or collective farms is because that is probably the only way the commissars will combat the hooligan problem. Happily, if that is the case, I shall be dead and hopefully playing par golf out there on some celestial links with Eamonn Andrews, Peter Jones, Bryon Butler and all the other old buddies from Studio 4A in Broadcasting House. We shall linger a year or two in the clubhouse recalling what glorious fun it was in the old days dashing back to the microphone, breathlessly putting over our reports and then repairing to The Stag just round the corner to spend all our fees and more at the bar.

It *was* fun in those days, too, and if I had to stop the watch at the year when the fun began to drain out of it, I think I would settle for somewhere circa AD 1970.

That, roughly, was the start of the sporting revolution which saw games become industries, patriotism buckle under financial pressure, agents shove their hands into the till, whole teams of players rebel against the established order, entire sporting nations manipulated by so-called statesmen, terrorists commandeer the televised arena to seize worldwide attention and murderous hooligans transform once-peaceful crowds into riotous assemblies.

Past 50 years of age the good-old-days syndrome takes its hold. I am aware the sun didn't shine *every* day in that 1947 summer when Compton and Edrich reaped their richest ever harvest of runs just as I appreciate that a Jimmy Hill *had* to come along to emancipate a soccer industry so anachronistically run by the wing-collared mill-owners that national idols like Lawton and Mannion were condemned to dole queue and scrap heap. Obviously a cantankerous old billionaire like Avery Brundage couldn't keep the lid on a boiling Olympic movement for ever just as the Rugby Union's snobbish middle-class vendetta against Rugby League had no hope of surviving the onslaught of social equality.

And yet were the inequities and schisms actually worse than the anarchy and rapacious greed which have replaced them? Were they worse than the Eastern Bloc's distortion of sport into War without bullets or the scientists' contribution to sport, namely the discovery and development of ultimate-performance drugs? Was there, even in boxing, a more repulsive figure than the csar-promoter Don King? And has any sport, in any era, ever so compromised its principles to throw up such ill-mannered brats as lawn tennis?

It has all occurred in the age of *Sports Report*, the age when sport changed within a violently changing world. In short, tell me that the climate of AD 2028 will have been cooled by one of history's periodic reformations − brought about, perhaps, by reaction to nuclear catastrophe or an AIDS epidemic − and I will hazard a guess that sport, similarly, will have come to its senses. But, frankly, I am mildly pessimistic.

Joe Davis: old style World Snooker Champion. Davis received £6.50 for winning the first World Championship in 1927 − a title he held for 20 years. He made his 500th century break in 1953 but did not manage a 'maximum' − the first official 147 − until two years later. Note the third-class travel.

Steve Davis: new style World Snooker Champion. Davis's ability and temperament made him a millionaire after television coverage of the sport attracted wealthy sponsors. He won his fourth World title in 1987 and was the first man to make a 147 break in front of the cameras.

Sport, spectacle and fun. The start of the London marathon at Greenwich in 1987.

I anticipate that a number of supreme sporting institutions will remain sublimely untouched: the Royal Yacht Squadron down at Cowes, the splendid coterie of friends who play Real Tennis at Hampton Court, the Valley of Peace Cricket Club just outside Christchurch, New Zealand, on whose acres no feminine foot has ever trodden, and Muirfield Golf Club in Scotland, whose elders in living memory denied the visiting American ladies' Curtis Cup team any access to the clubhouse lavatory.

The common denominator of these reactionary sporting backwaters is total lack of interest in money. I am hard-pressed to think of many others where such lofty indifference to the chance of coining the quick buck still applies. One body which would be extremely miffed at being omitted from such an exclusive roll-call is the Augusta National Golf Club in Georgia,

USA, whose paranoic obsession with 'tradition' is hilarious to anyone with sufficient perception to see through the hypocrisy.

For 51 weeks of the year the Augusta National is more impenetrable than Buckingham Palace. During the 52nd week it throws open its gates to the properly-dressed hoi polloi to allow them to become moving wallpaper at the annual televising of the Masters Championships. It is one of the most cleverly-marketed events in world sport. Their income from television rights − despite their decree that no commentator, on fear of expulsion, may make any reference to money − is astronomical. When the show passes on the old guys sit in the clubhouse gloating over the fact that the world has just lavishly subsidised their 'tradition' for another year.

It isn't evil. It is what has become known as street-smart. And it illustrates precisely how television, with its power to attract advertising and pirate advertising, otherwise known as the sponsor's logo, has changed the face of sport. Television was in its nappies when *Sports Report* took to the air. It is now the most powerful single influence on the business and it isn't going away.

The classic example of how television can transform a recondite sport into an unmanageable monster of conflicting interests is the oldest of all international matches, yachting's America's Cup. First raced for in 1851, it was won by the autocratic and extremely rich New York Yacht Club whose disdain for any form of commercialisation was probably the most honest aspect of its 132-year guardianship. When Australia won it in 1983 the entrepreneurs came racing out of the woodwork. Winning the Cup became a billion-dollar battle for television rights. The money men had taken over again.

It is this gold-rush aspect of sport which more than any other factor will determine its character 40 years from now. The most inviolable of entertainments, I suspect, will be horseracing, for one cannot visualise any generation rejecting a colourful vehicle for gambling. The most vulnerable, on the other hand, could well be soccer. The genuine world game, ill-served by administrators ranging from the astigmatic to the corrupt after its control passed into Latin hands, may well continue to thrive in the Third World. But its failure to capture big television audiences in the United States and the defection of millions of fans in Europe as the hooligans sank their fangs into a once lovely game could well prove critical.

The way of cricket is probably more clearly defined. Like it or not – and I don't – the bulwark of Test cricket has been swiftly eroded by the pyjama game, pop theatre which produces a positive result in a single day. To me, cricket played without slips and gullies is the step-brother of baseball but its mass appeal is undeniable.

Compare the crowds now at the traditional and manufactured varieties of cricket and the crystal ball clears. The day when it was heresy to hit a boundary before lunch on the opening day is already history.

Will the Olympic Games still be with us? If they are I have a feeling that the Chinese national anthem will be the tune of the month for no country, and certainly none of such gargantuan human resource, has emerged to make its impact so swiftly on the competitive stage in a single decade. But, again, a movement founded on idealism cannot survive it. Beset by political boycott and commercial assault its foundations were further weakened in the 'eighties when its premier sport, athletics, inaugurated its own World Championships. They were an instant and brilliant success with a vast international television audience and the huge television income which once would have gone directly into the Olympic coffers was retained by the sport itself. You don't have to be very bright to reckon that every sport under the Olympic umbrella now has the same ambition.

Paradoxically this could be the saving of the Olympic movement. Let the full-time professionals go about their perfectly legitimate business within their own sports and allow the Olympics to revert to their original *raison d'etre:* a quadrennial stage for the genuine aspiring amateur. At the moment the 'balanced' sportsman – the man who combines sport with a full-time career – has no hope of achieving Olympian heights against the commerce or state-subsidised performer who has done nothing but train for an event for up to four years. This is contrary to every concept in the Olympic Charter. I doubt whether such a radical reversal is possible. One can but hope because, as I fear the Seoul Games of 1988 will confirm, the Olympic movement in its present form is under terminal threat from forces beyond its control.

Prediction is simplified, of course, the moment one defines the word 'sport'

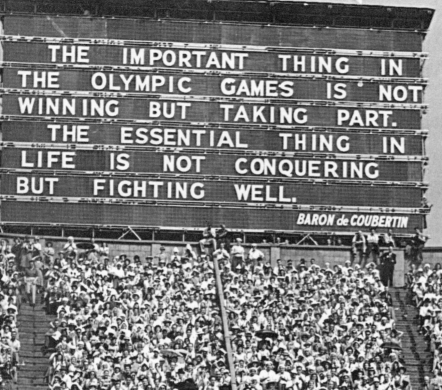

THE IMPORTANT THING IN
THE OLYMPIC GAMES IS NOT
WINNING BUT TAKING PART.
THE ESSENTIAL THING IN
LIFE IS NOT CONQUERING
BUT FIGHTING WELL.

BARON de COUBERTIN

somewhat more clearly. The old generic term is hardly of any value any more since the diverging paths of sport-for-sport's-sake and sport, the vehicle for spectacular high-performance entertainment, are already so distanced that they are almost at right-angles. How, for example, can one talk about 'sport' encompassing both English village green cricket and American Football's Super Bowl, the ultimate in manufactured performances?

If we re-introduce the word 'games' to differentiate between a recreational day in the sun and a heated night watching the latter-day Christians and Lions batter it out at the local coliseum we can probably come to some happier conclusion. Sport is at the mercy of social change but games are forever and I suggest that the trend over the next 40 years will be to get back to games. Remember *Chariots of Fire*? It was about a golden era of competition and extolled the virtues of high accomplishment born not only of determination but grace.

'Was it really like that?' they asked in their millions as they flocked, inspired, from the epic film of the year. It was less a question than an unspoken yearning for the restoration of standards and gives us hope that over the next 40 years *Sports Report* may be able to report that the good guys are getting on top again. Not in Russian, we trust, but in the excellent English that has made it the most literate radio sports programme in existence.

The Olympic flame arrives at Wembley Stadium in July 1948.

Postscript

Patricia Ewing
Head of Sport and Outside Broadcasts, Radio 1988

P.S. The applause faded to order. Eamonn Andrews, his *This Is Your Life* smile broadening, opened the Red Book. *'Sports Report'*, he said 'you were born on 3 January 1948 to the sound of this tune.'

Marjorie tried to edge herself into a more comfortable position in her seat at the back of the studio and nudged Evelyn. 'I've never heard of *Sports Report'*, she whispered. 'I've never seen him on the telly – have you?'

'No', murmured Evelyn with her eyes firmly fixed on the stage. 'That tune's familiar though. It's funny, but it reminds me of frying sausages and Dad in the corner chair in our old kitchen telling young Billy to keep quiet.'

'It reminds me', said young Billy, 'of trying to get out of the multi-storey car park by five o'clock.'

Dee-dum, dee-dum, dee-dum, dee-dum, dee diddely dum dee-daaah!